THE GREAT WALK
OF CHINA

The Great Walk of China

Travels on foot from Shanghai to Tibet

Graham Earnshaw

BLACKSMITH BOOKS

To the people of China, who have taught me so much.

The Great Walk of China
ISBN 978-988-19002-1-0

Published by Blacksmith Books
5th Floor, 24 Hollywood Road, Central, Hong Kong
Tel: (+852) 2877 7899
www.blacksmithbooks.com

Contents

PREFACE

THE FIRST STEP

I am walking from Shanghai to Tibet.

It is a great line, and it is true. My journey is not continuous; I walk when I have the time, usually once a month and always starting from the last place I stopped and always heading west. With every step, I cover an unbroken trail that began at the Bund in the heart of Shanghai, to (as I write this in January of 2010) the Sichuan basin north of Chongqing.

I have walked, with many twists and turns, well over two thousand kilometres since I began this venture in 2004, having passed through two municipalities (Shanghai and Chongqing), five provinces (Jiangsu, Zhejiang, Anhui, Hubei and Sichuan) and countless towns and villages.

People often ask me how I came up with the concept of a walk across China, and my thanks go to Edwin Dingle for being my inspiration. In the late spring of 2004, I was sitting in a Japanese restaurant in Shanghai and reading Dingle's book *Across China on Foot*, which tells the tale of the Englishman's 1909 trek. But Dingle didn't really cross China on foot; instead, he took boats up the Yangtze River from Shanghai to Chungking (now spelled Chongqing) and then, over a period of nine months, walked southwest through Sichuan and Yunnan provinces to the

Burmese border. The twenty-eight-year-old Dingle could neither speak nor read Chinese, so while the book is highly readable and fascinating in its descriptions of magnificent scenery, hotel squalor and the activities of foreign missionaries, it lacks a certain local depth.

As I feasted as usual on salmon sashimi and cucumber sticks, I thought to myself: I can do better than that, and over another flask of hot sake I mapped out the plan. I would walk due west from Shanghai towards Lhasa, staying as close as possible to the 31st parallel – Shanghai is at thirty-one degrees north, which is the same latitude as Marrakesh, Morocco. The Yangtze Gorges are at thirty degrees north, while Lhasa is at twenty-nine degrees, making the journey pretty much a straight line due west for four thousand kilometres. The expedition would have to be non-contiguous, because I lead a busy life, but the rule would be to always start from the last place I stopped, so that I would literally walk every step of the way.

The decision was made: I would walk to Tibet. I pushed my empty plates aside, turned on my laptop and opened up Microsoft Encarta (this was in the days before Google Earth). Looking at the vast map of China, my first question as I looked west of Shanghai was whether I should go north or south of Tai Hu, the almost perfectly circular lake about fifty kilometres from the city. North would take me through Suzhou, Changzhou, Wuxi and Nanjing, tracking close to the lower reaches of the Yangtze River. This route wanders through towns and cities that are well-known, well-travelled and well-integrated into the global economy, thanks to their export industries. Travelling to the south of the lake would take me through Pingwang, Huzhou, Changxing and Guangde: towns and cities I had never even heard of and knew nothing about. It was an easy choice; I would take the southern route.

I started the walk the very next afternoon: April 4, 2004. It was a bright and shiny late spring day. As I walked those first few kilometres, I wondered many times if I could really do it and whether the goal of walking across China was, pardon the pun, really a step too far. But I persevered and, after a few months, I became proud of the distance I had put between myself and China's largest city. For a long time I didn't tell anyone of my plan because I was worried that I would fail. Then, somewhere in the rice paddies of Zhejiang Province, I decided the dream could become a reality and I became for many people, including myself, the man who is walking across China.

As I walk, I am constantly reminded of the many reasons I decided to do this.

I bill myself as a China expert, and while I have set foot in every province and region of China at one time or another over the thirty years I have lived in and around this country, there are vast areas that I have never seen. The walk gives me some credibility to speak to the 'Real China', in a way that is at least closer to the truth than the view from central Beijing or downtown Shanghai.

I have always been interested in how China and the West interact, in all ways. Just about everything I have done seems to have been an exploration of how these two cultures fit together and for me, it is an unending investigation. The walk yields an interesting perspective on China/Outside dynamics because for just about everyone I meet out there, I am the first non-Chinese person they have ever seen, let alone spoken to. The fact that, unlike Mr. Dingle, I can also read and speak Chinese means that I can talk to people and I can read the signs and slogans and graffiti that I come across. I see things in a way that many non-Chinese would not, and perhaps in a way that many Chinese would miss because I have an outsider's perspective.

When I first came to Mainland China in 1978, this was a very closed country. Foreigners were not allowed to travel beyond a radius of about twenty kilometres from the centre of Beijing without official approval from the Foreign Ministry. Every road out of Beijing had a sign posted and a checkpoint that required foreigners to stop and turn back if they lacked a pass to proceed. My walk is a way to test today's limits, of proving how much China has changed and how much it has opened up to the world. It is, hopefully, a celebration of tolerance.

I have a problem with my leg. I limp, and have done so since I underwent an operation at the age of eleven to cut out a section of bone in my right hip joint that had been affected by tuberculosis. This, and later operations, resulted in my right leg being shorter than the left, leaving me with a lop-sided gait and an increasing stiffness of my spine. The walk is partly a message to heaven, declining to accept the affliction's constraints.

I suppose I am also a part of the tradition of English eccentricity, which is particularly strong in Englishmen resident in foreign parts, and often includes the habit of taking long walks. There is no point fighting this kind of thing.

There were other inspirations as well, including an 18th-century Chinese traveller named Xu Xiake, who wandered central China describing its sights in, amongst other tomes, *The Travel Diaries of Xu Xiake*. Then there was the great Isabella Bird, the intrepid British traveller of the late 19th century who wrote wonderful travelogues of Asia and elsewhere and passed along what became a key part of my route.

The only advantage of age is perspective, and at 57, I now have some of that. My first career was as a journalist for newspapers and news wire services, and while I am a journalist no more, I still look at the world as a reporter. People on the road ask me what I am doing and I say 'cai feng', which means to 'grab the wind', a metaphor for travel and experiencing the world. The phrase is also similar in sound to 'cai fang', which means to 'do reporting'. The trip is a bit of both concepts.

While walking across China sounds like a formidable concept, in a way, it is simply a series of strolls through the countryside. Or sometimes hikes – I walk up to fifteen or even twenty kilometres a day, depending on how many people I stop to talk to along the way. I do not camp out overnight. I sleep in little local inns, or in a hotel in the nearest town. I am not roughing it.

People ask if it is lonely on the walk, for I almost always walk alone, and the answer is: No! I come across people in every type of landscape. I say "Ni hao" to all, resulting in dozens of conversations each day I am out there, even when the weather is bad. I choose to walk alone because it creates the opportunity for conversations, and it is these conversations that are the point of the whole enterprise. I hand out my name card to everyone I meet and encourage them to contact me. I get telephone calls from farmers and tea traders in the middle of nowhere asking where I am and how I am doing.

I have learned to read satellite images, use maps, Global Positioning System (GPS) units and a compass. I have learned more about how to talk to strangers, and to make people feel comfortable talking to me. I have learned how to read directions from the sun and moon, and something of the cycle of plant life and how farmers think. I see and learn something new every time I go out there.

On the walk so far, I have already talked to thousands of people, taken tens of thousands of photographs and seen places that are hidden in their ordinariness or remoteness from most Chinese people, let alone people from other parts of the world. I have had the opportunity to experience the spontaneous hospitality of ordinary Chinese people, see the rapid changes that are taking place in this country at the most basic of levels, and talk to kids and old people, farmers and traders, madmen and nuns, about everything under the Chinese sun. I have planted rice, de-corned corn cobs, winnowed wheat and paid my respects along the way to Buddha and a number of other deities – nothing wrong with hedging your bets.

The walk continues, and while my original plan was to do the book when I finished it, I now have no idea when it will end. For me, this is not a race. I saunter on and stop whenever I feel like it to talk to a farmer or an old woman or a kid about whatever comes to mind. With China continuing to change at such a fast rate, I was concerned that the value of some of the observations would be diminished if I left it too long. This is only the first part of the story.

So to paraphrase a Chinese saying, a story of ten thousand sentences begins with one word. And that word, may Buddha have mercy on my soul, is "I".

CHAPTER I

INTO THE MOUNTAINS

I was nearly two years into the walk before I reached the mountains.

The road from Shanghai on the Pacific seaboard of China, at zero metres above sea level and sometimes less, through to the Tibet plateau in the heart of Asia involves two major 'steps'. The first is from the central China plain, where the average height above sea level is twenty-five metres or so, up to the Sichuan plateau with an altitude of around four-hundred-and-fifty metres. This is the range of mountains through which the Yangtze River has cut the Gorges, now dominated by a massive dam and reservoir. The second step, just west of Chengdu city, pushes the altitude up to more than four thousand metres. The paths up both steps are within one degree of latitude of Shanghai.

As I started out of Shanghai, I was out of shape and five kilometres a day was something to be proud of. Then my father died, I thought my right knee was collapsing, and I basically abandoned the walk on the shores of Lake Tai for nearly a year. But the urge to continue the project eventually resurfaced, and I picked it up again, and walked on through the rich rice lands of Zhejiang Province. I crossed into Anhui Province, making my way through many little towns until, on New Year's Day of

2006, I crossed the Yangtze River at Tongling, a filthy industrial city. I struggled on through the bleak Anhui winter, but when I hit springtime at the edge of the Dabie Mountains, the walk changed from a trudge to a romp. I haven't looked back since.

The countryside just to the east of the mountains is at roughly the same height above sea level as had been the previous five hundred kilometres from Shanghai – about forty metres. Then, suddenly, it changed.

On the satellite photographs, there is a clear straight line running NNE to SSW for a couple of hundred kilometres. To the right of the line are fields and flat land; to the left are mountains and forest. Highway 209, which is a paved but quiet country lane, crosses this line into the mountains.

The road up from the plain rises steeply to two hundred and fifty metres above sea level, making this leg of the journey a bit of a struggle, but I finally crossed a ridge, entering the world of mountain valleys, which, after so many hundreds of kilometres of flat paddies, was a startling and welcome change.

The Dabie Mountains region has the reputation of being one of the most remote and backward parts of China. The region is also a significant part of the Chinese Communist Party's mythology as its desperate rebels passed through the area in the late 1920s and early 1930s to escape the guns of the Nationalists. The rebels survived.

The air in the mountain valleys is clean and fresh in a way that is unknown on the plains to the east. I could hear the melodious sound of running water, a novelty for me, and within this there was a deeper silence, thanks to the muffling effect of the mountains and the thick forest cover.

I paused near two houses nestled below the road and sat down on a low wall. Before long, three women came over to find out who this stranger was. The woman was surnamed Zhu, she was in her late sixties, and she had two sons and an extended family of more than a dozen people all living in the same house with wonderful views of the deep valley in front and the steep mountain behind. She invited me into her clean kitchen, which had an old-fashioned wood-burning stove on which she made me a cup of tea with tea leaves plucked from a bush just outside the door. In the corner was a covered plastic tub of water fed by a pipe from a deep well. I dipped a small bowl into the tub and took a refreshing gulp. It tasted ... how to describe it? Soft?

"This is better than any mineral water in the city," her son proudly told me. "No chemicals. It's the best water for making tea."

A little further along the road there was a small group of women and children playing in a yard in front of some simple houses. I said hello, and they all crowded round. One of the girls was wearing a T-shirt decorated with faded, unreadable English.

"What does that say?" I asked the girl, but she looked back at me and shook her head, while one of the women laughed and said: "It says she's an idiot."

"Well, I can read English," I announced, "and I can tell you it says the opposite, that she is smart and has a bright future."

The girl looked from the woman to me, and wondered what was going on.

I continued at a slow pace: the mountains and valleys were easily the most beautiful country I had passed through since the start of my walk, and I wanted to make sure I experienced every view and took every photo, aiming for the perfect digital photographic equivalent of a classical Chinese painting with mountains, water, trees, and, somewhere in an insignificant corner, a humble human overawed by the wonders of Nature.

There was a steady sprinkle of human habitation wherever I walked; after all, this is China with a population of well over a billion, and people and their homes are never far away. Down on the plains of Anhui, there were almost no thatched farmhouses left, but the traditional tiled-roof design still dominated in these nearby mountains. Scattered amongst the vestiges of olden times were more modern buildings in the standard early 21st-century design, which is two stories with a flat roof.

As I walked along, a man on a motorcycle passed me, then stopped and came back. He was Xu Hongsheng (Red Life Xu), a chemistry teacher at the Chashui High School from the nearby town of the same name. We talked for a while, and he invited me to visit the school the next day and speak to the students. I accepted gladly and asked what time I should arrive.

"Six o'clock." I groaned at the thought of getting up so early but agreed, and off he rode.

I passed a temple with a dog that growled angrily and wouldn't let me inside. Shortly after I heard a waterfall, which must have been massive from the roar of the water, but wasn't visible from the road. All the while, I gloried in the relative lack of litter along the roads, which was a big change from the plains where the edges are generally lined with rubbish.

The next day saw a gloomy, grey start in the depths of the mountains, but by 6am, there were hundreds of teenagers from farms and villages covering a wide area around Chashui standing before the main school building. Headmaster Chen, Teacher Xu and I watched three children raise the Chinese flag as the national anthem blared over the PA through sickening layers of karaoke-style reverb.

The students were wide-eyed at the sight of this non-Chinese person standing before them, the first they had ever seen in the flesh. One girl shyly approached the front and mumbled her way through an essay about the importance of the Beijing 2008 Olympics, scribbled on a sheet from an exercise book. The reverb was horrible; no one was listening.

I asked Teacher Xu if we could turn the reverb down. He went inside, and suddenly it was possible to vaguely understand what the girl was saying. I was up next with Teacher Xu introducing me to the gathering as a foreign friend walking to Tibet. He handed me the microphone, saying: "Tell them that learning Mandarin is important."

Okay.

So I introduced myself, the red flag of Communist China fluttering above me. "The Dabie Mountains are no longer isolated," I told the group, "You are now linked into the rest of China, and China is now linked into the rest of the world. Languages are the tools we use to bind the world together."

Warming to the topic, I continued: "You and I can communicate because I speak and understand Mandarin, and so do you. With Mandarin, you can communicate with anyone in China. And beyond its boundaries is the whole world. English is the language that works outside China. First, make sure your Mandarin is good and then learn English."

I spoke for fifteen minutes. It was quite a responsibility, representing the world in front of hundreds of people, many of whom had never stepped beyond the mountain valleys. I told them about the many positive changes I had seen in China over the decades; about how optimistic I am about the future of China; and about the constructive role China can play in the world. "The world needs China," I said, "And China needs the world."

The students dispersed to the classrooms, and I asked the headmaster if I could visit a class. He had no problem with it, so we went upstairs to the senior class.

"Good morning," I said in English as I stepped in front of the blackboard.

"Good morning!" the teenagers roared back, beaming with delight.

"Shall I speak in English or Chinese?" They decided on Chinese.

One student asked why I was walking across China, so I told him I have a problem with my leg and wanted to send a message to the heavens. Another asked what I thought of China: "It is a place that is changing rapidly and opening up and full of promise and potential." Another wondered what I thought of Chinese education and did I like the Dabie Mountains. Yet another asked me to tell the class the most amazing thing that had ever happened to me. My brain raced for a couple of seconds before coming up with: "There was a day in 1980 when I was a reporter and I was in the Great Hall of the People and I stood right next to Deng Xiaoping." I paused. "He was short."

I asked if the school had computers they could use, and the answer was that yes, there were a couple, but access was strictly controlled: 'Going online' is apparently not good. I decided to be subversive. I pulled out my laptop computer and said: "This computer is linked into the Internet right now, and I want to show you my homepage." I clicked on earnshaw. com, and the site came up really quickly, thanks to the wonders of wireless technology. The students were amazed.

I wrote the address for the site on the board and said: "On this site, you will find a link to send me an email. I want you all to send me emails, okay?" They declared as one that they would.

Back on the road, I walked along a steep gorge lined with waterfalls, then passed through a break in the ridge called Dragon's Pass. Once through, I found myself in a wide valley dotted with farms and fields, mostly planted with rice or rapeseed, a fast-growing plant with bright yellow flowers used to make canola oil. This was the Chashui High School's catchment area.

Passing by a small house with lines of gravestones at the front, I was invited in for a cup of tea by an old and balding gentleman named Zhang Zuhua, who turned out to be the engraver of the stones. I asked the sixty-five-year-old how much for a gravestone, and he told me about one hundred RMB in total, stone plus engraving. "It is a very seasonal business," he explained. "Things are busiest after the Qingming Festival." This traditional rite is celebrated on the one-hundred-and-fourth day after the winter solstice, which had just passed. Mr. Zhang said he made a few thousand RMB a year, which he said was more than enough to live on in his village. "I have five children, but I live alone and take no money from them," he added in a satisfied manner.

I left Mr. Zhang and continued walking, but about fifteen minutes later, I realized I had left my mobile phone in the engraver's house. "Not to worry," I thought and kept walking, knowing it would be safe with him. Sure enough, a short while later I was walking through a bamboo forest when a motorcycle roared up with Mr. Zhang on the back seat behind a young boy. "I found you!" he exclaimed. "You forgot your phone!"

Every turn in the road offered views of terraced fields, old Anhui-style farmhouses, streams tumbling through rocks, and a rich mixture of vegetation: pine trees amongst bamboo groves, streams tumbling through rocks; fields painted with purple flowers; and seas of rippling wheat, corn, rapeseed and vegetables. No rice yet, but the paddies were ever-present, many of them with ranks of ducks methodically hoovering their way through the mush with fast staccato slurps.

By lunchtime, I was walking into the town of Chashui, which was little more than a long main street with houses and little shops ranged along the dusty Highway 209. The fields lay directly behind the buildings, and sometimes between them.

In the centre of town, Teacher Xu's wife ran a small knick-knack shop with a photo studio in the back, where she wielded a pretty impressive Nikon film camera with a 35-105mm lens. She was taking some photos of local babies sitting in front of pictures of Hawaiian beaches, their legs splayed out.

Teacher Xu rode up on his motorcycle, and I told him how beautiful I found the countryside. Grasping the notion, he told me: "You should invest here."

"Interesting you should say that," I commented. "I was just thinking this morning, as I was walking along, that a small six-star boutique hotel in the middle of Dabieshan would be a good idea. Then the rich people of Shanghai could come and experience Anhui village life in luxury."

I invited him and Headmaster Chen to dinner that evening. We would meet at 5.30pm, and it would be my treat, to thank them for allowing me to visit the school. "See you then," he said, and roared off back to the school.

The road out of Chashui took me up a gentle valley towards mountain peaks to the west. On the road's right, terraced fields in decreasing arcs traversed the valley, with each arc covered by a complex series of wooden trellises. Two farmers were digging away at the earth under one of the trellises and I shouted hello. One of them shouted and waved back:

"Where are you from?" I said: "England," and added, "Pleased to meet you," before continuing up the road.

The valley ended, the forest began, and I passed a woman with a massive basket of brushwood that she had collected and was in the process of heaving onto her back. I took some photos of her as she managed this feat, and she laughed with glee. As I worked the camera, I became aware of a man sitting astride a stationary motorcycle up the hill a ways, waiting and watching. I walked up to him and he greeted me with: "Hi, I wanted to talk to you. I saw you down below. I was working in the field." Presumably he was one of the two men working under the trellises, but he had cleaned himself up. He asked what I was doing, and I offered him my mantra that I was walking to Tibet.

"It's so cool to do something like that," he said enviously. "Well, thank you," I replied, "You are very lucky to live in such a beautiful place with such lovely air."

The young man said he wanted to show me some medicinal melon seeds and other produce that he grew, expressing the hope that we could perhaps do some business together, and help sell his wares. I said I doubted it, but he was a smart and polite guy and he was reaching out, so I invited him to join the little dinner I was organizing with the school people. He said his name was Xu, Xu Bing (Soldier Xu), and that he was a graduate of the Chashui High School, but that he was not sure it was a good idea for him to come to my soiree. To this, I responded: "Don't worry about it. I am the host and you are welcome to join us." We agreed to meet in Chashui at around 6pm.

As I continued on, the walk was becoming more like a climb. I passed through a valley with an extremely impressive terraced field that appeared to be more a work of art, and the sun was at a wonderful angle, highlighting the terraces. I stopped to take photos, and a man and a woman appeared over a balcony behind me.

"When were these terraces built?" I asked, thinking perhaps the Song dynasty, eight hundred years ago.

"I don't know, they were here when I was born," the man responded. "Maybe in Chairman Mao's time?"

Taking this to mean "a long time ago", I went further up the hill. Magnificent views stretched out down to the left over terraced fields and the valley below, and, near a traditional farmhouse stretched along the road, a pretty young woman with a small child came towards me, with an old man following. He was wearing the kind of blue Mao jacket that was essentially the only attire for males thirty years ago, but is now nowhere to be seen in the cities.

"Come in and have some water," the woman said.

I readily agreed and was given a small bench seat near the door overlooking the valley. This would be where their family had sat for decades; a southern aspect, with a good view of the road in either direction.

The old man settled in next to me and I gave him my card, although I wasn't sure whether he could read. Illiteracy is prevalent in the mountains, particularly among the older generation. On this leg of the journey, I asked many people to write their names for me; while most below the age of thirty have had some degree of education, I sometimes find people even in their thirties and forties who cannot write their own name. But this old man could read, and he glanced at me when he saw my Chinese surname.

"Yan," he said in surprise.

"Yes," I said (my Chinese name is Yan Gewen). "And your name?"

He stood up and went inside for a moment, then emerged holding a small red passbook, an old people's benefits certificate. There was his surname, Xu, and his given name, Yan, the same character as my Chinese surname. It is a rare character, the name of a famous politician from the Warring Kingdoms period of Chinese history more than two thousand years ago, named Yanzi or Yan Ying, who is known for having been short of stature and smart of brain.

My Chinese surname was chosen for me by a teacher in Hong Kong the first day I started to learn Cantonese in 1973, while my full Chinese name was decided upon some years later by the kung fu novelist Louis Cha. I patted Xu Yan on the shoulder and said: "We are the Yan brothers." He smiled happily at the small coincidence.

Xu Yan was born in 1927 in this very house, and had lived here all his life. "So you were here when the Communists came?" He nodded. "Liberation," I said, to test his reaction. It is a word I usually strictly avoid due to its reference to the 1949 Communist victory. He shook his head, stating bleakly, "It was not a liberation."

Mr. Xu showed me round the house, which had a long dark corridor, mud brick walls, rooms with tiny windows, and rafters high above in the darkness strung with stored produce. Suspended from the roof over the main corridor was an entire room: the grain store. The kitchen was medieval in design, but everything was spotlessly clean and orderly. "How is the house in winter and summer?" I asked. "Cool in summer and cold in winter," Mr. Xu said, "But we wear lots of clothes to keep warm." To prove his point, he showed me that even on a spring day, he was wearing at least five layers including two sweaters.

We discussed the harvest. "Last year was good, but I don't know about this year," he said with the cautious pragmatism of the peasant.

As we chatted, a man rode up on a motorcycle and stopped outside the door. The bike had a big wicker basket on the back and he took off the cover, revealing dozens and dozens of tiny baby ducks.

"How much?" I asked as everyone from the house gathered around.

"Three RMB [$0.40] for a pair."

"Wow, that's cheap," I replied.

"No, expensive!" Xu Yan's family corrected me earnestly.

"Right, expensive!" I said quickly. "Outrageous!" I added to the duck seller.

I said goodbye to Xu Yan and his family and walked on accompanied by a man of around sixty who was a relative of Xu Yan's. "There is a small waterfall up here, come and have a look," he said.

As we walked slowly up the hill, I looked round and I saw Xu Yan coming up after us. I went down to meet him, and we, the Yan brothers, walked to the waterfall together arm in arm. He was really happy. We took a photograph together, both of us beaming.

CHAPTER 2

DRINKING GAMES

The day's walk was over and I returned to Chashui for dinner. I called Teacher Xu, who asked me to come to the school gates at 5.30pm. Arriving promptly, Teacher Xu led me inside to a conference room where I found a delegation of five men waiting for me, three of them in suits. Leading the delegation was Mr. Cheng Zhihua, secretary of the Qianshan County Communist Youth League, who looked about thirty-five years old. Accompanying him were his assistant, Mr. Huang, Teacher Xu and two vice-headmasters. Headmaster Chen, I was informed, was not available.

Mr. Cheng formally welcomed me to the mountains by saying, "This region is poor."

"I think it is very beautiful," I replied.

"We welcome people from all over the world," he responded, so I asked how many other foreigners had passed this way. "There was an African man from Cameroon a few years ago, but apart from that, you're the first foreigner to visit the region." I said it was my honour.

"We are looking for investment – investors – and maybe you would be interested?" he asked.

"I am just walking through," I replied. "I am not here looking for investments. But I do think the mountains are beautiful and there should be big potential for tourism in the long term."

"We think so too," he said. "There are several local hotel projects under construction, but not high class. There is no foreign investment in them."

I suggested they should be cautious about developing lower level hotel projects to avoid the kind of damage to the scenery and environment inflicted on other places such as the once-beautiful town of Guilin.

"Mr. Yan referred to a six-star hotel idea?" prompted Teacher Xu.

"I think such an idea would be great in theory, though in practice it would require a lot of patience and money and support from the local government. Outside investors are convinced about the future of China tourism, but the Dabie Mountains are very remote, and there would be a reluctance to invest."

"Thank you for your frankness," Mr. Cheng said. "Now it is time for dinner."

"My treat," I said. "Let us go to a local restaurant and have a simple meal."

"I have arranged dinner at the best restaurant in town, a banquet for two hundred and fifty RMB," Teacher Xu announced.

"Wow, two hundred and fifty RMB!" I said. "You have a Grand Hyatt here? I had dinner the other night for just forty RMB including beer."

"Only forty RMB? Impossible," Teacher Xu said.

"Our treat," Mr. Cheng pushed.

"No no," I said.

"Yes yes," they said.

It was the old Chinese banquet-hosting ploy of push and pull. I decided to cave in, even though it meant no dinner for Xu Bing. I sensed they had expected me to insist but I wasn't interested in playing their game – there were more people than planned, and two hundred and fifty RMB for a meal in Chashui was outrageous.

We drove off from the school and thirty seconds later we arrived at the local inn at which I had previously eaten for forty RMB and taken a room. We went upstairs and the toasting began. Everyone drank 'baijiu' (the Chinese spirit that's from eighty to one hundred and twenty proof and is usually made from sorghum grain), except for one of the vice-headmasters who gained my respect by bucking convention and drinking beer out of the baijiu shot glasses.

The drinking culture in China is fascinating. All the strengths and genius of Chinese culture are revealed within it, as well as a few of the shortcomings. But it's the strengths that predominate.

It is social manipulation on a scale and sophistication far beyond anything Western culture has developed. In the West everyone basically drinks alone. When a group of people gathers together to drink alcohol in Europe or the United States, they may clink glasses and say cheers once at the beginning, but after that each person drinks alone, sipping alcohol when they choose with no regard to what is happening around them. In China, no one drinks alone. Every time the glass is raised it is used to manipulate a relationship in some way. The aim is to toast each person around the table in turn, including a special look and a few words, which provides the chance for manipulation. Of course, as in the West, the aim is also to get drunk, but there's an added layer of social interaction that comes from thousands of years of perfecting the drinking culture. The West has a lot to learn from China in the 21st century.

My new friends were toasting each other like mad, and with each salutation a glass was drained. I chose to sip my drink, which drew disapproving glances. Teacher Xu was the worst, making a big point of wanting me to drain the glass each time. On principle I declined, telling him my drinking capacity was clearly no match for his. I can drink large quantities of baijiu when necessary – if it is an important dinner in an outlying province and it is necessary to gain the respect of my dinner companions – but I don't enjoy it, because a baijiu hangover is about the worst I have ever experienced. Actually, the only good thing that can be said about baijiu is that every glass tastes better than the last.

There was no way I wanted to become baijiu-drunk and have to sweat the stuff out the next day on the road.

"Mr. Yan is a cautious drinker, like myself," Mr. Cheng said, to head off Teacher Xu. He toasted me and we continued to sip the alcohol.

Still strictly business, Mr. Cheng said investors would be able to enjoy special tax breaks for several years, and tasked his assistant Mr. Huang to visit me in Shanghai to give me materials on investment policy and opportunities in the region but as soon as he realised that I was not going to invest in any of his proposals, he stood up suddenly and said that while it had been an honour to meet me and all that, he had to leave to get back to the county seat about fifty kilometres from Chashui.

"Stay with him for a while," he said to Teacher Xu as he left.

Teacher Xu, who I now noticed was pudgy and unfit at only twenty-nine years of age, continued to toast me, although he said at one point that he had drunk so much that if he drank much more he would explode. "That would be unfortunate," I said, but he kept up the toast rate, and began pushing the investment line in a self-serving way. "Your plan of a six-star hotel is excellent, but you will need assistance here, and a lot of help from the local government."

"I am sure that is true," I said. "But, remember, I am just walking through."

He said that being a teacher is very important and that while he'd had opportunities to develop his career outside the mountains, he had decided to work in the Chashui High School in order to help the local people.

"We play an important role, developing the patriotism of the students. Connections with the outside world are important, although I don't like Japanese people," he said.

This is a comment that always annoys me. "Why don't you like Japanese people?" I asked.

"Because of the way they treated China in the war."

"But it wasn't the Japanese of today, it was their grandfathers," I pointed out.

"Nanjing massacre... Yasukuni shrine..."

"This is all history and government policy," I said. "The British fought the Opium Wars with China. Do you think I should apologize to you for that?"

"Um, well, the Japanese government won't admit the errors of the past."

"That is the government. What has that got to do with the ordinary people? You think I support every policy of the British government because I hold a British passport? Should I blame you personally for the Chinese government's activities in Sudan?" I was warming to the theme. Bloody baijiu. "Your students deserve a balanced education. To condemn Japanese people in this way is to return to the mistakes of the Cultural Revolution. In those days, as you know, Teacher Xu, people were imprisoned and their lives ruined because they had a 'family background problem', meaning their grandfather had travelled abroad, or something equally irrelevant."

We eventually ended the impasse by agreeing that everyone in the world is equal.

Xu insisted on opening yet another bottle of beer, even though it was clear I didn't want it and he couldn't handle it. We drank half and then he said: "You should now go upstairs to rest." I insisted on going down to the door with him to see him off. "Really not necessary, you go and rest," he ordered me. "I am waiting for someone," I replied.

"Who is it?"

"Someone I met."

"I had better stay here and see him to make sure it is all right," he said, playing the role of the nosy official.

"Teacher Xu, I am grateful for your concern and good wishes, but I am an adult and I wish you a good night." I presented him with my hand to shake.

Xu Bing, damn him, chose that moment to arrive on his motorcycle and Teacher Xu went over and said a few words to him, then turned to me and said: "It's all right, I know him."

Teacher Xu disappeared into the night, and I smiled at Xu Bing and apologized. He brushed it aside. "Let's have a drink and a talk somewhere," I suggested. It was only 8pm but all was dark on the main street. Things close down early in a small Chinese mountain town. "Let's go upstairs."

The serving girl was unhappy because she wanted to leave. "One bottle of beer, two glasses, you go home, and I promise to turn out the light," I said. She seemed content with this deal.

Xu Bing and I talked for a couple of hours. He was a peasant boy, but the contrast between his simple open honesty and the selfishness of Teacher Xu was refreshing.

He was twenty-two years old and, following graduation from Chashui High School at the age of seventeen, he went to Shenzhen to work in a factory for two years. Then three years before our meeting, his mother died unexpectedly and Xu Bing's father had to undergo a heart operation. His younger sister was devastated, and he had to hurry back to look after everything. He nursed his father back to health, worked the fields and arranged for his sister to get a job in Shenzhen. His father, now better, was the man I saw working under the trellises in the fields that afternoon. "I have a girlfriend now," Xu Bing told me, "I expect to marry her one day, but I don't know when I will have enough money to manage it."

Xu Bing's excuse for talking to me was the medicinal melon seed idea he had brought up when we first met, but what he really wanted to talk about was life and responsibility and his father and his puzzlement about things in general. He expressed amazement at what he knew or guessed of my life and I gave him a pep talk, telling him how lucky he was in so many ways and how the secret to success is persistence. It was a pleasure to talk to him, to get to know him. He made me ashamed with some of his statements: "If I have some money and I spend it to buy some clothes for myself, I don't feel as good as when I am buying something for my father or my girlfriend," he said.

The next day, he would be back in the fields digging dirt, while I would be on the road and Teacher Xu would be in school. But in terms of being a human being, he was doing better than at least one of us.

It was raining when I set out in the morning, which was a big contrast from the sunny skies of the day before. I ran across the road from the inn to a little shop selling shoes and bought a pair of plastic Wellington boots for seventeen RMB (about two US dollars).

It was mostly light rain as I walked through the mist-coiled mountains that evoked classic Chinese scenes: layered ranks of mountain ranges, each one paler than the one in front, fading into a pearly glow.

Every corner I turned showed me something new and beautiful in its own way: an overhang of brilliant red flowers, or an Anhui farmhouse with chickens outside and an old woman sitting silently in the doorway, watching. Or maybe a view out over terraced paddy fields, or a three-wheeler scooter truck, with a couple of pigs in the back, churning black smoke into the sweet wet atmosphere.

I was pretty high up, about seven hundred metres above sea level according to my GPS unit, compared to three hundred metres for Chashui. At one point at about 11am, the rain turned into a storm and lightning flashed and the thunder clapped right above my head, then off to the left, then over to the right. As the rain cascaded down, I sloshed past a peasant house up on a rise, and a man called out: "Come up and have some water." I accepted his invitation with great relief.

His name was Feng Tianbei and he said he had seen me several days before on the road about thirty kilometres to the east. A rice farmer, he had two children aged twenty and eighteen, both studying in Beijing.

"But having two children was against the law then, right?" I asked.

"They didn't enforce the policy too strictly up here in the mountains," Mr. Feng said. "But nowadays people only want to have one. The girls won't agree to have more."

His children's studies were being financed by loans from the Industrial and Commercial Bank, which the children will be responsible for paying back once they graduate and start work. He invited me to sit on a special heated stool, which I found in all the peasant houses in this little corner of Anhui, and which I have never seen anywhere else. The circular, wooden stool has a semi-circular seat punctuated with two slit holes, while below is a metal brazier for coals – absolutely brilliant in its design.

Mr. Feng's wife was serving lunch, and I was invited to join them in their repast. I had some white rice, which Mr. Feng himself had grown, while they ate a full meal of meat and vegetables. "And how is your life?" I asked him. "We are poor," he responded, but then Anhui farmers always say that. I pointed to the richness of his life – the beauty of the scenery, the fresh air, fresh food. "The scenery is not beautiful," his wife said, adding: "This house is awful." She was right – the house was pretty awful. There were holes in the walls and holes in the roof. It was nowhere near as nice as Xu Yan's house.

I asked about electricity, which had arrived in the region in about 1991 (the phone service was installed in 2001). They had a black-and-white television, but no refrigerator. "We grow our own food," Mr. Feng said. "And if I had the money, I would build a new house," which he said would cost him around seventy thousand RMB (US$8,000). My impression was that most of the ordinary farmers in this region of Anhui Province have an income of somewhere between one hundred and three hundred RMB a month, which seemed to be enough to live a basic life.

The rain stopped and I walked on to the little town of Nishui. Xu Bing had said he would come out to see me on the road before Nishui, but he hadn't showed up, which given the heavy rain was understandable.

There is not much to say about Nishui. It is just another one-pig town, but it does have a little 'supermarket' which had its lights off to save electricity. I bought some batteries and chatted with the owner, asking him which products sell the best. "Milk powder for babies," he said. "But mother's milk is better, right?" I said with a smile. He didn't respond. I directed the question again to a lady in her early thirties sitting by the door. She shook her head strongly in disagreement. The shadow of sore nipples hung in the air for a second, and I thought that with luck the milk powder on sale in Nishui was actually real, as opposed to the stuff that killed forty babies in Henan Province the year before.

On the outskirts of town, I saw a faded slogan painted on the wall over a small shop that said: 'No matter how tough it gets, don't make it tough for the children'. Got to agree with that! The standard of rural slogans has changed dramatically, and for the better, since I first came into contact with them in the 1970s when the walls of villages used to be plastered with phrases like 'Long live the Great, Glorious and Correct Communist Party' and 'Long live Mao Zedong Thought'. Now the predominant slogans are for birth control or promotional lines for motorcycles and mosquito coils ('One Spot Red' is the main mosquito coil brand in this part of Anhui, with the character for Spot written on a red spot. It looked cool on the brown mud-brick walls).

I went up to the counter of the little shop, which measured about two metres by one metre, where a man with a big smile sat behind a counter stocked with fruit, nuts and seeds. Behind him were shelves loaded with alcohol, cigarettes, instant noodles, soft drinks and various simple and cheap household goods. His name was Mr. Jiang, and he was slightly drunk and chain-smoking, but gentle and courteous with the few customers who came up and bought things as we talked. He invited me to sit on a stool behind the counter and for a while I looked out at the world from his perspective.

When Mr. Jiang was ten years old, his left foot caught an infection which then spread up his leg. His mother thought he would die, and she introduced him to smoking cigarettes to ease the pain. He didn't die, but his leg was ruined. "I have been smoking ever since… it's been twenty-six years," he said as he looked out at the muddy street. He had a wooden crutch even more basic than Long John Silver's, but told me walking was painful for him and that he didn't go very far very often. "But I hobble two kilometres to my parents' house twice a month." His father was seventy years old and his mother was in her late sixties.

"I have a problem with my leg too," I said. Mr. Jiang pulled up his trouser leg and showed me the withered useless appendage, covered in purple blotches, with a handkerchief wrapped around the top of his painfully skinny thigh.

"I still have pus coming out of it," he said. "It hurts a lot." Painkillers?

"I have tried them, but they have no effect." I showed him my right leg, which by comparison was in great shape.

Chatting about his business, he said he did about six hundred RMB in revenue a month or twenty RMB a day, and turned a profit of about one hundred RMB. Jiang slept on a bed space behind the shelf next to a small black-and-white television that was his only source of entertainment. He said there was no hope of any improvement in his life, no hope of marriage or of children.

I looked around for something to buy. "Which is better, the apples or the pears?" I asked.

"It depends what you like. The pears are pretty juicy."

"I'll have a pear," I said. "How much?"

"A gift to you," he said.

"I won't take it if it is free," I said.

"I won't give it to you if you pay."

We looked at each other and smiled. Of course, I let him win. He pulled out a penknife, peeled the pear and handed it to me. It was delicious.

I bade farewell to Mr. Jiang and walked on through the afternoon. The rain had stopped, but the road ascended back into the mountains and everything was soon covered with a thick mist. By 5pm, it was time to end the walk because I could see nothing in the mist and there was no one to talk to.

The next morning was dry, but cloudy. I started out from the last place I had stopped, enjoying the sounds and smells and sights and looking for a place to sit where I could write out my notes on the past couple of days. The birds were calling, the air was sweet after all the recent rain, and the mountain views down into valleys filled with terraced fields and toy farmhouses were spectacular. The bamboo and pine mix of vegetation that enraptured generations of classical Chinese poets and artists captured my heart as well. I sat down on a road marker in the midst of this nature wonderland and started to write.

Along the road came a man who, when he saw me, mooed in the way

I had learned many mutes do. He was dirty, his eyes were askew, his brain was damaged, but he recognized me as someone different, an outsider, and he was amazed and excited. It seemed there were quite a few mentally impaired people walking the mountain roads, as I was coming upon at least four or five per day. Following a couple of little incidents, I had learned to tell the difference between the dangerous and the harmless. This man was harmless, but he could say nothing, and there was nothing I could say to him in any language that he could understand. I smiled at him and tried to find a way to wordlessly express something positive. He mooed again, did a sort of a jig in excitement and then tore himself away from the engagement and walked on.

I resumed my writing, but a few minutes later I had a couple of salt-of-the-earth farm labourers inspecting my camera and asking where I came from. A few more people appeared, including a father and his son. The mute came back. It was becoming a town hall meeting, so I stood up and we all walked off along the road, the people gradually peeling off into the fields. Finally, the only people left were myself and the mute.

We passed a farmhouse with noisy chickens presumably in the process of laying the free-est of free-range eggs. Then the mute started mooing urgently and pointing to a path off the road. I shook my head to indicate I was staying on the road, and he headed off down the path by himself.

I stood and thought about it for a minute. The road was winding and twisting but perhaps he was trying to tell me it was a shortcut down to the road at a lower level. I decided to trust him and left the main road to head down the little path.

It was the right call. I found myself at the top of a peaceful valley, bordered by lush forest cover, every inch in between organized into neat paddy fields. They were ploughed and waiting, this being only mid-April. There was a babbling brook and a small path beside it leading downwards. The mute was now far below, but he turned and saw me in the distance and mooed, presumably acknowledging the fact that I was not as stupid as I had appeared when I at first rejected his guidance.

A kilometre or so down the valley, I came back to the road, which led me across a bridge where I took photographs, including some of a boy riding on the back of his bike, his hands stretched out around the seat to the handlebars. A little further along, as I stood entranced by a perfect wooded and terraced hill amidst the paddy fields, a boy came up to me accompanied by a couple of his friends. They were all surnamed Chu, and all lived in a collection of houses about two hundred metres up the gentle slope, looking out across the fields towards my favourite hill. The people working in the fields were their parents and relatives.

The boys said "Good morning."

"What else can you say in English?" I asked and they parroted the phrases "how do you do?" and "thank you". The boy on the bike answered all questions with the word "yes". One of the men in the fields shouted to the boys, asking who I was. "He's English!" they shouted back. I turned and shouted as well. "Your sons are very smart! Congratulations!"

One of the men laughed and shouted back: "Okay!"

I said goodbye and walked on, but another ten minutes later they all came tearing after me again. They wanted me to take a photo with them and for us to exchange names. They invited me to one of their homes for a meal. I said I was honoured, but I would continue to walk (I could easily have had three or four meals a day for free from these hospitable people in one of China's poorest regions).

They had a quick discussion, then said: "Well, can we walk with you?" I said, "Sure!" and as we walked, we talked about all kinds of things. I asked them about their little village.

"Everyone is surnamed Chu," said Chu Jun (Army Chu), aged fourteen. "People have sons, and the sons marry and the families divide up, but we all stay together."

"What about the daughters?"

"They usually get married and move away, but they sometimes come back and visit their parents."

"How many people altogether?"

"About twenty to twenty-five families."

"You go to school?"

"Yes. Junior high school. The school is terrible."

"What will you do when you graduate?"

"Go to university!" said Chu Bingbing (Soldier Soldier Chu), aged fifteen.

"And then?"

"Find work outside."

"You won't come back to live here?"

"No," he said.

"Then who will work the fields?" I asked.

"Our parents."

"Well, not forever. Right?"

"Er, right." He thought about it for a second. "Well, maybe we could hire people to work the fields."

"Or we could sell the fields," added Chu Jun.

What was interesting is that the only possibility not considered by the boys was working the land themselves. This was the shift in China's population from the country to the cities in action, at its most basic level.

Two other boys joined us from the fields: Chu Kui, aged fourteen but looking more like eight, and Liu Da, aged maybe six and who was too shy to talk to me but bounced around me the whole time listening to the conversation while playing Tetris on a small hand-held machine. "He's introverted," Chu Jun explained.

They asked me lots of questions too. "Are there fields in England? What do English people do with the bodies of dead people? What religion are you?" I told the boys I had no religion.

"But what religion do other people in England have?"

"Many people in England are Christian," I said. "How about you?"

"I guess we are Buddhists," said Chu Jun.

"I like Buddhism," I said. "It is peaceful."

Chu Jun pointed to diminutive Chu Kui. "His father is a Taoist priest."

"Taoism! I like that as well," I said.

I recited the first three words of the Taoist canon, the Daodejing: "Dao ke dao (the way that can be followed...)"

Chu Jun completed the phrase. "Feichang dao (...is not the true way)."

"Ming ke ming," I continued (the name that can be named...).

"Feichang ming (...is not the true name)," Chu Jun completed the couplet.

"What's the next line?" I said. "I can't remember it."

"I can't remember either," he said, and we both smiled.

We were walking down a hill, and on the slope ahead of us on the right, placed by the heavens with perfect timing, was a shrine. It was small and simple, with walls painted white and a peaked tiled roof. Over the door were four characters: 'Whatever you ask for, there will be a response (you qiu bi ying)'.

"There used to be a vicious dog guarding it, so you couldn't go in, but the dog has gone," Chu Jun said.

We walked up the steep steps and went inside. There were two circular straw mats on the floor in front of a shelf on which were placed three statues of the Buddha in different incarnations, with an incense burner in front of them.

"Do you want to pay your respects to Buddha?" Chu Jun asked me.

I said yes. He pulled a couple of sticks of incense from a box by the burner, lit them, and handed one to me. We knelt down together. "Now make a request," he said to me as Liu Da continued battling the Tetris blocks beside us. I made one and Chu Jun took my incense stick and placed both sticks into the incense ash in the burner. We went back outside into the sunlight, with the wide valley laid out below. I felt good.

CHAPTER 3

ANHUI IN MAY

At Yuexi, the most westerly town of any significance in southwest Anhui, I was faced with the prospect of returning to Highway 318, which starts in Shanghai and goes west all the way through to Lhasa. On occasion, I walked along the highway, but I much prefer mountain country roads, and I was concerned about returning to the busy thoroughfare.

To my great delight, however, the section of Highway 318 west of Yuexi was far more like a country lane than a highway. The road wound picturesquely up and down mountains and valleys, one macadamized lane in each direction, fading at the edges into soft shoulders where paddies and chickens, pine and bamboo forests, children and farmers all interfaced with this tenuous link to the outside world. One of the reasons this stretch of 318 was so quiet was that there was a new expressway away to the south, raising a pleasant prospect: the construction of China's national expressway network is simultaneously creating a national network of backwater country lanes.

I stopped at a small 'doctor's surgery' – a simple hut with 'Doctor' Wang in attendance. There was a woman of about thirty years of age lying on a sofa with a drip stand beside her, a needle stuck in her arm. I asked her why she was on a drip, and she said: "I've not been feeling too well." The way she said it suggested to me that she was not sick at all and that the drip of, presumably, glucose was just a pick-me-up. "How much for the bottle?" I asked. "A few RMB," she shrugged.

The next day I met a doctor who had two 'drip stations' in his small country clinic. It was all a bit ominous: Are Chinese people becoming addicted to indiscriminately prescribed and administered intravenous drips?

I continued on, walking a road that tended gradually higher and followed a broad valley west of Yuexi, with a rank of magnificent peaks on the left guarding the heart of the most inaccessible and scenic parts of the Dabie Mountains. I passed through one village where two men virtually accosted me in the mistaken belief that I was a journalist. They wanted me to write an article about what they described as the outrageous conduct of the local officials who they said had promised to pay compensation cash for flood damage and then had never handed over the money. "We are poor," said one of the men, just as his mobile phone rang.

"You don't look so poor to me," I said.

"There are people who are much poorer in the mountains," interjected a woman who had joined the group, undercutting the man's argument.

A little further along, I stopped at a small shop to buy a bottle of water, a regular excuse of mine to start a conversation, and chatted to a group of six girls, all aged about ten years old, plus a younger boy. They told me they all went to the local primary school, and I asked them all to write down their names for me, which they did.

This part of Anhui had lots of slogans on the farmhouse walls stating pro-female themes such as: 'Daughters are Descendants Too'; ' Daughter is as Good as a Son'; 'Look After the Girls'; and 'Reduce Infant Mortality Rates'. Their purpose, of course, was an attempt to halt female infanticide, which was an issue in places such as rural Anhui in the desperate days of the 1980s when the government was vigorously pushing through the one-child policy. The policy now is one child only if the first-born is a boy, two if the first-born is a girl, and I have the sense that the days of forced abortions and female infanticide are, thankfully, over.

Judging by the places I walked through, China's rural population has stabilized and in some areas is falling rapidly due to the shift from big to small families and the movement of people into the cities. Every family I met seemed to have at least one son or daughter working in Qingdao or Shenzhen or Ningbo.

I met a sixty-nine-year-old man who looked after a village temple and I wondered who would take his place when he eventually went to meet Buddha. When I later visited the home of one of the Chu boys, who I'd met in a village near Nishui, I found his father was away on business until the end of the year and his mother was helping an uncle with planting, while Chu Bingbing (Soldier Soldier Chu), an only child of fifteen, had been left in the huge, dark farmhouse all alone. One of his relatives told me that in the past the Chu family had split away, with brothers setting up new houses in nearby valleys. "So will the next generation divide up in the same way?" I asked. The man laughed and shook his head. "The next generation? With the number of children in this generation, there will be no splitting up any more."

About ten kilometres west of Yuexi, I met an old peasant as he stepped out of the fields holding a basket full of rice seedlings he had just picked for replanting later in the day. He had a pair of rubber boots and heel-less socks in his other hand and I offered to help him carry the seedlings basket. He shook his head.

Chu Nansheng was seventy-one years old and he told me he had five children. As we walked together, it soon became clear to me that he was somewhat drunk. Not so much drunk, perhaps, as floating gently in a mild alcoholic haze.

It may be that a relatively high proportion of males in the rural 'real China' are drunk much of the time – baijiu is cheap, the farming life is often monotonous and having a bit of a buzz is not going to have much of a negative impact on work performance in the paddy fields.

Walking through rural China, you see that it's not religion that is the opiate of the people – it's baijiu among the adults, and television among the children. I almost always saw the television on and images from other worlds beaming in through the satellite dish. The children sat transfixed in front of the screen for hours on end, learning about life from Hong Kong gangster movies and low-grade Chinese television dramas while outside the authentic drama is unfolding in the fields and streams, amongst the people and their chickens, ducks and pigs.

While I am willing to admit that television is not inherently bad, and can provide valuable exposure to all kinds of knowledge, the quality of what is shown on most Chinese channels is usually awful. The children can read – the spread of basic education throughout rural China is one of the great triumphs of the past thirty years – but they don't read much. At least, I saw no sign of books visible in the houses I visited.

But back to peasant Chu Nansheng, slightly drunk and very hospitable: he led me off the road down a dirt path, over a little brook, past two houses and into his courtyard. A woman, one of his daughters-in-law, was there with a child in one arm and some crunchy rice cakes in the other. She offered me one and it was delicious, reminding me of the brown burnt bits at the edge of an English rice pudding made by my mum. Peasant Chu was missing several teeth, had bristly grey hair, bloodshot eyes and a cigarette hanging out of his mouth. He invited me into his room, which was on one side of the courtyard, and sat me down by the door while he went into the kitchen and brought out an enamel cup inscribed with the name of a distant state factory and the year 1992. He rinsed it out, threw the water out of the door, and offered me a tin of tea leaves. "You pick some out, my hands are filthy," he said. So I made myself a cup of tea and, as he squatted down outside the door and sorted the seedlings, we talked.

He told me he had lived in the village all his life and was admitted into the Communist Party in the 1980s, adding that he was one of fifty party members in the district. He also said he had three sons and two daughters.

"Against the regulations," I said.

"Not by so much," he replied. "Premier Zhou Enlai said 'one is too few, two is good and three is a little too many.' Plus if you have daughters there is more flexibility." He came into the kitchen and showed me faded photographs of his children in a small photo album, the same as any kept by parents and grandparents all over the world. One of his sons, he said proudly, was one hundred and ninety centimetres tall. One photo showed a son posing with a pretty wife and a little girl well on the way to becoming pudgy, the result of city living. In contrast, the village children I met were all trim and in pretty good shape. No obesity (yet), and some were amazingly agile, leaping from bridges or running straight up mud banks. The children of rural China eat plenty of vegetables and meat – simple, basic food and not high quality – cooked on stoves that are often medieval in design. But in terms of a healthy, balanced diet, the average Anhui village child may now be ahead, in health at least, of his or her cousins in the coastal cities.

Peasant Chu showed me a document from the local party secretary naming him as a model comrade. "The young people don't understand the history of it any more," said another old man who had dropped in to check out the foreigner.

Chu then wrote out an inscription for me: "The state depends on the people, the people depend on food." That's true, I thought: The cities depend upon Peasant Chu. The farmers sell their rice, and sometimes their pigs and ducks, to wholesale traders in the closest towns and, from what I could tell, the buyers were now mostly private companies, not state-run monopolies as had traditionally been the case. The farmers only sell their excess, so they have the choice of not selling if the price isn't right.

Leaving the elderly gentlemen, I strolled back to the road, which then arched up steeply towards the head of the valley. The sun was now shining brightly, the rice terraces magnificent in design and well prepared to accept the rice seedlings that were being planted all around me. The road became a series of twisting hairpins, back and forth and back again, edging up the steep mountainside towards a break in the ridge, which was surely... I puffed... up there... somewhere.

Pine trees became more prevalent, but the rice terraces were just as packed into every inch of land with terrace walls now sometimes two metres high to cope with the steep grade of the slope. It was a tough climb from Yuexi (at three hundred and twenty metres above sea level) to the top of the rise at six hundred and eighty metres, but the view back down the valley, all the way to Yuexi in the far distance, was stunning. It was also a first for me, in that I could look across an entire day's walk, from start to finish, and spot the places I had been from a new three-dimensional elevation.

I walked through the gap in the ridge and immediately felt a difference. Crossing a ridge can really provide perspective as there's a different quality to the light, the air, the sounds and probably the vegetation (if I had been looking at things with the eye of a botanist).

The next day I returned early to the commanding point at the head of the Yuexi valley hoping for some of that 'cloud-sea' action that stirs photographers' blood. And there it was, the long valley blanketed with clearly differentiated layers and banks of mist. Charming. If only my photographic skills had been up to capturing it properly.

After the long uphill walk the previous day, this morning was all downhill. The Chinese proverb – uphill is easy, downhill is hard – may make sense as a metaphor for success and failure, but as a practical fact, it is definitely incorrect. I stopped and talked with a man on a motorcycle who I had seen the day before. His surname was Chu (no surprise there) and he had a pile of bedsheets in lurid colours, plus piles of trousers and other clothes. Chu Tianting, a modern-day tinker, said he lived in Yuexi and travelled each day through the valleys selling his wares.

I also spent some time sitting with Doctor Han Jixin, who had manned the same simple country clinic since 1970. His workplace was like a miniature piece of the Cultural Revolution captured in a *China*

Reconstructs magazine article from 1972 and preserved in a time warp. For example, on the wall of the main room of the clinic was a massive poster of a very healthy-looking Chairman Mao.

Doctor Han was a holdover of the concept of that era's 'barefoot doctors', who were trumpeted as the answer to mass rural medical needs, just as acupuncture was then lauded as the answer to all ailments – better than nothing at all, I suppose. But Yuexi, only twenty kilometres away, now has a large hospital, the biggest building in town, for patients who need more than an intravenous glucose drip.

Doctor Han administered both Chinese and Western medicines, and had a large apothecary next to the clinic's main room, complete with an impressive number of built-in drawers, each carefully marked with its contents. He said his patients – the local peasantry – pay two RMB per visit, plus the cost of the medicine. He showed me the bill on the top of the pile and it was for two RMB plus twenty-one fifty for medicine. "Do your patients usually want Western or Chinese medicine?" I asked. "More and more want Western medicine," he said, "Although the older people still believe in and ask for the Chinese medicines." Like the other doctors I met, Doctor Han had two intravenous drip stations set up, but all was quiet this Sunday morning: no peasants lying down with needles in their arms.

The walk in the sunshine was gorgeous. There was a stream accompanying me almost the whole way, its banks lined with rice terraces and farmhouses in strategic locations, as if the buildings were guarding the fields. From each farm's placement, I could tell which fields they 'controlled'. Many faced out proprietarily over a bank of terraces below or stood defensively in front of ranks of terraces heading up the hill behind. I passed a group of men using rocks to re-build a rice terrace wall down a fast-moving section of the stream. They stopped to look at me and I gave them a thumbs-up sign. They waved in response – contact made! – and I shouted: "You are working hard!"

"Okay!" one shouted back in English, clearly a well-known word.

A little further on I saw a little girl standing on a terrace wall while some people worked nearby in the field. I took a photo of her and said hello, but the poor thing burst into tears. Two other youngsters came up to comfort her, and I tried to make friendly expressions but a woman arrived on the scene and asked sharply: "What are you doing?"

"Sorry, I was taking her photograph."

"Why?"

"Because she is pretty."

The woman's expression changed to a smile.

"Are you her mother?"

"Yes."

"I could tell," I said.

The girl was still sniffling, but her first contact with a foreigner was over, and it hadn't been too painful.

In this part of Anhui, the pigsties were more luxurious than any I had seen. They typically had a front yard, a house and a pond. All small of course, and nothing compared to the idyllic life P.G. Wodehouse created for Lord Emsworth's prize pig, the Empress of Blandings, but overall it seemed to be a pretty ideal situation, at least until the animal's inevitable fate. One example of porcine accommodation was nestled next to a hill and had a cave dug into the hillside for the pig to sleep in and while away the day. Just then, a few children came up to me and I tried asking them about the sty's resident, but they were very shy so I said goodbye and walked on. But within a minute or so, they ran up and said: "There's a temple down the hill, would you like to visit it?"

I followed them down a path to a relatively large old-style village temple that had obviously been constructed in the recent past and had white walls and grey ornamental flourishes on the roof. The temple's courtyard was quiet and cold. There was no incense burning in the brazier in front of the altar, but several long and burning incense coils in the shape of bells curled down from the rafters, emitting thick streams of smoke into the still air.

Five Buddhas graced the altar, the centre deity being of black stone and clothed in heavy yellow robes. Five circular straw mats were placed in front of the altar: a table nearby with incense, candles, and a bamboo cup with *I Ching* sticks and wooden blocks for fortune telling. The children raced through the courtyard and knocked on a side door, and out came the temple's old caretaker, Mr Liu, aged sixty-nine. He told me the temple was twenty-three years old: "There was another temple here before, built in the Qing dynasty. But it was destroyed and levelled during the Cultural Revolution. Then it was rebuilt."

"Why was it destroyed?" I asked.

"Chairman Mao said to destroy old things," he said.

"Was it outsiders or local people who destroyed the temple?"

"Local people," Mr. Liu said, and looked down, the pain of dealing with the consequences of that destruction still painfully obvious in his expression. I asked if there was anything rescued from the old temple and he pointed to a huge calligraphy board suspended high on the wall next to the altar. It was faded, but in the strong, proud calligraphy of olden times, it stated clearly: "Buddha's Law knows no limits".

"It is dated the fourteenth year of the republic (1925), so let's see, that's thirteen years before I was born," Mr. Liu said.

"I should clean up," he added and grabbed a broom and started to sweep the floor. I took some pictures and asked if I could pay my respects to Buddha. "So you know about our customs?" he asked.

"I am learning. Can you teach me?"

He went inside and came out with a small plastic transistor radio-like device. It was coloured brown, with the character for Buddha stamped on the plastic. He turned it on and it started warbling the 'amitofo' chant that is the most basic part of the Chinese Buddhist ritual. Actually, blaring would be a better word to describe the raucous noise that obliterated the peace of the place. I prepared some money in my pocket – twenty-five RMB – and pulled a small incense stick out of the box on the table. Mr Liu stopped me and walked over to a side table and brought back a pack of three thick incense sticks. He lit two candles on the altar table as the children sang along with the amitofo song, burned the plastic covering off the incense sticks and handed them to me. He taught me how to place the sticks between my hands and bow three times to Buddha.

I took some more photos of the incense coils and started to leave, but Mr. Liu became agitated. "You must give some donation," he said anxiously. Damn. I had forgotten, so I pulled the money out and placed it on the table next to the *I Ching* sticks. I don't think he wanted the money; rather, I'm sure he felt that Buddha would not respond favourably unless money was handed over (Buddha in the Chinese context totally understands the concept of capitalism).

I had arranged to visit another of the Chu boys, at the bridge where I had first made contact with the Chu children. He and the other boys, plus a little girl, led me off the road and across a stream, using five stepping stones to cross the water. I handed my camera to one of the boys to take across as I'm not the steadiest of people on my feet, and leather boots are not ideal for fording streams.

We went over the stream, along a path, then into a small cluster of mud brick houses, right at the foot of the perfect little hill I had first spotted. The simple, poor homes had pigsties and cow pens, and chickens and ducks running around. We went through a doorway, plastered on all sides with colourful New Year couplets, and into the kitchen, which had a packed dirt floor, an old wood-burning brick stove and an old calendar featuring Deng Xiaoping on the wall. All was dark inside: the windows were tiny and broken and were boarded up to keep the warmth inside. Chu Jun's mother came out to greet me, plump and jolly with a big smile. I walked through to a large room beyond the kitchen, which had a double bed and a television. "Who sleeps here?" I asked.

"I do," said Chu Jun.

"Just you?"

"Yes."

Wow. He turned on the television and all the children stopped talking and ignored me in favour of the show, a costume drama. It seemed to me that the story and the characters were irrelevant and that the children were just staring at the screen out of habit. I sat there for a minute and then asked Chu Jun if he would go outside with me and explain the fields. He pointed out who owned which field, including a small fish farm on the right. His family's fields were on the other side of the small valley. "What's the name of the stream?" I asked.

"It doesn't have a name."

"How about the cows and the pigs, do you have names for them?" No.

He pointed to a tiny figure working in a field. "That is my father," he said and then called him over. He was a thin man who looked about forty years old, and together we went back inside the family home. He offered me beer and baijiu and of course, I asked for the beer and he poured it into two cups inscribed in English with the words 'Cuddly Bear'.

"How is the harvest?" I asked.

"We are poor."

"You seem to have the basics," I replied, looking around. "Food, shelter, electricity, baijiu… Chu Jun is smart, I hope he does well in the future."

"We could use your help on that."

"Well, we must keep in touch," I said.

He said he planned to pull down his house later this year and build a new one. "Good idea," I said. The house was not in good condition.

There was a shout from across the fields and Chu Jun's father shouted in reply. "That's my elder brother, he wants me to go and help him," and with that, he shot out of the door and I saw no more of him.

"Chu Yuehua wants you to go to his house," said Chu Jun, so I gave a bag of fruit to Chu Jun's mother as a parting present, said goodbye, and we walked back across the stream and up a hill to a much larger house of the same design. We passed a new two-storey red brick house under construction, and I asked Chu Jun about the difference between the new and old houses. "The old ones sometimes collapse after heavy rain," he said after some thought. "Are there any good things about the old houses?" I asked. "They don't cost anything to rebuild," he replied.

Chu Yuehua's father was clearly unhappy about being called out of the fields, but he came at his son's bidding to meet the foreigner and we sat in a clean living room with a poster of Chairman Mao waving in front of a modern, multi-storey building in Shanghai that was built at least two decades after his death. The wonders of Photoshop provide a brilliant way of keeping Mao current for today's farmers.

Chu Yuehua's aunt appeared and asked who I was, but before I could respond she asked: "You want to buy my necklace and bracelet? Real ivory." I said no.

"I bought them last year from a man who went to Africa."

I asked how much she had paid and she said two thousand RMB. She took off the necklace to show me. The beads were uneven and unlikely to be plastic.

"Poor elephant," I said.

"They were bought in a shop," she pointed out.

The children and I travelled even further up the hill to Chu Bingbing's house, which was huge and empty with chickens and ducklings in separate baskets outside the house in the courtyard. It was exactly the same design as Xu Yan's traditional farmhouse, with a long internal corridor, a grain store suspended under the roof, and the kitchen at the back of the house.

We sat in the living room, bags of food suspended from the roof and walls, but we had little to say: I had run out of questions and they had no questions to ask me. The small group fidgeted, unsure of what to do next, so I gave them name cards and told them to send me emails or text messages and to contact me when they went to Shanghai. The aim was to put the onus on them to take a step, to reach out beyond the glow of their television sets.

"Will we meet again?" asked Chu Jun.

"Send me an email," I said.

CHAPTER 4

A Peasant's Life

As I descended further from the ridge, the slopes of the valleys became more gradual, with more acreage devoted to larger paddy fields that were now planted with small rice seedlings growing quietly in the rich muddy water.

I arrived at Laipeng, which is a town larger and more compact than Chashui, though much smaller than Yuexi. It was arranged in the shape of a 'T' along the road and then along the banks of a significant and rock-filled stream course that hit the road at a right angle. There were two mobile phone network pylons on facing hills above the town, and the main street ran down quite steeply to the stream. I saw a woman washing clothes in a trickle of water, but the dimensions of the watercourse indicated that when in flood, it would be a large and fast-running river.

The road I took passed a number of farmhouse compounds, all with large and imposing mud-brick gateways set at an angle to the road and raised up several steps. The valley widened out and on the hillside opposite, beyond the stream, I saw a farmhouse sporting a slogan from the Cultural Revolution, the first I had seen in the seven hundred kilometres from Shanghai: 'zili gengsheng, jianku fendou!' – Self-Reliance and Struggle!

– with the required exclamation mark there, too. This phrase used to be plastered on walls all over China to make Chinese people feel better about the fact that their country had no allies except for Albania and North Korea. To come across this slogan now was like unexpectedly meeting an old friend.

I walked into the little village of Huadeng (Flower Lantern). It was very hot and the sky was a burning blue above. I was having a conversation with some locals about the weather (I was, after all, born in England) when a tiny mini-van pulled up in front of me, with a police light on the top. Given the size of the van, I was amazed when five men piled out of it, three of them in uniform. The shortest of the uniformed men walked up to me, fumbling with his wallet to pull out his identification card. I said hello and smiled.

"So you speak Chinese?"

I nodded. He held a plastic card right up close to my face.

"This indicates my identity," he said.

"It does," I replied.

"What are you doing here?"

"I came to have a look."

"Where did you come from?"

"Yuexi."

"Yuexi?"

"Right."

"When did you enter China?" he asked.

"I live in Shanghai."

"So how long have you lived in China?"

"Many years."

"Can I see your documents?"

I handed him my passport. They looked at all the visa stamps and the young leader exclaimed in surprise: "When you visit a place in China, you must first get permission from the local Public Security Bureau. Do you know that?"

"You mean this is a closed area?" I asked.

"You need to get permission. Do you understand what I am saying?"

"So the concept of closed and open areas – is that still used in China?"

"You need to get permission from the Public Security Bureau when you go to various areas."

He gestured for me to move to the side of the road. I moved half a step in deference to the uniform then got into chatting mode with him, saying: "So let's see. In the 1970s, this area was closed, right? In the 1980s, some parts of China were open and some were not open. But this is now the 21st century. Right?"

"You need to get permission, do you understand?" he repeated.

It seemed pretty ridiculous to me. The road I was walking along was identified on the map as National Highway 318.

"So is this a closed area?" I persisted.

He dodged the question. "Where are you going to stay tonight?"

"In Yuexi, at the state-run Dabieshan Guest House."

"Wherever you stay, you must register with the Public Security Bureau," he told me. Registering at a hotel is a legally accepted equivalent for registering with the Public Security Bureau. "You cannot stay overnight anywhere without registering."

He was on reasonably solid ground with this point. I agreed, and he handed back my passport. "Where are you going now?" he asked.

"I will continue along the road. This is such a beautiful area," I beamed. I held out my hand to him and he shook it. "Shall we all walk together?"

They clambered back into the little van, which sped off and I saw no more of them.

Beyond Huadeng, two streams met and then headed off together southwards. The road passed over a large arched bridge at the confluence, and then headed slowly back up in elevation along a valley. The fields were wide; the cloudless sky was even wider. Many farmers were out in the fields completing the rice planting and I stopped to take some photographs of two men methodically planting the seedlings. The closest one glanced up and saw me. I said hello.

"Hello," he said back, smiling and open.

"It looks like hard work," I observed.

"Come in and try it," he replied.

Well, how could I say no? A small group of people gathered by the roadside as I walked along the narrow path between the paddies, and took off my socks and shoes and shirt. I rolled the camera and my wallet into the middle of the package, rolled up my trousers and plunged in.

The mud was warm and thick and much deeper than I had expected, and I wobbled in surprise, but managed to avoid toppling over. The young man, Mr. Wang, who I noticed had a mobile phone on his belt, came over and handed me a small sheaf of seedlings tied with a sliver of bamboo. He pointed out the tramlines – absolutely straight single rows of seedlings planted along the whole length of the paddy about a metre and a half apart to guide the rest of the planting work.

"Plant five seedlings across between the tramlines. The seedlings should be equidistant, left and right and up and down," Mr. Wang said, guiding me.

I pulled a seedling out of the bunch and found it tricky to not rip out the delicate roots as I did so. Then I stuck it in the mud. Repeat, and repeat.

The planting is done one horizontal line of five at a time, then a step back to lay another line. I found it really hard to get straight lines, and I often found deep holes in the mud where I wanted to plant a seedling.

"Shift some mud over," Mr. Wang said. He watched me for a while, then went back to his own planting, leaving me to it. I did a few more rows, the sun beating down on my bare back, and then straightened myself and looked around.

There I was, knee-deep in mud in a rice paddy in the Dabie Mountains working alongside the farmers. No longer on the road observing a scene, but rather a part of the scene itself; I felt as though I was in an alternate universe. It felt peaceful, and basic, and clear in the requirements and the goals – finish off the planting, move on to the next field, go home and wait for the harvest. I wished the Public Security officers would come by right now and find me in the mud, but they didn't.

I suddenly wondered about bugs and leeches wallowing around in the mud between my toes, but it was too late to worry about it, and I decided that as the fields had been dry until recently, there was unlikely to be much in the way of wildlife down there. In any event, I did not catch foot rot or any other ailments from the experience.

Farmer Wang pulled out his mobile phone and snapped a picture of me in the mud, and I asked him to take some photos with my camera. I finished off another sheaf of seedlings and decided I had had enough. I had done a few bundles, maybe two hundred seedlings in all; enough to get a sense of how it is done without getting a sore back. I waded over to the edge of the paddy and washed my feet in the clear water channel that separated the paddy from the walkway between the fields. Wang and his companion took a break and came over to sit with me. They offered me cigarettes, as all the men do in this part of China, and as always I declined.

"It's hard work being a farmer," I said.

"Not at all," said the other older man. "It is very simple work. Being an official (ganbu) is much harder."

I asked Mr. Wang a few questions about himself and gave him brief answers to the obvious questions he had about what I was doing there.

"What do you usually do in the evenings?" I asked.

"Drink baijiu with my friends," he smiled.

"Would you have dinner with me this evening?" He agreed, and I asked for his mobile number. I punched it into my mobile and called it, and his mobile rang immediately with the sound of a little girl reading out the numbers of my mobile phone. "That's very cool," I told him. I had never come across that before, and had not expected to experience a moment of techno-envy in the paddy fields.

"That's a China Mobile number you have," he said.

I nodded. "Okay," I said. "You keep working, I will keep walking, and we will meet again this evening."

That afternoon I passed a little field shrine with a padlocked door, with six idols on the shelf inside, all with their heads covered in red cloth. It was called the 'Good Fortune and Benevolence Shrine'. Nearby, I met a boy wearing a bright red T-shirt inscribed in English with the words 'dead rock star'.

"Do you know what that means?" I asked. He looked down at it and shook his head. "It says you are a dead rock star." The boy squinted back at me with a look that said: Who cares?

As I ascended the valley the size of the paddies shrank, bamboo spinneys appeared and hillsides began to take on rows and rows of tea bushes. Tea is important in this part of Anhui, and every house seemed to have a cup of local green tea waiting for me.

The shadows reaching across the steep slopes at the top of the valley lengthened and the bugs started to come out and harass me. Fortunately, by this point I had reached my target for the day: the six hundred and sixty kilometre milestone on Highway 318 at one hundred and sixteen degrees and eight minutes east of Greenwich. I did some calculations and worked out that at this rate of progress, it would take me seventy-two years to walk around the world.

Once I had returned to Laipeng, I called Mr. Wang and invited him to come over to the Pingtan Inn, which was where I was staying that night. It sounds dramatically grander than it was; it was just a single shop front on the outskirts of town. Facing onto the street was a counter, a television and a sofa. Behind the front room was another room with a dinner table and a parked motorcycle, while upstairs was a dormitory room with bed spaces for rent. I asked the innkeeper to set up a little dinner table in the front 'lobby' just off the street.

Mr. Wang rode up on a motorcycle and we sat at a little kindergarten table on tiny stools. The innkeeper was from Fujian and had set up the hotel to service engineers working on an expressway being built somewhere in the region, but things had not worked out, and there was a sense of desolation about the place. There were no other customers, and clearly none had been expected because they had to go to the shop down the street to buy food to cook for us.

Mr. Wang told me his story. His full name was Wang Quanwang (王全望), which is interesting because each character includes the basic element 'wang', which means king. Wang was born in this area with three older sisters but no brothers. He graduated from high school and his father sent him to work in a town to the east of the mountains as an apprentice. He hated it so much that on the third day, he cycled all the way back home, seven hours pedalling up and down the hills along the same road I had travelled. He went instead to the coastal city of Quanzhou in Fujian province, looking for work. The people of China still often operate on a clan network basis, and just as every other taxi driver in Shenzhen seems to be from the town of Mudanjiang in Heilongjiang, so Quanzhou is apparently a first call point for people from this part of Anhui.

As soon as Wang arrived in Quanzhou, he bumped into a direct sales outfit running a pyramid deal designed to scam cash off poor migrant workers from other provinces. He and two others from the Yuexi area were invited to a revivalist hard sell meeting, but Wang saved himself by missing the meeting due to a mix-up. The other two were convinced of huge riches awaiting them if they would first cough up some cash, and ended up losing the RMB equivalent of around one thousand US dollars each.

Wang could not find work in Quanzhou, so he went south to Xiamen, then on to Zhuhai in Guangdong province, next to Macao, then finally to Shenzhen where he found a job working in a local hotel. He rose through the ranks to become lobby manager and met a local Anhui girl there through the clan network. They soon married and had a daughter together. His wife was still working in Shenzhen, while their daughter was with her grandparents at home near Laipeng.

"I'm back home for a few months to oversee the demolition of our old family house and the construction of a new one," Wang told me. "The structure of the new house has been completed and the interior decoration and fitting work is about to begin. When it's all done, I'll go back to Shenzhen."

"Are you planning to have more children?" I asked him.

"Our first child was a girl, so we would be allowed to but my wife and I have decided not to," he said. Wang went on to tell me that his father was bitterly against their decision and wanted a grandson.

"So what will be the outcome?"

"We are gradually working on him," Wang said with a smile.

I asked about the status of land ownership and he told me that each person is allotted a fixed plot size by the village.

"Is the land owned by the individuals, the families or by the state?" I asked.

"By the state."

"Do the farmers feel a sense of ownership?"

"Well, the land is handed to the families to work."

"Can you sell the land?"

"No."

"Bequeath it to your descendants?"

"Yes, but with the same terms. Plus the government has the right to take it back to build a road or whatever at a ridiculously low price."

I asked if there were ever land disputes between the farming families, and he said that such disputes had been a regular occurrence among people of his father's generation and above.

"But for our generation, we figure, whatever, it's not worth worrying about."

"I guess the difference is that your generation is focused on moving beyond the farm, going out into the world?" He nodded.

I asked about food. Wang said his family grows its own rice and vegetables and has chickens and ducks and several pigs, but no cows or buffalo.

"So what do you buy at the shop?"

"Chili sauce… salt… not a whole lot more."

"What about electricity?"

"Our family pays about twenty RMB a month for power."

I asked about his new house. "Three bedrooms, each with an en-suite bathroom," he said.

"Sounds pretty grand," I replied, and Wang invited me to go to the new house for dinner on my next visit. I said I would be honoured to join them.

After we finished dinner, Wang rode home on his motorcycle through the deep darkness of the countryside while I spent the night at the little inn in Laipeng. It was far more convenient than making a thirty kilometre trip back to Yuexi, and it was also pleasing to overnight in a hotel that did not involve registration – another blow struck for freedom.

I started out early the next morning and by 7.30am I was having my first conversation with two farm labourers and a woman with a cow. The road continued on upwards, and I walked for a while with a man who was carrying a wooden plough over his shoulder. The plough was a primitive and ancient device with around ten iron spikes of ten centimetres in length and while it wouldn't cut much depth, apparently it's all that's necessary to churn up a rice paddy, which is soft and soggy for most of the year.

Then I topped a ridge, and began a downhill stroll in the sunshine. I saw a pretty girl with freshly-washed hair hoeing a vegetable patch as I descended into a hamlet. There was a small store and an old man and a middle-aged woman sitting outside and I went over and said hello. The woman, Ms. Ling, patted a stool for me to sit down. There were four of us – Ms. Ling, her twelve-year-old son and the old man who turned out to be deaf. I asked his surname, and Ms. Ling held out three fingers horizontally. I guessed Wang. She nodded.

"How's business?" I asked.

"Not good," she said.

I asked about the traffic, the number of cars moving past her door on Highway 318, which was still a small country lane.

"More and more. Far more than before."

"Do they ever stop and buy?"

"No, we only have local business."

I looked at the shop entrance, and it was easy to see why no one stopped – the interior was very dark and it looked like a farmhouse, not a shop. I wondered if she would eventually figure out the concept of advertising and put up a billboard to get passing drivers to stop.

As we talked, a very short old woman dressed in a blue peasant smock walked up to our group and said something to me that I didn't catch. The Anhui dialect can be pretty incomprehensible. I looked at Ms. Ling who told me "Shenjing bing" – she's crazy, mentally deranged. I looked back and the old woman was staring intently into my eyes and talking at me using clear sentences and structure.

"Do you understand what she is saying?" I asked Ms. Ling. She shook her head.

The lady moved round and sat down right beside me on the bench, still looking at me. These crazy people in the mountains seemed to be attracted to me and it may be because, like them, I am different.

I wondered what the best way is to communicate with these people who live partly in our world, and partly somewhere else. In my normal life, I rarely came across people like this. How to break through to them? How to dig through to the sentient core hidden under the damaged mental layers?

I started to talk to her. I looked straight at her and answered her in standard Chinese with phrases that seemed appropriate based on what she seemed to be saying. "Really?... That is interesting... I didn't know that... Why did you do that?... Do tell me more..." And she talked on and on in response. Ms. Ling watched the conversation in growing amazement.

"Do you understand what she's saying?" she asked. I shook my head, and smiled ruefully.

Ms. Ling said I was the first foreigner that had ever been through the little hamlet and I was the first non-Chinese person she had ever spoken to. "But I have seen foreigners on television, of course," she added.

I took my leave of the group in front of the shop and walked on, taking photos of the delightful scenery. I snapped a man in a bright yellow jacket walking through the paddy fields carrying two empty wicker baskets on a pole over his shoulder. He came up to me out of the fields and I said "Hello" and asked his surname. He told me it was Ling.

"Were you born in this place?" I asked.

"Our family has been here for more than ten generations," he said proudly.

"Where had the family come from originally?"

"From the plains southeast of the mountains, near the Yangtze River."

We walked along together for a way. I asked about the history of the road we were on, Highway 318, and Mr. Ling said that the road had been upgraded to a road from a path in 1958 and then widened and upgraded into its current country lane status in the late 1960s. We came to a group of little houses by the road.

"Would you like to drink some water?" he asked. By "water", he meant tea.

"Yes please," I said, and followed him into his poor mud brick house. There was a medieval stove, chickens wandering around the earth floor, and his wife sitting at the table. She accepted my arrival without comment and we all chatted for a while.

Mr. Ling was born in the Year of the Horse (1954), and was therefore two years younger than me (I was born in the Year of the Dragon). All the years in Mr. Ling's head were part of the twelve-year animal cycle, and we then had to work out the year according to the Gregorian calendar, which I am more used to. Mr. Ling's father died in the Year of the Dog (1958) at the height of the Great Leap Forward famine period, when Chairman Mao's directives led to failed harvests and millions of people starved. The Dabie Mountains region was among the worst hit, and I had heard stories of men waylaying travellers to eat them. Mr. Ling's father had died not of starvation but from a lack of medical attention for some ailment.

"It was a hard time for this region," I said.

"It was the hardest time for our nation," he replied. From his tone, he seemed to bear no grudge.

His wife was taking medicine for some brain-related problem. They had three children – one daughter, who was a teacher in a school in Laipeng, came home reasonably regularly; another daughter was working in Ningbo; and their son was at university in Beijing.

I gave Mr. Ling my name card and told him I would be going to Beijing the following day. His son, Ling Qixin, called me the next day and we chatted for a while, but he could not come out to meet me as he was preparing for exams. However, I did get an email from him, written in English, which said:

Dear Mr Graham,

How are you doing? It's a pity that we can not see each other last time when you stayed in Beijing. I'm looking forward to see you and take a pleasure talk. Now let me introduce myself for you! I'm a lucky fellow because I can enter the campus, what is other teenagers can't do that. Not because I'm outstanding but lucky. You know my hometown is badly off and out-of-the-way. Lots of boys or girls discontinued their studying when they were young. So I became the first collage student in my hometown fortunately. Three years ago, I arrived Beijing with lonely and studied in Beijing Information Technology Institute. My specialty is Accounting. But to my family, it's difficulty to afford heavy tuition fee and living expenses in metropolis. My English is very poor, please don't care my lovely mistake! I'm really looking forward to hearing from you!

With my best wishes!

A Chinese Boy, Lingqixin

I said goodbye to Mr. Ling and his wife and ambled on up the hill, away from the farmland and towards the forests. I passed a pool of water fed by a small waterfall, the water as clear and clean as any I have ever seen. I met a man walking along the road, middle-aged with a 1980s Chinese university student sort of haircut, a black bag on his shoulder, and a plastic water bottle in his hand. He was clearly not a farmer so I asked him about his profession.

"I am a vet," he told me. "I look after the cows and pigs and chickens around here."

"So is there any mad cow disease?" I asked.

"No."

"Any avian flu?"

Also no.

We said goodbye and he added: "I wish you good fortune."

Thank you.

I passed the six hundred and sixty-six kilometre marker on Highway 318, and there was no sign of the Devil in any of his incarnations. I climbed over the ridge and Mingtangshan, one of the prettiest peaks of the Dabie Mountains region, was on my right. Several farmers had told me that there were plans to turn a part of the mountain into a tourist resort, but on that day, it looked untouched and magnificent.

On this stretch of downward road, dug into the side of the mountain in the 1950s, I was stopped at least every ten minutes to be offered a lift, or by people wanting to chat, or just shout hello. A black Santana with a male driver and three girl passengers stopped and offered me a lift. I explained that I was walking.

"Why?"

"To look at the flowers. Looking at the flowers from a car is just not the same."

"We want to talk to you," one of the girls said.

"Come and walk with me for a while, then."

There was no interest in walking for these middle-class wannabes. They drove off and one girl stuck her head out of the window and shouted: "You know the way?"

I spread my arms in amazement. "Three One Eight!" I shouted back in

Mandarin. It was the only road in any direction.

The previous year in the flat canal lands of Zhejiang province, there had been one weekend in April when the grass by the roads had been a seething mass of white butterflies. On this day, I saw hordes of black and brown butterflies, mostly in the shade of the rockfaces along the road. A mother and her young daughter flashed by on a motorcycle. The girl looked at me and I raised my hand to wave, but I was holding something and all I could do was raise one index finger. The girl raised her index finger to me in reply, then turned to her mother, and was saying "One finger…!" as they disappeared round a bend. Who knows – the one index finger greeting could become a fashion in Anhui.

A cool guy with his head shaved and driving a tiny white van stopped to talk to me and said he was a tea trader. His name was Zhou Xuefa and he invited me to visit him when I got to his village, named Baimao, somewhere ahead of me.

The road was winding down a long valley, and peaks to the west were noticeably lower. There was a growing sense that the mountains were coming to an end. Beyond them lay the Yangtze River plain of Hubei Province.

CHAPTER 5

END OF ANHUI

The weather forecast had promised rain and thunderstorms, but I was determined to keep walking and so, with a couple of extra pairs of shoes in my bag and umbrella in hand, I resumed the walk along Highway 318.

As in any other country, people like to stay in on rainy days, and this means that on such days, there are less people for me to talk to and brighten up my day. On the other hand, the rain and mist give a whole new dimension to the already breathtaking mountain scenery. And while humans may avoid the rain, nature continues to go about its business, and the stillness brought on by the lack of people draws the eye to the life that makes up the scenery: the rice was now quietly growing, needing no attention; and young ducks and chickens were everywhere; grey water buffalo and brown cows walking along the roads with their masters, grazing by the roadside, or sleeping. One cowherd told me that an adult buffalo is worth around two thousand five hundred to three thousand RMB; younger ones are worth less. "They eat one hundred jin of grass per day," he added. That's fifty kilos of food. "What a load of bullshit!" I exclaimed to myself in English.

As I made my way into the little town of Baimao (which means 'white hat'), I saw two girls under a tree blowing on the edge of leaves, making them vibrate and produce a sound.

This, I suddenly remembered, was something I used to do when I was seven or eight years old. I had completely forgotten about it, and to see it being done here on the other side of the world, was a shock, and it was extraordinary to me how such little games and pastimes spread from one continent to another and stay alive through the generations and cultures.

I pulled a leaf off the tree and placed it against my lips. After a few tries, I managed to emit a light farting sound – nowhere near as professional as the noises the girls were able to produce. I gave up and the girls walked with me down the main street of this little town. One of the girls asked where I came from. I said I was from England, and she replied:

"Your country is very beautiful, right?"

"China is more beautiful," I said, the misted mountains, the paddy terraces, the plunging valleys and streams that surrounded Baimao fresh in my mind. This setting is wonderful by any scenic measure, but she couldn't see it. The girl frowned and shook her head. "It's not beautiful. It's filthy. Look at the rubbish," she said, pointing to a piece of crumpled paper on the road.

"Well, why don't you pick it up?" I asked, and she pouted.

A little later that day, I was standing on the balcony of a house with a local official and we looked down together on a pond with a dozen white ducks motoring through water that was heavily covered with rubbish. I told him about my little conversation with the girl and said I thought it such a pity that so much litter was just left all over the place. He seemed embarrassed to have a shortcoming pointed out to him by an outsider, but nodded and said: "Yes, we should do something about it, but it is not easy."

The answer may be to return to the campaigns of the past. Smash litter! Take picking up rubbish as the key link. When the Communist Party really wants to do something it can get it done, even at the grassroots level – they did it with birth control, and, if they wanted to, they could do it with litter.

I was making slow progress on the walk. While the weather was far from ideal for an outdoor stroll, a light warm drizzle is not without its charms, and the misty landscape compelled me to stop and take photos constantly. The countryside here is dotted with the old-style Anhui farmhouses that might look ancient, but were mostly built in the 1980s.

Quite a few conversations in this area went like this:

Self: This area is very beautiful.

Anhui area resident: Yes, but we are poor.

"Poor?" I would ask at this point. "Do you own a mobile phone?" Most of them do. Of course, they are poor compared with myself or with middle-class people in Shanghai, but in my view, their lifestyle provides its own luxuries that those in the city find it hard to acquire: fresh air; security; peace of mind; and deep roots into the landscape – contentment that they were not even aware of.

One little boy wanted to know how much money I had – IN TOTAL. I put my hand in my pocket and pulled out two coins. "Two RMB. How about you?"

Two girls came up to me in a restaurant and asked if they could be photographed with me. I said sure, and reached for my camera, but they each had their own mobile phone camera, and happily photographed one another with the foreigner.

As I walked past a doorway, a girl called out "Hello!" in English. A young man came out and invited me into the house to sit with them. The girl introduced herself as Chen Baolian, a Chinese language teacher at a primary school. She had been practising calligraphy and pages filled with characters were on the table between us. She told me that she was planning to move to Shanghai to study at a teachers' college for a master's degree in Chinese teaching. "And after that, will you return to Baimao?" I asked. She shook her head.

"This is a backward place, a closed place," she said in English. "I know you find it beautiful, but for people like me, we have to leave."

I told her that her English was pretty good, but she disagreed, saying it was self-taught. I replied in English that being self-taught was the best way. "Otherwise it is in one ear and out the other." She looked puzzled, so I gave her a Chinese version of the phrase.

"Oh!" she exclaimed. "We say exactly the same thing in Chinese!"

Dusk was settling as I walked on, and I passed a big old farmhouse with a family group sitting outside the door. The adults were enjoying the cool of the early evening, while the children played in the dust in the wide yard at the front of the house. I took a couple of photos of the children and everyone laughed. I walked over to the doorway and was offered a tiny stool to sit down with them. It was a lovely twenty minutes: I played with the children and chatted with the grandparents while the young mothers sat silently watching me. But there was a hole in the group; the fathers of these children, the husbands of these young women, were noticeably absent. I was told that they were away in the coastal cities, working in factories or on construction sites.

It was time to look around Baimao for a small hotel to spend the night in. My requirements in terms of a room are simple: electricity to charge my gadgets, a door that can be locked securely and a window that would be difficult for someone to climb in through. If there is ever any doubt about the matter, I set a tea cup on the window sill for any intruder to knock over and I always put my wallet and passport under my pillow. Many of the inns had only multi-bed dormitory rooms, which were intended for use by truck drivers passing through and, in such instances, I rented the entire room. This may not have been necessary because in fact, I rarely saw any other guests in any of the small town inns I stayed at. The fact is that virtually no one goes to these little places unless they know someone there, in which case they already have somewhere to stay. Hot water was nice to have, and clean sheets were always welcome. Coffee was out of the question, and the toilets tended to be pretty foul, but it was all worth it – there is something wonderful about going to sleep in a peaceful small town in central China and waking up to hear the bustle below in the dawn grey.

Once I had established a base in one of Baimao's small hotels that was set up in a school compound, I phoned the tea dealer, Zhou Xuefa, who I'd met near the six hundred and sixty-six kilometre mark, but there was no answer. I asked a young woman in a shop at the entrance to the school if she knew Zhou, and she said: "Yes, everyone knows him. In fact, his wife is a relative of mine."

She made some calls on her mobile and found him. "He'll be over soon," she told me, and I sat in the shop entrance and waited. I asked the woman what products sold best and she said snacks for the children. Another woman brought her baby over to see me, but the poor thing took one look at me and burst into tears. Perfectly understandable.

Mr. Zhou arrived wearing a silk Chinese-style shirt, which was pretty rare and meant 'I am different, I am a star'. He had a crew cut, smiling eyes and exuded confidence. Beside him was a shrunken sidekick, a teacher surnamed Xu. We went two doors along to a little restaurant and Mr. Zhou suggested we go to a room upstairs, but I said no, let's stay on the ground floor close to the street. It wasn't a security concern; I just wanted to watch the passing scene. My new friends had already eaten, but we started to drink beer as some simple food was prepared for me (my usual beancurd, vegetables and rice).

"I was planning to be away in Yuexi, but I cancelled my trip," Mr. Zhou said. "It is fate. Do you believe in fate?"

"I believe in coincidence," I said. "It may be the same thing."

Teacher Xu said he'd seen me on the road. In fact, I found I was becoming a 'known person'. Many people I met had already seen me walking, or had heard about me from someone else. This was partly a function of the mountains, which feel much more like discrete and cohesive communities than the plains, where anonymity is the norm.

"So, Mr. Zhou, how is the tea business?" I asked.

"Prices are lower this year because of unusually warm weather," he said, adding that his buyers were usually his friends, so he felt uncomfortable about taking too much profit. That sounded unlikely.

"He is 'Big Brother' to the people in this area," Teacher Xu confided in me. "He knows everyone and everyone respects him."

Zhou said he had got married at the age of seventeen, which is far younger than the usual age.

"Was this a marriage of necessity?" I asked.

"Yes, my girlfriend was pregnant. I don't know what happened."

"I think you do," I said.

I saw blackboards in a couple of villages I passed through with detailed information of the rules regarding births and parentage, but there was a sense that the age of strict controls was over. Mr. Zhou said he was planning a second child to celebrate his thirty-sixth birthday.

"But isn't that against the regulations?" I asked.

"Well, yeah, but you pay the fine and no problem."

"How much?"

"Not much. Maybe ten or twenty thousand." He looked down through the cloud of cigarette smoke for a moment and I guess we were both pondering whether ten or twenty thousand RMB was "not much".

Zhou talked about his son, who was seventeen years old. "He is a real disappointment to me," he said. "He only got around four hundred points in the exams and he should easily have got five hundred points or more. I was really angry. Maybe you could talk to him. He wastes his time. In fact, I think he might have a girlfriend."

"A-ha!" I said. "Like father, like son. Just teach him to use condoms and he'll be okay." That comment was a little too personal and he ignored it, moving on to the topic of power. Mr. Zhou said he'd been invited to join the Communist Party and was studying the documents and teaching materials.

"What are the Three Represents?" I asked, referring to the main political slogan of that time. "Quick!"

He stumbled and mumbled, unable to recite them. I laughed and said: "Don't worry. I met the political news editor of the People's Daily in

Beijing recently and asked him the same question and he could only name one of them."

"It's very difficult to become a party member," said Teacher Xu, with a touch of reverence.

"Why would you want to become a party member?" I asked Mr. Zhou.

He fidgeted. "Well, to do something for the people," he replied.

The basic idea, I guessed, was that he was well-known and well-connected and that the party preferred to have people like him as insiders rather than outsiders. I asked if he could still run his business as a party member.

"Oh yes." He talked at length about the heavy responsibility of party membership, but there was a fake touch to his words that reminded me of other party members I had met in Shanghai who used their positions for their own personal benefit without any moral qualms. Of course, he agreed, party membership also brought with it expanded networking opportunities and alternative business possibilities.

The next day, when I visited Mr. Zhou's house in a village a few kilometres beyond Baimao town, I found a copy of the party handbook with a hammer and sickle symbol on the cover that looked crisp and untouched. Under the glass on his desk were photos of Mr. Zhou in his twenties: he was a long-haired ruffian.

The house was a three-storey storefront with a big backyard next to a school. The open ground-floor area was for business, but it was empty except for the desk, a scale for weighing tea and a disgusting mouldy sofa. It didn't feel as though business was good. His wife wandered past, knitting as she went, but she wasn't introduced. She smiled shyly at me.

Also there was a friend of Zhou's, a local official named Wang Quanwen, which translated as 'Full Text' Wang. His son was with him and I asked if his son's name was Summary Wang, but the joke didn't register. Never mind. I asked Mr. Wang about the population of the area.

"The whole of Yuexi County has a population of just over four hundred thousand and Baimao village has twenty thousand or so," he said. "We now have a population growth rate of zero. Births are balancing out deaths."

"So if you add in the people who are leaving to seek work elsewhere, the population is falling?"

"Right."

"Will there be enough people in ten years' time to look after the fields?"

It was not clear.

Mr. Wang was thirty-five years old and he was born in a village to the east of Baimao, close to Mingtang Mountain, which I had passed a few walk days before. After graduating school at the age of twenty, he'd been assigned to local government work and now received a salary of fifteen hundred RMB per month as the deputy village head of Gufang, a village just to the north of Baimao. I asked him about his work.

"It's lots of things. I spend my time racing round sorting out disputes and solving problems, all kinds of things. But it is a lot easier than when I started. In the early years, my job was to collect agricultural taxes and it was very difficult."

Mr. Wang was required to go round to each household and get them to pay up. How much? Around fifty to eighty RMB per person per year, but many of the farmers were unwilling to pay. "So what did you do?" I asked.

"Usually I'd seize the water buffalo, but it's different now."

The agricultural taxes were abolished in 2005 and the whole relationship between the government officials and ordinary farmers changed in an instant.

"Instead of taking money from the farmers, we now distribute money to them," he said.

Mr. Wang seemed to be a good man – calm and intelligent – and I guessed he was respected by his flock, a modern-day version of the 'Fu-mu-guan' – father-mother officials who had managed the grassroots for the emperor since time began. His son, Wang Zhaozhou, was eleven years old and seemed quietly smart. He wrote out the three characters of his name with speed and neatness. I asked him what he wanted to be when he graduated, and he immediately said a scientist as if he meant it. This surprised me as it is rare for Chinese children to have a clear idea of their own futures. I gave him my card, with the usual instructions to call me when he arrived in Shanghai.

It was time for lunch so Mr. Wang, his son, Zhou and I went to a simple restaurant.

Zhou's son turned out to be an introverted, pimply, gangly kid looking for a way out. A pregnant girlfriend could be his unconscious strategy; who knows.

We talked at lunch about the development of the region and I expressed my view on the potential for high-end holiday villas in a natural village environment. To this Official Wang said: "I will give you a plot of land near Mingtangshan to build on. I mean it. It belongs to my family."

This raised the interesting question of land ownership of which Official Wang's understanding was different to that of Wang Quanwang near Laipeng.

"The ownership issue is not clear," said Official Wang. "Deng Xiaoping said things would stay as they are for one hundred years. That means people effectively have ownership over the land, but it's not clearly stated. They own it, but they cannot sell it, although they can sell usage rights, which is effectively the same thing."

I said that leasehold as opposed to freehold would in the end become a drag on the economy. People and companies want freehold with full rights to hold land and property in perpetuity and bequeath, sell or hold as they please, one generation to the next.

"That is in effect what we have now," Official Wang said. "But a formal change is linked to the political system."

Understood.

The political system had made itself felt earlier that morning. I had started out at 6.30am, the mountain road silent in the mist except for birdcalls, roosters crowing and the very occasional three-wheeler mini-truck puttering by as I strolled along. I came upon an old woman sitting by the road watching her two cows grazing on the vegetation on the roadside slope, which reminded me of the 'two cows' joke I used regularly in the 1990s to test Chinese people's sense of humour. The joke goes like this:

Two cows are standing by the road, and one says to the other: "What do you think about this mad cow disease?"

"I am not worried about it," says the second cow.

"Why not?"

"Because I'm a rabbit."

In Chinese, it is necessary to emphasize a couple of times that both animals are cows, otherwise the joke doesn't work.

I walked round a bend and a little police van heading east passed me and screeched to a halt. I kept walking and a policeman ran after me, calling: "Hold on! Wait!"

I stopped and the policeman asked me what I was doing. I said, "Walking west to Tibet." He asked to see my passport and looked at several visas that had expired before calling into his headquarters to enquire about what to do with a foreigner whose visa had expired. I sighed and took the passport off him and pointed to a visa that was still valid. He went back to the van and disappeared.

I passed a cow in one of the distinctive Anhui cow stalls that have a central bamboo pole, round wooden lattice platform heaped with rice straw at just the right height for the cow to snatch. The beast was mooing in great distress, while its master tried to calm her as he held onto a rope looped through a ring in the cow's nose. A little further along I came upon a dam and a reservoir, which was a still slab of water with steep slopes extending up from the water level. I saw a man kneeling in a bucket that was set in the middle of an inner tire and he was paddling across the placid surface of the reservoir with a fishing net.

The country broadened out and I passed a couple of shrines on the heavily wooded slopes of the valley. Then the road headed back up into the mountains, up towards a ridge called Caoling that marks the dividing line between Anhui and Hubei Provinces and is a word in Chinese that's a delicious expletive.

And then I was at one hundred and fifteen degrees and fifty-one minutes east, thirty-one degrees and forty minutes north, the point at which Highway 318 crosses the provincial border. Goodbye Anhui. Hello Hubei.

CHAPTER 6

PUTTING AWAY THE GPS

I began a new walk with a new driver to take me to the starting point. Mr. Guo met me at Wuhan airport and on the drive east I told him a little about the project.

"You're weird," he said, and he meant it.

"Guojiang (I am not worthy)," I replied.

"Why do you wear old clothes like that? It's ridiculous."

"Because I'll be spending the day with farmers and pigs and water buffalo. You think I should wear a suit?"

"Well, no, but look, the trousers are ripped."

"They're comfortable."

"And the leather boots are all wrong."

"Well, I wear them all year round," I said. "And I am not mountain climbing."

"Why are you doing this? It's a waste of money!" He was puzzled rather than antagonistic.

"To understand more about China. And I may do a book."

"And the people you meet will be in it?"

"Yes."

"Including me?"

"Yes. So be careful what you say," I laughed.

He asked me what I did on the walk and I told him I talk to people.

"Ah! Ni! Hao!" He said the words 'ni hao' in a fake 'foreigner-pronouncing-the-tones-wrong' way.

"No," I said, rather annoyed. "NOT Ni! Hao! Precisely not that." Idiot.

"So you gather stories about the people you meet?"

"Not every one. Many people have nothing to say or I don't learn anything interesting from them. But yes, lots of stories about China."

As we drove through a town on the way to the mountain where I last left off my walk – the border between Anhui and Hubei Provinces – I said: "There are no restaurants up ahead. Do you want to buy something here to take with you?" He said no, the correct macho answer, and as soon as we arrived at the last place I stopped, he said: "I'm hungry."

"I have bread and chocolate, would you like some?" He said no again, but he complained every time I saw him, completely ignoring some of China's most beautiful scenery and the cleanest of air. Instead, he sat in his car, smoking and listening to Chinese pop music at heavy boom box volume.

The walk started from the border and I immediately noticed a difference in the quality of the road. Anhui's thoroughfare had been in far worse shape and I generated a mental memo to the party chief of Anhui Province: *Dear Sir, in order to improve the perception of people crossing between Anhui and adjacent provinces by road, I suggest the local government spends some money on fixing up the roads to a distance of 50 metres from the border line. More, if possible.*

The superior Hubei mountain road was all downhill, a narrow lane with views out over steep valleys, with swift hairpin bends and rockfaces. The little farms were nestled in such secluded valleys two hundred metres below that I wondered how often representatives of authority actually paid visits to the inhabitants. I imagined no more than a couple of times a year, at best.

I came upon a small shack by the road with a tiny counter visible through the window with a few items for sale. I went over and saw a boy in his late teens sitting inside watching television. It was Channel V, the Star satellite music channel broadcast out of Hong Kong, which was theoretically banned. I bought a bottle of water and asked him: "So, how's business?"

"I don't know. This is my dad's shop. Probably not too good." He kept his eyes on the television for most of the time he was talking to me.

The terrain was gradually levelling out and all around me were large butterflies, mostly yellow and black. I was lucky enough to get a good shot of one just as it was sucking the juice out of a purple flower. In focus, too!

That long walk downhill was my reward for the hard climb upwards in Anhui, but the heat was suffocating, relieved only slightly by a breeze blowing up from the valley floors.

And then, suddenly, the mountains were no more. I walked down a slope past a deserted checkpoint and was once again on flat land. To the right was a little village, Xinpujie, which means 'New Relay Station Street.' (The word 'pu' in place names usually refers to the original role of the settlement and the other parts of the word indicated it was a place for official messengers to change horses.)

In front of me Highway 318 stretched into the distance, looking wide and new and treeless with bright green paddies on both sides. I was hot and thirsty, and relieved to see that there was a shop just off the road. In the back, a few guys were playing mahjong while nearby a woman sat with a man who looked slightly abnormal. Behind the counter was a man sitting at a desk with an intravenous drip in his arm. "Hello," I said. "Why are you on a drip?"

"I hurt my arm," he said, and showed me his elbow that had a fairly big scratch on it, but nothing too serious. "Ah. So… how many bottles a day?" I asked.

"Three." I went over to take a look and the bottles were labelled

'Glucose.' I regularly saw huge piles of such bottles, empty, by the road. The 'patient's' wife changed a new bottle for him as I watched.

I engaged the couple in conversation. "The shop isn't doing well," he told me. "The best-selling items are soft drinks." I asked a question of the strange-looking man, but the woman stopped me: "He's a mute."

I bought a towel – one of the most expensive items on display – for seven RMB and started out again in the heat.

I was now in Yingshan County on the eastern edge of Hubei Province. Yingshan is one of China's top four counties for tea production and the scenery was lush with swallows swooping and diving over the mid-life rice plants beside the road. I walked for a couple of kilometres along this section of Highway 318, newly built and raised above the level of the paddy fields, with no trees, houses, ducks, chickens or children in sight. It was tedious.

"Okay, this is clearly a new road, so there must be an original Highway 318 somewhere nearby," I thought. I looked over the paddies to the right and saw a few old farmhouses and realized: "That's it!" I walked along a thin, straight path from one road to the other, not entirely sure of my way, and came upon a peasant surrounded by extremely green mid-growth rice plants. He was deep in the mud, sprinkling ash over what would become a high-yield field. I said "Hello" and he had a big smile and spoke in easily understandable Hubei Chinese.

"The field is lovely," I said.

He looked around. "You're right. It is beautiful. Would you like to go to my house for some water? It's just over there." He pointed beyond the new road, but I shook my head.

"Not right now, maybe later," I said, not wanting to get too far behind schedule. "How is life here?"

"We are poor. I'm just building our new house. I have two sons, both working in Shanghai. Sometimes I go out myself to work as well."

"When do you go?"

He laughed. "I go when I feel like it and I come back when I feel like it."

"It sounds very relaxed."

"No. We are poor." But he said it with a smile. I gave him a name card and asked him to write out his name, which he did, adding a mobile number. I invited him for dinner, but he shook his head: "We're busy right now, but next time for sure."

As I was talking to him, a younger man came up to us and I greeted him, but the farmer said: "He's a mute. He can't speak." I nodded.

I made my way through the paddies to where I thought the old road lay, having to jump over a couple of irrigation channels on the way. I am not the steadiest, most athletic person on the planet, but I managed it just fine, and finally clambered up a slope to find myself back on the '318' I had known and loved since Yuexi, but this stretch was even more quiet and quaint.

The first building I came across featured a slogan from the 1980s: 'Resolutely Implement the Spirit of the Eighth Plenum'. The Chinese Communist Party holds 'plenums' (major meetings) once or twice a year, while more important Congress meetings are held every five years. In the 1980s the slogan would have been significant, but it was now a museum piece. The people of China have been relieved of almost all the superficial political nonsense that was inescapable in the 1970s and much of the 1980s, but the old slogans are still daubed on farmhouse walls all over China. On one wall, I saw a slogan from the late 1990s praising Communist Party Secretary-General Jiang Zemin and another that was surely tongue in cheek: 'Improve the quality of sleep'. This being tea-producing country, another slogan stated: 'Talk tea talk, read tea books, take the tea road and reap tea riches'.

Further along, near Simaoling Village, I saw several AIDS-related slogans painted on walls. I asked a man about them and he said he knew of no AIDS in the area. In contrast, some villages in central China, particularly in Henan Province, are known as AIDS villages because of the disease's high incidence caused by people donating blood for cash, a trade made by blood collection teams with disastrously low hygiene standards.

The old road was neglected, peaceful and beautiful; a forgotten rural backwater sleeping in the sunshine. I saw children, mothers and old people, but virtually no men of working age. I went into a little shop and found three women with a bunch of youngsters aged between one and five. I bought a bottle of water and the shopkeeper said: "Take a seat," pulling up a little chair to the table where a young woman was reading a newspaper with her son standing on her leg, head shaven and looking as serene as a Buddhist priest.

I asked the lady if her baby was a boy or a girl and her glance reflexively shot to the open split in the trousers of her child. My hand shot to cover my own crotch, and they all laughed.

Two young children were playing on the floor with a plastic device that started to play the music to 'Old MacDonald Had a Farm,' so, for fun, I sang the nursery rhyme for them in English. When I'd finished I asked: "Are there Chinese words to that song?"

"Yes," the woman with the Buddha child said, looking up from the newspaper. "Something about a duck."

I gave my name card to the ladies and one of them, clearly pregnant, said she'd spent some years working in a factory in Shanghai.

"Why did you come back?" I asked. "To have your child?" She nodded.

We chatted about the village and one lady said there used to be wide bamboo forests in the area, all now chopped down. "You should have seen it in the old days," she said.

I walked through more little villages with a few motorcycles and a couple of tractors passing me by, but that was it. The shadows stretched out over the old road, the sunlight rosy pink as it hit the ground. As dusk approached, farmers carried pails of water to their vegetable patches. I passed a shrine looking out over a wide expanse of paddy field; there was no name on it, no inscription, but there were three deities inside, each in its own tiny alcove, three straw mats in front of them, and a board showing who had donated how much for the construction of the shrine. The average donation was twenty RMB.

It was not clear who the idols were, perhaps Buddhas, perhaps some other deities. There was an incense burner in front of the altar, but no incense burning. I knelt down before the centre idol and said: "I don't know who you are, but if you can help me in any way, I would be grateful." I said it in English, so I am not sure my words were understood, but I left two RMB on the altar and walked on.

The hillside rows of demure tea bushes set in the midst of dynamic upstart live-fast-die-young rice paddies provided many pleasing views. With virtually no vehicles, the scene was quietly peaceful or, rather, other noises became more obvious, including a distinctive birdcall that I heard continuously for the next couple of days. I heard this tune so often, I came to recognize it amongst the chatter of the other bird species. The bird's song had four notes: High-mid-mid-low and repeat. It was very harmonious and, being an amateur musician, I tried setting chords against it in my head.

Outside many of the farmhouses sat wide, shallow wicker baskets filled with wheat grains, while in some places the 'un-winnowed' wheat plants were heaped in piles across the road for cars to run over and help with the separation process.

I came to a tea factory that was dark and dirty with piles of tea on the floor, machines turning, and a huge clothes dryer-type machine churning the tea.

"Can I buy some tea please?" I asked the manager, Mr. Zhou, who was wearing only a pair of white shorts. "Of course," he said and picked up a huge empty sack. "No, no," I said. "I just want a little. Do you have a plastic bag?" One was found and I was invited to stick my hand into a barrel to grab some tea. I asked him if they do any tea-making by hand, but he said: "Not nowadays."

I descended into the little town of Yangliuwan – Willow Bend – and passed a couple of men, one of whom confidently said to the other: "He's from Xinjiang."

I stopped and corrected him. "I am not from Xinjiang. I'm from England."

The man looked at me. "No," he said. "Xinjiang."

"Okay," I said, and walked on.

I crossed the East River over a long bridge just outside of town. On Google Earth, the river appears to have a reasonable flow of water, but on the day I crossed, it was dry and bleak, a vast sandpit with one lonely worker under a parasol in the midst of what was effectively an open mine.

I passed a sign warning of severe penalties for unauthorized gender checks (authorized checks are made on women to see if they're pregnant and stop them from aborting female foetuses), then out into the country again amidst fields of tea and rice and more tea. The rice appeared to be doing well, but it was very hot, and several ponds I passed were close to dry. I followed a crazy bag lady for a while in the late morning heat, humming the tune to the Noel Coward song 'Mad Dogs and Englishmen,' and then I came upon a grouping of city vehicles and well-dressed men with mobile phones and city shoes. There was a construction site nearby, next to a tea-covered hill that had recently undergone a partial mastectomy to create a piece of flat ground. "Hello," said one of the engineers in English, and that turned out to be the only English word he knew.

"What is happening here?" I asked.

"A new freeway will be constructed to the south and they need to use this land to build new housing for the displaced peasants."

I stopped at a small shop with three people sitting outside, two men and a woman. I bought a bottle of water and they invited me to sit with them. "What 'danwei' (work unit) are you from?" one of the men asked.

I laughed. "Wow, that's a question straight out of the 1980s," I said.

The other man laughed too. "That's right! We should now ask: What's your profession?"

I asked about business in the shop – it wasn't good. "The new Highway 318 was built three years ago. Before that, there were buses going up and down here all the time. Now, there's almost no traffic and the vehicles that do come by are from around here."

It reminded me of how I tended to idealize everything: I looked at the road and saw a pleasant and peaceful country lane, while they looked at the same road and saw a lifeline discarded to their economic detriment. But they didn't appear to be too worried about it, sitting contentedly outside the shop, whiling away the day.

A little further along I came upon two men digging in the dirt by the side of the road. They invited me to sit for a while in the shade under a tree and I accepted as it was indeed extremely hot. The men were building a new home because their current house had been taken from them by the government to build the expressway. He didn't seem too put out about it: "The home cost seventy thousand RMB and they're giving me seventy thousand in compensation, which is reasonable, but the price of building materials has gone up and it will cost me one hundred thousand RMB to build the new house."

A motorcycle drove up, its rider dressed smartly in a China Unicom shirt. He dismounted, shook my hand, and said his surname was Hu, which was no surprise at all as this area was clearly Hu-land, just as the area of the mountains to the east of Yuexi was Chu territory. Mr. Hu asked me where I came from and where I was going and, after briefly explaining my mission, I told him how much I appreciated China Unicom's excellent data reception service, which allowed me to be online throughout the whole region. I asked him about signal strength and he said Unicom was superior to China Mobile.

"That may be true," I said. "But China Mobile is way ahead in terms of propaganda. The whole district is plastered with slogans such as: 'Successful people use China Mobile'."

He invited me to his home for a meal, one of half a dozen such invitations that day, but I declined politely. I had to continue my walk.

I was walking through Simaoling Village when I fell into step with an older man carrying a pretty girl aged three or four. We talked for a while and then we came to his turn-off. "Come and have some water," he said, repeating the words of hospitality that were repeated from one end of the Dabie Mountains region to the other.

I followed him down a narrow path and the noises of the road, such as they were, faded quickly. We passed two other farmhouses and then came upon his house, where all was quiet in the sun. The wind whispered through the bamboo; there was a birdcall or two. A farmer's wife laughed to her friend as they picked tea down below. We entered the farmhouse, which was the standard design for the region with its high ceilings and dark interior. Above, there was a mezzanine area across most of the room upon which, through the gloom, I could see firewood stacks. Chairman Mao gazed down on us benevolently from the back wall, facing the door. There were no floorboards in this simple residence, just packed earth.

The farmer's name was Hu (as expected) and he was a member of the fourth brigade of Simaoling Village. The brigade concept is a holdover from the communes into which all of China's countryside was organized, by order, in the 1950s. He brought me a mug of water, no tea leaves. It was a metal mug and very hot. I sat under Chairman Mao's image and Mr. Hu sat before me with his granddaughter Zhenzhen on his knee.

His wife was gone, perhaps she had died, but he had two grown sons, and he said he had paid a two-thousand-RMB fine for the privilege of having the backup. Zhenzhen's parents worked in factories in Shanghai. The mother had left eight days after giving birth to Zhenzhen and she and the child's father returned just once a year to see her, at Chinese New Year, so the old man was raising the child alone.

"You have good fortune," I said. "To be able to watch her grow is a wonderful thing." He nodded, but in the quiet house there was also great loneliness. I asked if Zhenzhen had any little friends, but the answer was no. Zhenzhen didn't say a single word to me or to her grandfather during the entire time I spent with them; they clung to each other like casualties in life, the shadows of absent individuals darkening the scene.

I asked about the harvest. "This year will be tough," he said, "because it's too hot and dry out there."

"Why do you have a picture of Chairman Mao on the wall?" I asked, but he seemed puzzled by the question and said simply: "Most houses have Chairman Mao on the wall."

I said farewell and walked back to the road, continuing on through the rich green tea and rice country. The ladies were out in their straw hats, picking tea or washing clothes in ponds while the rice plants, stretching off in all directions, formed a brilliant emerald ocean under the sun. But then I came across a cheerless slogan on an old red brick farmhouse wall: 'AIDS spreads through sexual contact, blood transfusions, or mothers giving birth to children'.

It was a brilliant summer's day and this truly was a delightful country lane. I photographed a random playing card lying on the road – a nine of clubs featuring a naked lady. The mature trees along the way suggested the road had been built in the 1960s. Women were spreading grain out on the road for cars to drive over, helping with the winnowing process, so I walked across the piles too, doing my little bit to help.

The tea fields were immaculate, laid out in closely parallel hedgerows and, in one beautiful corner, I saw a shrine in a spinney of trees, looking out over an expanse of tea fields and rice paddies, as I liked to imagine it had for hundreds of years (with a short Maoist intermission).

I passed a farmer fast asleep on the road's surface in the shade of the trees, his straw hat and sandals beside him, and then came upon a stone-carving workshop with several huge white statues in various stages of creation, including a Buddha and two Confucian scholars. The lady in charge had been resting in the shade, but jumped up when she saw me. I asked her how much the statues cost, and she said thirty thousand RMB each. Who was buying them? "Schools," she said and then invited me to stay for some tea, but I declined and walked on.

Within a kilometre or so, a car pulled up and the driver said: "Are you Yan Gewen?" I said yes. "My boss asked me to offer you a lift to the next town."

"Please thank her, but I am walking, and if I take a car any part of the way, then the journey loses its meaning."

"Just go a short way with me," he urged. "It's so hot today, no one will know." I declined as politely as I could.

Half an hour later, a motorcycle pulled up, ridden by the man I'd met earlier that day building a new home. He'd come ten kilometres to offer me a ride, and while it was most impolite to decline, I had to.

For the first time, I was carrying a Global Positioning System (GPS) device with me and I watched the latitude and longitude coordinates change with each step. It was useful, but in some ways annoying. The numbers became an obsession and in the heat I began doing all sorts of calculations: A degree is divided into sixty minutes, then again into sixty seconds, each further divided on my GPS 'toy' into tenths. It took eight steps for the tenth number to change once, but I was heading generally in a west-southwest direction, not due west. If I were to go due west, I guessed it would be an average of seven steps per tenth of a second of longitude. I decided to use eight steps as my average: Eight times ten equals eighty steps per second of longitude (at least at this latitude, which is thirty-one degrees north of the equator), then eighty times sixty equals four thousand eight hundred steps per minute of longitude. I multiplied this figure by sixty to make one degree and ended up with a total of two hundred and eighty-eight thousand steps per degree of longitude, assuming there are no corners. But there are always corners.

So after a day of watching the damn numbers and calculating my insignificant progress per step across the invisible lines of the grid that covers the surface of the world, I vowed to leave the GPS in my pocket and only use it once a day to receive a satellite positioning fix. To use it all the time would surely lead to madness. It would also be a distraction from the beauty of green paddy fields.

CHAPTER 7

RED TOURISM

The air was fresh and the ground was soft after an early morning rainfall. It was warm, but pleasantly so: perfect weather for a summer's stroll in central China.

The previous day the first-ever passenger train had left Beijing for the city of Lhasa, which was at that point still the intended destination of my walk, and the official media was full of the event. Several farmers I met referred to the story, a reflection of the power and penetration capability of the state media into this remote corner of China. They spoke with the pride with which all Chinese viewed the completion of the line, which was an engineering wonder by any measure. A railway line constructed across land that's five thousand metres above sea level is truly amazing. The highest I'd been so far on the walk was about nine hundred metres on a couple of ridges in the Dabie Mountains and I was now in the lower foothills of the mountain range at an altitude of only about two hundred metres, and this height was falling as I approached the plain.

I first visited Lhasa in 1982 on one of the first group trips taken by foreigners since the Cultural Revolution. It was a week of glowing blue skies and of numerous incidents that showed the clear disconnect between the Han Chinese on one side and the Tibetans on the other. Lhasa was two separate towns sitting uneasily next to one another – the Han expat enclave and the old city, nestled under the Potala Palace. I and the other foreign journalists on the trip were taken to the Jokhang Monastery in the centre of the city and we watched the pilgrims crawling on their hands and knees, prostrating themselves every step of the way. We were also taken to the Ganden Monastery, once the largest of the Lamaseries (schools of Buddhism) in Tibet, but now a shadow of its former self after massive destruction at the hands of the Chinese Army and the Red Guards. We were allowed to speak to the monks in controlled settings and, while I can't now be absolutely sure, it is possibly not apocryphal that one of them, when asked how things were during the Cultural Revolution, told us it was the worst thing he had experienced in all his 'lives'.

I carried my Martin acoustic guitar with me everywhere in those days and I lugged it up all the stairs in the Potala Palace, through the rarefied air, to the roof and there I played a song, with Lhasa and Tibet stretched out below and the wide Tibetan blue sky above. I used to say that I sang 'Hello Dalai,' but it's not true. I sang Chuck Berry's 'Maybelline.' I have no idea why, but it seemed right at the time.

Memories fade over time, but some images have stayed with me: The crystal clarity of the air; a woman sticking out her tongue to me in greeting; the smell of yak butter everywhere; the otherworldliness of the official Chinese guesthouse in which we stayed (the only hotel in the city at the time). But the most unforgettable memory was that of a Tibetan 'sky burial'.

On our first morning in Lhasa, at about three o'clock and well before dawn, I sneaked out of a window of the guesthouse with British diplomat Will Dennis. The front door of the guesthouse was locked and there were no guards in sight. We headed out of town, but as we walked beyond the houses, we began to pass pilgrims coming into Lhasa, some walking and some crawling. We walked in the dark to a hillside behind the Sera Monastery, where we understood sky burials were performed almost every day. We probably walked for two hours, with me wondering about the possible effects of altitude sickness, which many people report. The condition is caused by the thin, oxygen-light air, but I felt totally fine, even though we'd been at that elevation for only a few hours before we started out on our adventure. The last part of the trek was a long trudge up the mountainside on a winding dirt track with the way ahead lit by a tiny campfire.

We reached the saddle of the hill and saw a 'Liberation Truck' on the left, lower side of the slope and the campfire on the right, higher side, around which were crouched a group of Tibetans, the relatives of the dead. They invited us to sit with them and we made friendly faces at each other as they didn't speak any Chinese and my Tibetan was non-existent. They offered us the disgustingly sweet milk tea that's made using the yak butter of which the whole of Tibet stinks. Further along in the darkness was the outline of a large rock on which were two whitish rolls. The rock was shaped like a flattened pear, the thin ending pointing outwards, with indents and pockmarks covering its surface.

After a while, a very short but obviously strong man arrived carrying several long knives. He was greeted with respect by the Tibetans and was evidently the Sky Burial Master. His torso was bare and he wore baggy shorts. He stepped onto the rock, carefully unwrapped the bundles and began to carve up the bodies.

I'd been worried that I would find it nauseating to see human bodies being cut up, but in fact I felt only curiosity, largely because the Tibetans themselves – the relatives and the Master – treated it like a normal, natural sort of event.

The sky was beginning to lighten. To the right, the rocky hillside curved up sharply towards a ridge high above us, while on our flat section of the mountain we became aware of a flock of huge birds watching the proceedings. They were massive vultures, the best-fed birds in the world. As the Sky Burial Master continued his work, the birds gradually moved down from the ridge towards the rock, flying and hopping, catching a bit of exercise before breakfast. The rocky outcrops were covered in the flags and wisps of material that Tibetans use to make shrines and there were small fires on some of the closer outcrops, sending thin trails of white smoke up into the still atmosphere.

The Master was cutting the bodies up in a definite and precise way. There was no obvious blood, because it's drained out of the bodies before the sky burial takes place. The Master carved the flesh into bite-size chunks on the thinner part of the rock, took the bones out, smashed them into depressions in the rock surface and then used an instrument to crush them into powder. By now the dozen or so vultures had hopped onto the fat end of the rock and were waiting expectantly for the first course. My memory is that the birds stood taller than the Sky Burial Master; I don't know if that's possible, but they were huge birds.

The Master took the pulverized bone fragments and scattered them onto the flesh chunks, then fed them to the vultures. The reasoning is that the vultures must eat the entire body to ensure the spirit of the dead person rises to heaven along with the white smoke, so the bone must be mixed in with the more tasty bits.

It was now pretty light and several Chinese wearing the standard blue Mao jackets of the era arrived to watch the spectacle. The Tibetans shooed them away, not allowing them anywhere near the campfire. The Chinese moved back a little up the hill and watched from a distance, but the Tibetans were clearly unhappy about their presence.

The ceremony was nearing its end and the bodies had almost been completely eaten when a jeep came roaring up the mountain below the sky burial rock, twisting around and up towards where we were standing. Two Chinese policemen jumped out, obviously extremely pissed off, and ordered myself and Will into the back. We were driven at a hurtling speed down to Lhasa, given a stiff talking-to and were made to promise that we wouldn't tell the other people in the party what we had seen.

The next morning, several of our companions, including some of the toughest and most resourceful foreign correspondents in the world, tried to leave the guesthouse to go to the sky burial site, but they were stopped before they even made it out of the door. Towards the end of our visit, word leaked out among our colleagues that we'd been to see the sky burial and they were extremely jealous.

Back on the road in Hubei Province, the rice was growing well, turning the paddy fields into brilliant carpets of emerald green. The weather was dry and the farmers were shaking their heads and making dire predictions about the harvest, but to my untrained eye, the rice plants looked healthy.

I came upon an old and wizened man, with a face and costume that could have been from the 18th century, resting by the road. He had a curved machete in his hands, a traditional peasant hat on his head, and a brown shirt – that could originally have been any colour at all – thrown over one side of his skeletal frame. I sat with him for a while and while his thick Hubei accent made it difficult to communicate, I ascertained that his surname was Zhang, that he was "a little short of eighty", that he had lived in this district all his life, that he had two children, and that he was interested in how much my camera cost.

As I continued on my walk in the hills, I saw many elaborate gravesites with large gravestones set amid plenty of tea and wide swathes of rice. This was rich farming country. I approached a turn-off to the Yingshan county seat and came upon a large gate and a sign proclaiming I had arrived at the 'Yingshan Hot Springs Mountain Resort.' I walked through the gate and a gatekeeper came out, gruffly asking "What do you want?"

"Ah," I thought, "A state-run place."

"This is a hotel, right?" I asked the man.

"Yes."

"So you take guests, right?"

He mumbled something unhappily, but I ignored him and walked up the shaded drive to a series of modern villas and a main hotel building. It had all the makings of a quiet and discreet weekend retreat for Communist Party leaders.

There was a notice board in the garden explaining the concept of 'Red Tourism,' a concept that essentially means people visit places that played a significant role in the Chinese Communist Revolution. This part of Yingshan rated highly in this regard as it was one of the places where the communist guerrillas established 'liberated zones' in the 1920s. The rebels were surrounded and attacked by the Nationalists and were eventually forced out of the area. The sign stated that Yingshan was the starting point for the Red Fourth Army Long March and that the Red Twenty-Eighth Army fought guerrilla skirmishes here. This hotel was clearly where Red Pilgrims stayed, enjoying the hot waters and at least pretending to have an interest in Red History.

The gatekeeper reappeared and told me to stop taking photos in the garden. "But this is a hotel and I am a tourist," I protested mildly, continuing to snap away.

"It's not allowed. You just go into the hotel."

I complied; no point starting a fight. "Who owns this place?" I asked as he escorted me to the front entrance.

"The Wuhan City Commerce Office."

A weekend resort for the Wuhan party leadership. Very nice. I walked into the cool lobby, passed billiard and ping pong tables, and was told by the receptionist that a standard room would cost me one hundred and sixty RMB. I asked to see the accommodations, which turned out to be three-star level, which was well above the standard of other hotels in this part of China. I said I would return later and walked back to the road.

A little way along, the quiet tree-canopied lane annoyingly merged with a newer thoroughfare that was dead straight and uninteresting. I walked along it for a kilometre or three in stifling heat; the clouds had dissipated and the sun was beating down onto my head. Sweat flowed into my eyes, which wasn't helping my photographic skills.

I came to an intersection and to my left was the resumption of the old '318,' while straight ahead a sign pointed to Wudang Mountain, a familiar name to me even though I had never visited it. Years before, I had translated a Chinese kung fu novel – *The Book and the Sword* – by the most popular author in modern Chinese literary history, Louis Cha. Known by his pen name Jin Yong, he is possibly the most pirated novelist on Earth. The first kung fu hero to appear in the book is Master Lu, a member of the 'Wudang kung fu sect' which 'stressed the use of Internal Force Kung Fu', and here I was at the foot of the mountain where Master Lu learned to use the Golden Needles!

With kung fu images dancing in my head, I turned back onto a peaceful, winding and shaded lane. There was a slope on the right and paddy fields on the left. A vehicle passed me every ten or twenty minutes, so it was just me, the cicadas and then Mr. Rao.

I came upon the old man as he sat by the road looking out over the terraced fields and I stopped for a chat. Mr. Rao was seventy-one years old and had been a farmer all his life, except for eight years in the late 1950s and early 1960s when he was a mechanic in the Chinese Air Force, stationed in Harbin. He was a rarity among the men I met in that he'd never been married and had no children.

"Why did you never marry?" I asked him.

"I couldn't afford it," he said. "When I came back from the air force, I had to look after my parents and my sister, and there wasn't enough money to take a wife." I asked if he regretted not marrying.

He shook his head. "The only advantage of a wife is that there is someone to look after you when you're old. Other than that, having no wife is better in all ways." He seemed pretty certain of this, presumably having seen some dragon-like wives in action among his neighbours over the years to reach such a conclusion.

I asked him about the road we were on. "Construction began in 1965 and it was finished in 1968," he said, which would make the trees shading us about forty years old.

The conversation turned to his land and he pointed to one of the terraces below us.

"That's mine," he said. "Each family has a piece of land for themselves. That way, everyone has food to eat. Things are good now. In the old days, there was the collectivization and the 'Big Pot of Rice' (the commune life), but people didn't have enough to eat. It was not good. Then Deng Xiaoping changed the policy and now everyone has enough food." And with that he rubbed his stomach.

I asked Mr. Rao what he did in the evenings. "I watch television and read books." What kind of books? "Religious books." He drew out the first of the two characters for religion in the dirt with his stick.

"Which religion?"

"Buddhism," came the reply. "There are many temples and shrines near here. There's a Guanyin shrine over that hill," he said, pointing.

I continued up the gently sloping valley with the cicadas going crazy. At the ridge at the top of the valley I came upon an old building from the 1960s with a sign stating 'Little Father-Son Ridge Forestry Check Station,' which was an attempt at halting illegal logging in the mountains. I looked through the door into the gloom and was instantly transported back to the Cultural Revolution.

A man in a vest and blue trousers was sitting in a rattan easy chair, a fan blowing on him, and on the khaki green wall behind him was a row of pictures. There they all were, lined up: Marx, Engels, Lenin, Stalin and, on the extreme right, Mao.

"What do you want?" he asked suspiciously, but after a few minutes of chatting, he warmed to the novelty of having a foreigner in his little office and offered me water and a seat. He said his surname was Jiang – the 'jiang' of Xinjiang, meaning border.

"Why the pictures?" I asked.

He looked at me and said nothing.

"You believe in them?" I asked.

"Yes, I believe in them," he replied.

Mr. Rao reappeared from down the road and just then I heard the four-note bird call again.

"What kind of bird is that?" I asked.

"You like the sound if it?" he asked.

"Yes. What bird is it?"

"We call it…" But I missed the name. "It is a seasonal bird. When we hear its call, we know it's time to start the rice planting."

I passed over the ridge and began walking downhill, which was much easier than uphill in the heat. I came upon another old man, a woman and a middle-aged man with crazy eyes all sitting by the road while three cows belonging to the woman grazed in an empty plot of land beside the road.

"Your land?"

"Yes," said the woman.

"Why not grow rice?"

"Too dry this year."

An old woman who said she was eighty-seven years old joined us. In age, stature and frame, she reminded me of Daisy Kwok, my friend in Shanghai who died in 1998 at the age of eighty-nine. Daisy was the daughter of the man who had founded the Wing On department store in Shanghai in 1918, when she was nine years old. She led the life of the rich and famous for several decades but after the Communist takeover, she lived the life of an outcast, downtrodden for having had the misfortune to be the daughter of one of Shanghai's richest men. But she survived the indignity of it with good grace and calm wisdom and would have become friends with her poor sister in the Hubei countryside.

The cows escaped and crossed the road and had to be brought back and then the old lady fell asleep sitting on the roadside. Life with all its tedium was as usual for them, but I needed to head on, walking past a stone quarry; past a sign saying 'Girls are descendants too'; and millions of mid-life rice plants, glowing in the sun.

I came to a small field shrine and paid my respects with a lighted incense stick and a few RMB. At the bottom of the hill, there was a substantial bridge over a river. Just before the bridge, on the right, was a little shop, and I stopped to buy some water at which point a dozen people gathered to see the foreigner. "Where are you from?" they asked.

"England (Yingguo). You are from Yingshan and I am from Yingguo."

Someone asked what I was doing, and I said I was walking from Shanghai to Tibet.

"I have just crossed the Dabie Mountains," I said. "I was looking for the Red Army. But I couldn't find them." That generated some amusement.

"That's because they've all retired," one of them said.

I pulled out my wallet to pay the one RMB for the water, and a man with a big smile said: "Ying bang (pounds sterling)."

"Right," I laughed. "Yingguo ren zai yingshan yinggai yong yingbang." An Englishman in Yingshan should use pounds sterling.

It was the last time I could use the Englishman in Yingshan joke, for the bridge proved to be the border between Yingshan County, the home of tea, revolution and moveable type, and Luotian County, home of I knew not what yet.

Dusk was approaching, but I continued through the late afternoon with the river course, dry and sandy, on my right. The air was warm, the cicadas were chirping, and I stopped occasionally for conversation. One was with a man sitting outside his house; a huge, three-storey villa that he'd built himself – he was a house builder by trade – for seventy thousand RMB. He had a wife and two children all working in Shanghai and the new house was very empty. He gave me some tea, my first taste of the rich, green Luotian brew, which was welcome, except that it was even hotter than I was feeling.

I stopped at a shop and met a woman and her two daughters sitting with an old man of no relation. I said I was from England and the man asked how far that was from Hong Kong, which was an interesting view of how the world is put together.

"England used to bully us," the woman said with a nervous laugh.

"British imperialism, the Opium Wars …" I said.

"… the Eight Nation Army," she added. The Eight Nation Army was the Boxer Rebellion relief force that trashed Tianjin and Beijing in 1900 on its way to raise the siege of the foreign legations in the Chinese capital.

I decided not to apologize for the activities of my ancestors. "Well, England is now small and China is becoming strong," I said.

"But England is more prosperous than we are," she said.

"There are poor people and rich people everywhere," I said. "You have television, telephones, fresh air and good food. Are you poor?"

"Well, maybe not so poor," she allowed.

The next morning, I almost immediately bumped into a field shrine. There were Buddhist elements about it, but the main deity in the altar alcove, flanked by a toy horse for its personal use, was an idol I'd never seen before. It didn't look like a Buddha, although Buddha comes in many forms.

I walked into the little town of Shiqiaopu (Stone Bridge Relay Station), and stopped by a pond for a minute to watch the women doing their washing. I imagine that most clothes in rural China are still washed by hand in streams and ponds. The task is clearly a ritual with the women, who enjoy a little time to exchange gossip in the open air, away from their dark and stifling farmhouses. In contrast, I have never seen a man washing clothes in any river, stream or pond across the long stretches of China I have crossed.

Stone Bridge Relay Station turned out to be a lively market town, but I was through it in minutes and walking over a bridge, which was disappointingly made of concrete, out of the town and back onto another delightfully shaded stretch of country lane. Whatever else you can say about the Cultural Revolution, they had the right idea in the 1960s about planting trees along roads.

I came upon a flock of beehives, the brown wooden crates that in China constitute a honey farm. I'd seen them many times as I walked across Anhui Province, each with dozens of bustling hives about a metre in height and a temporary tent off to one side where the honey men live. I decided this was the time to find out about the honey trade, so I introduced myself to the beekeeper.

Mr. Wang Qiudong (Autumnal East) was from Juzhou in Zhejiang Province, far to the east. He was forty-four years old and was taking care of eighty beehives. He said he moved the honey farm depending on the seasons, maybe four or five times a year. He'd been working with bees for twenty years and had been all over – Sichuan, Shandong, Inner Mongolia – searching for good hunting grounds for his bees. The honey men are the gypsies of China, always on the move, always apart from the local culture; transients with a different agenda.

He reckoned each hive had four or five thousand bees, which meant he had something close to half a million bees under his care. The bees lived for about one month each and, in normal circumstances, travelled within a radius of about five kilometres in search of pollen. The queen bees (which have the same name in Chinese) lived for seven or eight years and were bred separately by the beekeepers.

The 'sweet gypsies' appeared to have a pretty consistent approach to life, as all the honey farms I'd seen were almost identical in terms of the hives and the tents. The collapsible shelters are made from a dark-coloured waterproof tarpaulin containing a stove, a bed, a big tub full of honey, and lots of plastic bottles to hold the honey sold as retail. Mr. Wang offered me some royal jelly, but I turned it down in favour of some ordinary honey. The price was eight RMB for a jin; or about a third of a litre. I had a taste of the honey on a bread roll later that day and it was deliciously sweet, but very runny, and while I prefer a thicker consistency, it was easily the freshest honey I'd ever eaten.

Mr. Wang said he made eighteen hundred RMB in a good month, much less in poor months. The difference depended on the weather as beekeepers are as dependent on the weather as taxi drivers are in Shanghai. Their customers are mostly local residents, but they also sell in bulk to traders who collect and consolidate the honey and resell it on the international markets. He said he planned to give up the wandering honey life when he reached fifty and retire in his hometown of Juzhou.

Mr. Wang showed me the beehives, opening one up to reveal a series of wooden slats with the honey combs growing in the darkness. Somewhere in the middle was the queen bee, but I couldn't see her. Each hive had a small opening, a tiny door, and it was up to the bees to decide when to go out and for how long. No curfews in force here.

There are no known illnesses for the bees, Mr. Wang told me; there is no apicultural equivalent of foot and mouth disease or avian flu. The only problem they have is that occasionally a bee will ingest some pesticides along with the pollen, causing a few deaths in the hives.

As I talked to Mr. Wang, a couple of other gentlemen joined us, including a hearty old man named Ye Dingwu ("my name rhymes with one hundred and five"), who asked me where I lived. I told him I lived in Shanghai and asked if he'd ever been to that great metropolis.

"I've never been anywhere," he declared. "I've been here in Shiqiaopu all my life. In the old days, in the time of Mao Zedong, no one was allowed to move, everyone had to stay where they were." He made enclosing motions with his arms. "Now the policies have changed and we can go anywhere, but not me. I'm too old now to go anywhere." He said this with a smile, challenging me to disagree, which I did, as he was thin but healthy of body, quick of mind, and more alert than most people a quarter of his age.

I continued to walk under the hot midday sun up a long and gently sloping valley to a ridge named Mengmengshan. "What does it mean?" I asked a man at the top. "It's just a name," he said. It was the 'meng' of Mongolia with a dripping water radical at the side, and my dictionary later told me that Mengmeng together means misty.

I met some people loading logs onto a truck. Each log, they told me, weighed eighty jin (forty kilograms). With Mr. Jiang at the forestry station in mind, I asked if they needed a license to ship the wood out, but their reply was evasive. "Where is the wood going?" I asked. "To a coal mine," they answered, "To shore up the mine's shafts."

I passed a blind man walking down the hill, all alone in his own black world as he felt his way along the edge of the sealed road with a stick. A long and thin expanse of water, set in a north-south direction, appeared on the right, while the road headed south down one side, then turned at the tip and headed up along the western shore. I stopped near a house to look down at the lake and enjoy a cool breeze coming off the hills to the west and a man came out and sidled over to see who I was. We shook hands and I asked: "Does this lake have a name?"

He gave me a look as if to say that's a pretty stupid question: "Yes, it does. This is Phoenix Pass (Fenghuang Guan)." I later learned Phoenix Pass played a crucial role in Chinese history two thousand five hundred years ago, during the Warring States period, when it was the eastern border crossing for the kingdom of Chu. But on that day all I learned from Mr. Zhang was that the lake's water was clean and the fish in the lake were delicious because of low pollution levels (there's a growing awareness among the farmers of China that they are lucky not to have the pollution of the cities).

I asked the man about his home, which was an old traditional farmhouse. "How long has your family been here? How many generations?"

"Uncountable," he said. "Far back into time."

Perhaps one of Mr. Zhang's ancestors had been a Chu Kingdom border guard at the pass.

"How much has life here changed in recent years?" I asked.

"A lot," he replied, brightening markedly. "Changes that could not have been imagined. We no longer have to pay taxes, instead the government gives us money. Who would have guessed it?"

The abolition of the agricultural taxes in 2005 instantly removed the tension of centuries. There were still slogans on walls all over the countryside warning people not to beat up, surround, shout at and otherwise harass tax collectors, but it was all a thing of the past. The government in Beijing has found the perfect way to keep the peasantry on-side: Stop hassling them, hand out a bit of cash, and give them the opportunity to be mobile so that they can go out and earn some money to bring back home. As a result, the peasants are happy and all is peaceful under heaven. Relatively speaking.

The water lilies were in bloom and the cicadas were going absolutely crazy in the heart of summer. I walked beside the reservoir, up to the top of a ridge, which was also the point in the valley that had been dammed to create the reservoir. The dam wall had a huge 1970s-style inscription on it: "Water management is the foundation of agriculture". The cows and water buffalo were sunbathing in the fields, languishing in the crippling heat. I met few people on the road that day, with an exception being three farmers on motorcycles (looking nothing like Hell's Angels) who stopped to join me under a tree. One of them told me the story of Phoenix Gate.

"Once upon a time, before the reservoir was constructed, there was a little town there named Zhangjiawan (Zhang Family Riverbend). In the town lived a rich man who employed a worker to bring water to the house but, strangely, the water in the tub would disappear very quickly. One day, the rich man discovered that there was a phoenix living in the rafters of the house and the big bird was using the tub as his drinking fountain. The rich man decided to chase the phoenix away but the phoenix had just given birth to a baby phoenix, so it had no choice but to pick up the baby phoenix with its beak and fly off towards the mountains. Just as it was flying over Mengmengshan, the phoenix, in a moment of carelessness, let go of the baby phoenix, which had not yet even opened its eyes, and it fell to earth and died. From then on, the place was called Phoenix Gate."

Every corner of China has, no doubt, little fables like this that are known to the local people and no one else. Let's hope the stories survive.

CHAPTER 8

COUNTRYSIDE POLITICS

As I walked on, two boys fell into conversation with me and invited me for tea at their house, where I met their mother and sister. We chatted in their cool, concrete-box living room, which had wooden armchairs lining the walls and a television in the place where an altar would have been a generation ago.

The boys were Liu Huan, aged fifteen, and Liu Yang, aged seventeen. The latter was dressed in cool basketball dude type clothes and sported a dyed, spiky haircut. The mother, sitting next to Liu Yang, also had the same shade of dyed brown hair.

"Is there a genetic connection?" I asked.

"No, dyed," they answered seriously, then: "Oh, ha-ha."

We discussed the concept of poverty versus wealth, with them taking the view that they were poor, and me taking the view that they were pretty well off by many measures. The girl said she was twenty years old and was in the middle of a three-year secretarial course. I asked what on earth they could spend three years teaching her in a secretarial course. The answer was vague, but included "how to file documents" and "how to answer the phone." I suggested that instead of taking the course, she should just leap into the market and learn on the job, but she seemed convinced that she needed three years to learn how to answer the phone.

Like all the youth I met, the two boys said they planned to leave home as soon as possible and were hoping to attend university. Liu Huan said he wanted to study computer science, although, as far as I could tell from his answers, he had touched a computer maybe only once or twice in his life. Liu Yang said he wanted to found his own company.

"What kind of company?" I asked.

"Any kind," he said.

Further questions indicated the only volume business in Luotian was the production and shipment of Chinese chestnuts. The boys showed me some by the road that would be ready to eat in just a few weeks.

The kilometres went by quickly and I arrived in the late afternoon at the county seat of Luotian, a town markedly bigger than Yingshan and strung along each side of the Yi River (Yi Shui – the Waters of Justice – indicating there had to be a story behind the name). The waterway was a shallow dribble in an impressively deep and wide channel, suggesting occasional massive flash floods. On the edge of town I came upon a group of men who were studying the geography of the local rice paddies using a map laid out on the ground. I asked what was happening and the answer was that the fields had been earmarked for redevelopment into residential and commercial areas. These fields were growing their last rice crop. That was it, forever.

I walked on and stopped at a small shop on a corner with several people sitting around outside. I joined the group and asked about the rice fields behind and they all confirmed this would be the last crop. They asked me how I felt about that. I shrugged. "That green is the most beautiful colour in the world," I said. "But development is inevitable, so I don't know." They agreed. The town was growing and it could not be stopped.

Earlier in the day, a man on a motorcycle had stopped and offered me a ride. Of course I declined, but I took his mobile phone number and arranged to meet him for dinner. We met in the early evening at an open-air food market in the centre of Luotian town. The stalls were lined up and down the middle of the street and each mini-eatery consisted of plastic chairs, little tables, bare light bulbs strung overhead, raw food laid out in plastic containers, and a wok at the ready. I chose a stall, Mr. Hu arrived with his wife and we ordered some food, including my usual – beancurd and eggplant.

Mr. Hu said he was a salesman with a Luotian company that made parts for construction equipment. I asked if the company was state-owned or private and he pondered this for a while before saying: "Basically private." I love China; so grey.

The company was a state enterprise, which had sub-leased its entire operations to a private businessman, and had monthly revenues of about one million RMB. Mr. Hu wasn't paid a salary and was responsible for all his own costs, but he did receive a commission on sales. He said he did around one hundred thousand RMB worth of business a month, with a take-home income of a few thousand RMB.

As we talked, a sudden rain shower drenched us, and we raced to the cover of the buildings. The chairs and table were moved over, along with the wok, and we resumed the dinner sitting on the steps of an office building.

After a number of conversations on the subject, I discovered that Luotian is known for three things: Chinese chestnuts ('banli'); a peasant rebellion at some point in history (no one was sure when) led by a guy from Luotian who proclaimed himself emperor; and Lin Biao, the general and right-hand man for Chairman Mao in the late 1960s. He was born near Luotian and had an airfield constructed in the county to facilitate his commute to his home village. The airfield had recently been converted into an economic development zone.

Lin Biao is generally viewed today as a brilliant general who degenerated into an evil dwarf of a political schemer, using the increasingly senile Mao and the chaos of the Cultural Revolution to advance his own power. The political machinations and in-fighting led to a crisis that resulted in him suddenly flying out of Beijing in 1972, apparently on his way to Moscow. But the plane crashed in Mongolia, killing all on board. Was he fleeing after a failed coup attempt? That's the official story. I asked the people near the soon-to-be-retired fields about Lin Biao and one said: "There are different views on him. Some people say he was good, some bad."

"What do you think?"

"Good."

"Okay."

"It's not clear how he died," said another guy.

"In an air crash," I said. "England played a role in that."

There was a puzzled pause.

"The plane he was in was a Trident jet, British-made," I added.

Mr. Hu, the salesman of construction equipment parts, insisted on paying for the dinner, which for the three of us, including lots of beer, came to forty RMB. I made the mistake of asking him about the chestnuts, which resulted in him buying some for me. He also insisted on joining me for the start of the walk the following morning.

It took me about forty-five minutes to walk through the town, which was bubbling as Chinese towns do at that time of day. Scattered along the street were breakfast stalls selling noodles, dumplings and onion cakes. I chose a deep-fried onion cake, which was pretty disgusting, and then started my walk from the little shop at Three Li Bridge (Sanliqiao), where I had stopped the day before. ("Where is the bridge?" I asked. "There is no bridge.") Along the streets, there was a lot of construction work in progress and in the distance I could see apartment blocks rising from the dusty hills.

Suddenly, a man appeared in front of me on a motorcycle. "I'm a reporter with Luotian TV and I heard about you last night," he said breathlessly. "Can I do a report on you?"

"Sure," I said.

He hefted his professional television camera onto his shoulder and I resumed my walk, looking around and taking photos as he filmed me first from behind, then in front. Gripping television, for sure. Then he came over and said: "Can I interview you now?" We were in the middle of town on a nondescript piece of road, so I suggested we do the interview near the more picturesque bridge in the centre of town. He agreed, and with the river channel in the background, he turned on the camera.

"I would like to know your goal for this trip."

"The purpose is to understand China better."

"When did you come to China?"

"Many years ago. My first visit to Mainland China was in 1978. Just before the Third Plenum of the 11th Communist Party Congress."

"Why did you decide to embark on this cross-China 'Walk to Tibet' project?"

"I read a book written by an Englishman. In 1909, he walked across China and the title of the book was *Across China on Foot*. But, in fact, he didn't really walk across China. He walked from Chongqing, south-west through Szechuan and Yunnan to Burma."

"It was 1909, so it was Edgar Snow?"

"No, it was the end of the Qing Dynasty. Edgar Snow was an American, it was a different era, and that's another story."

"He wrote about China's Communist revolution."

"He wrote about what the translator told him. He couldn't speak Chinese. That's the difference between him and me. Whatever the translator told Snow, that's what he wrote down, whereas I can communicate with you by myself."

"Okay."

"I am walking from Shanghai to Tibet. I come out during the weekends or when I have free time. Each time, I start from the place where I last stopped. So I really am walking from Shanghai to Tibet, just not each day, every day."

"Then during the trip you have returned to Shanghai?"

"Yes, I'm flying back to Shanghai tonight. I have to work tomorrow."

"Oh. And then when you have time you will fly back and continue?"

"Basically, each month I have six or seven days of walking. My goal is to walk into Lhasa in August 2008. To crawl into Lhasa."

"So right across China, right?"

"Highway 318."

"Your entire journey will be along Highway 318?"

"A lot of it is along Highway 318, as long as it's in a westerly direction. For instance at Anqing, Highway 318 curves too far south, so I didn't take '318' at that point. After I pass Yichang, I think it goes south again, so I will continue going west through the Three Gorges."

"During your trip across China, do you have any interesting stories that you can share with us?"

"I have many interesting stories. Being interviewed by you is a very interesting story."

"You arrived in Luotian yesterday?"

"I arrived in Luotian last night."

"Where did you stay last night?"

"Dabieshan Hotel, here in town."

"And now your plan is…?"

"I returned to the last place that I stopped and now I am continuing. My purpose is to talk to people, communicate with people. I have talked to hundreds of people, thousands of people in Anhui, Zhejiang and Hubei. Ordinary farmers, children, everyone …"

"You arrived in Luotian yesterday. Today, you may leave Luotian. Do you have any comments?"

"The people I have met here have been very, very kind. Many of them want to invite me back to their homes for tea or water. That gives a very good impression. It's obvious that people here are very hardworking. Luotian is like other cities in inland China; its connections with the outside world are getting stronger, and people here know more and more about what is going on outside of Luotian. That, I feel, is a very good direction. Also, previously, perhaps not many Westerners have travelled to Luotian. But in the future, more will definitely come here."

"What do you feel is the best thing about Luotian?"

"Of course, it is the scenery. The fields are very beautiful. Green, the green is everywhere. It's a wonderful green. The air is very sweet, very nice. This is the difference between big cities and the countryside – the air quality. Of course, Luotian has pollution, too, and it's evident. But it's not as bad as, for example, Shanghai, where the situation is more severe."

"So, speaking to the entire Luotian audience, they see you as a stranger, they don't know you, right?"

"Right."

"So, you need to first introduce yourself and then talk about your journey. Okay?"

"Understood."

"Now, tell me your name."

"I can start? My name is Graham Earnshaw, my Chinese name is Yan Gewen. I was born in England and I am now fifty-three years old. I live in Shanghai; I have lived a relatively long time in Shanghai and greater China. My first trip into this part of the world was in 1973, before the opening up of China. After the Third Plenum ended, I came to live in Mainland China. At that time, I was a reporter in Beijing. I have basically been in greater China ever since. There have been a few periods of time when I have lived elsewhere, but for the most part, Shanghai is my base. I have a business in Shanghai. I can speak Chinese; I can read Chinese. I have a keen interest in China, Chinese society, Chinese culture. That is why, about two years ago, I came up with the idea of walking from Shanghai to Tibet. As it happens, they are almost on a straight line, around the latitude thirty degrees north: Shanghai, the Three Gorges, and Lhasa. So, when I have the time, I come out and walk. Every time I start from the last place I stopped. Each time I always walk towards the west… west, west, and more west. My goal is not a time-related one, not a speed-related one. It's not a matter of getting from point A to point B in a certain amount of time; that's not my goal. My goal is to have a better understanding of each place. For example, Luotian: Every day I have a chance to talk with local people, I say hello to everyone, and they say hello to me. Then we talk, we communicate. Communicating and sharing is very important. My goal is to better understand your situation; Luotian's situation. What are you like? What are you thinking about? And you may be curious about me as well. What am I like? What am I thinking? What do I think about Luotian? I can tell you, Luotian is a very beautiful place. The air is very sweet. A very nice place. I feel that this place is definitely developing. It is not as developed as Shanghai, but that is a positive thing, not a negative thing. Shanghai is not heaven, and Luotian is not so poor. In other parts of the world, it is the same. In England, for instance, there are people who are poorer than some people in Luotian. And there are some people in China who are richer than I am. That's the way it is."

"Okay. Very well said."

"Thank you."

I followed the River of Justice out of the town and saw some guys fishing on the opposite bank and cows grazing in the almost-dry channel. Further downstream, there were sand-dredging boats at work with huge pumps sucking up the river's floor and piling the sand on the shore.

Through the trees, I spotted a highly unusual bridge crossing the river. Built on wooden stilts, the one metre wide and two hundred-metre long structure was covered in earth and weeds. I had to walk across it. I had seen nothing like it anywhere.

The bridge shook as I stepped on it and it was a disturbing process moving forward, but I concentrated on looking straight ahead and tried to ignore the flimsy feel of the structure. The water rushed underneath and I finally stepped off the bridge onto the opposite bank where a woman in a pink blouse was waiting for me.

"That's five mao," she said.

I handed over the money (half of one RMB) and asked her how old the bridge was (she didn't know), when it had last collapsed (last year sometime), and who used it (farmers taking their goods into town to sell). My questions answered, I turned to re-cross the bridge.

"That's another five mao," she said.

I saw a tarpaulin-covered shelter below on the riverbank and went down to see who was at home, finding five men resting from the heat, lying on bunks surrounded by rusted metal, with a big plastic bottle of water in the middle of a table. They invited me to take a seat.

"What are you doing here?" I asked.

"We are digging sand," said one man who was dressed somewhat better than the rest of the group in a dark blue sports shirt.

"And then? Where are you going to sell it?"

"To steel plants for iron-smelting," he replied.

One of the men was cutting up a watermelon and offered me a slice. It was very sweet. Another was struck by the fact that I was a foreigner and said the first thing that came into his head: "Mixi mixi."

"That's what Chinese people say when they pretend to talk Japanese," I said. "Nothing to do with English."

"The Chinese have a poor impression of Japanese people," said an older man.

"It seems so, yes," I replied.

"Not seems so. How can it be 'seems so'?" he said indignantly. "But the English are considered friends."

"Really? The Opium Wars don't count?"

"The Canadians are also friends," he replied, dodging controversy.

"Really?"

"You don't think so?"

"You mean relations between the countries? What about between the people?"

"Right, right, right," he said. "But we Chinese are pretty stubborn in our views about that period around the time of liberation. The Japanese were the worst in that era."

"The Japanese involved in that war are all dead now," I replied. "They have passed on."

"They are dead, but their sons and grandsons still adhere to the same things," he said.

"Well, if you're going to include their descendants then, sorry, you're going to have to hold me responsible for the Opium Wars."

"No way!" the man said with a laugh. "You can't be held responsible for that. You wouldn't be distributing opium here, would you?"

"No," I said. "We're out of stock."

He laughed. "Even if you had stock, you wouldn't be able to import it."

I took another piece of watermelon.

"These little Japanese," said the man. "They've got some money, but there is still the militarism."

"How do you like this place?" the man asked.

"It's good," I said. "A fun place."

"What's fun about it? It's no fun."

"The scenery is good, the air is good. Fresh," I said between bites.

"Are the girls beautiful?"

"They are. Anyway, this place is very different from elsewhere. Are you all from Luotian?"

"Locally born and bred," said the man. "When you were learning Chinese, did you find it hard?"

"Of course it was hard at the beginning. But I live in China and I'm surrounded by Chinese, so it was not so difficult."

"So which do you think you have a better command of, Chinese or English?"

I laughed. "My mother tongue will always be the strongest. That's always the way."

"Enemy," said the man in English. "Enemy. I can't say it accurately."

I did a double take "Huh? What does 'enemy' mean? If it's an English word, then maybe you mean enemy," I said using the Chinese translation.

The man smiled.

"Is that what you wanted to say?"

He nodded. "Yes, that's what I was saying."

"Who taught you to say that word?"

"When you were walking towards us, I told them all to shout 'enemy' at you. But they didn't."

"Okay, my brother. So why did you tell them to shout 'enemy'?"

"Because I was reminded of the Opium Wars, and I remembered Lin Zexu, and thought of opium." Lin Zexu was the official in Canton who in 1840 or so had opium supplies seized from the foreign traders and dumped into the sea, sparking the war.

"Well," I said. "I forgive China for all the bad things it has done wrong in the past. I forgive you all."

They laughed at that.

"Every country has done bad things," I added.

"Well, that's true," the man allowed.

I changed the subject. "You guys are here all day. What about at night? Do you go home?" The man nodded. "How many hours do you work here every day?"

"We get here at five in the morning. Why don't you live with us here for a couple of days? What do you say?"

"Not enough time," I replied ruefully.

"Come back and have a meal with us," he insisted. "Experience the life of us Chinese workers. You are a friend from afar."

"Ah, so you treat me as a friend and not an enemy. Thank you!" I said.

We all laughed.

"But if you were Japanese, then we'd slash your tires and all of us here would be singing the song 'The Big Knives Chop off the Heads of the Devils.' Do you know the song?"

I quickly scanned the song catalogue in my head. 'Brown Sugar', 'Around Midnight', 'Summertime'… it didn't seem to be there.

"No, I don't know it," I said. "But individual people have nothing directly to do with their country's history and government policy."

"Well in our opinion, they do," said the man.

"Opinions are opinions. But I don't think you should assume someone to be bad. Who knows if someone is good or bad? There are bad people in China and there are also good people. I'm assuming you guys are all good."

They laughed.

"There were good Japanese people during World War II," the man agreed. "There were those who opposed the war and who helped us to fight Japan. You English also had a flying group that helped China, American and English pilots flying over Mount Everest from Burma." He was talking about the Flying Tigers, led by Claire Chennault.

"That's right," I said. "They flew into Chongqing."

"Right, into Chongqing. Not so many English pilots, more Americans. Anyway," he sighed, "War can't be avoided. Are you aware of the Eight Powers Military Force?"

"Of course I am," I said. This was the allied expeditionary force that marched on Peking in 1900 to relieve the siege of the foreign legations.

"Your ancestors were a part of it."

"Yes," I said. "May I take this opportunity of formally offering you my sincerest apology."

"No!" the man protested, missing the irony. "It's not necessary, really."

"Really, I must," I said.

"Do you return home every year?" the man asked, meaning to England.

"I live in Shanghai, so 'return' means there, not England," I said.

The concept of 'return' in China is extremely deep and often it took a while for people to understand that I no longer considered England to be my home.

"The concept of 'return' is becoming out-dated," I said. "For instance, more and more Chinese people are emigrating to America, Canada and Australia. Where do they 'return' to, China or Australia? It's becoming harder to figure it out."

"You've lived in China a long time," the man said. "How many years?"

"My first entry into the Chinese world was in 1973 when I arrived in Hong Kong. At that time, the Mainland was still closed. Then, in 1978, there was the Third plenary session of the Eleventh Central Committee and the windows were opened and in came the flies."

"Ha! You're calling yourself a fly? Deng Xiaoping's remark at the time was that if you open the window, it's hard to stop flies coming in."

"Right, that's what he said."

"So are you one of those that flew in?"

"I'm an English fly," I said.

"An English fly! Ha!" He liked that.

"It's harder to learn Chinese than English," the man observed.

"Why?"

"Because Chinese is complicated."

"I think, in terms of grammar, English is even harder," I said. "Chinese grammar is very simple. What is hard for foreigners is the writing."

"Yes, writing Chinese is definitely harder than English. In English you have just a handful of letters and everything you write uses just those few characters."

"Right," I said. "Twenty-six characters."

"How old are you?" he asked.

"I'm fifty-three, but the way you count makes me fifty-four."

My host offered me another piece of watermelon, but I'd had enough.

"What animal year sign are you?" he asked.

"Dragon."

"So, you use animal signs in England?"

"No, but we have star signs. I am a Capricorn."

"China uses that too," he said.

"Right, and China uses blood types as well."

"What do you do for a living?" he asked.

"I have a small company in Shanghai," I said. "Business is okay, thanks to the Party's benevolence."

He laughed. "I'm sure you're a good boss," he said. "You've got a sense of humour."

"Maybe. But when you have to fire someone you have to fire them."

"Do you smoke?" he asked, offering me a cigarette.

"No. You have an extra one for me. So, how long do you rest at midday?"

"We're resting for longer than usual today because the truck we use is off doing something else," he said.

"Do you have to pay a fee to the government in return for digging the sand here?"

"Well, of course!" he exclaimed.

"You pay the county government?"

"Yes."

"Which steel factory are you transporting the sand to? Wuhan?"

"The sand is processed in Wuhan, although we do some processing here too, and we also deliver to some other places. China's a good place, right?"

"China's a good place," I agreed. "There are plenty of problems, but the overall trend is good."

"The system is no good," the man said.

"What's wrong with the system?"

"This one-party system isn't good," he said. "It should be multi-party rule. It would be good if China could solve that problem."

"There's something in what you say," I said. "The one-party system doesn't allow for any competition or supervision."

"Right, exactly," he said.

"They're not afraid. In any multi-party system, the politicians are always scared that if they do not do a good job ..."

"...that if they don't do a good job, then another party will take over," the man completed my sentence.

"Right. The Communist Party calls itself great, glorious and correct. I'd say great and glorious might be okay. But correct? Not necessarily all the time."

"Right, that makes sense," the man said. "That slogan was used in the

Mao era, maybe around 1973 to 1976. Once Deng Xiaoping took power, it dropped out of usage."

"Deng Xiaoping was a great man," I said.

"You've lived so many years in Shanghai. What about Jiang Zemin?" he asked. Jiang had been the mayor of Shanghai and stepped down from the Party's chief post in 2003.

"What's your opinion about him?" I asked in return, dodging the question.

"Why won't you give your opinion?" he challenged me. "Anyway, what we say about Jiang is that he seems pretty obsessed with women."

"What about Hu Jintao?" I asked. "Are he and Wen Jiabao doing a good job?"

"They're doing okay."

"I agree," I said. "Hu Jintao doesn't shoot off his mouth, unlike Jiang."

"I'd say the policies are okay. But when it comes to implementation at our level, then it's different."

"The scrapping of the agricultural taxes was a good thing for you all, right?"

"Right. That was an improvement. But now school tuition fees are a heavy burden on us. College fees remain more than a normal family can afford."

"How much?" I asked.

"It costs about twenty thousand RMB a year to support one university student, meaning that it's difficult for even two workers to support one college student."

"Look at us," said another of the men who wore big glasses. "We are merely members of the powerless masses. We make a few hundred RMB per month. Not like him," he said, nodding at the boss, who was doing most of the talking. "He makes over a thousand. He is our boss. Did you notice that?"

"But look at your glasses," I said to the worker. "They are big, just like Jiang Zemin's. You must be the boss."

"I'm a potato head. A nobody," he said.

"So what do you think of our Mao Zedong?" asked the boss.

I decided not to dodge the question. "I would say that he did a good job up to 1949. I'm not sure about the seventy percent and thirty percent assessment of him as I'm not Chinese. But I do think the damage caused to China by the Cultural Revolution was huge. Look at culture and simplified characters, for example. I think he really used them to try to separate you from your own past. I think that's a terrible concept. How could anyone attempt to cut a people off from their own past? It's hard to understand."

"Unacceptable," the boss agreed.

"It was arrogance," I continued. "Mao thought he could replace Buddha, so there were Chairman Mao portraits hung everywhere. I feel that someone who tries to take the place of Buddha doesn't necessarily have a normal state of mind. What do you think?"

"What do I think?" repeated the boss. "My opinion is the exact opposite of yours."

"The opposite? Please explain."

"The way we see it, he was the founding emperor of our country."

"I know that," I said. "What he did – saying the Chinese people have stood up – that was good. The colonialist era was no good for China and no good for the world. China at the time was too weak, so Western countries and Japan could do what they wanted in China. Chairman Mao said that had to be changed, that China must be treated on the same level as other countries. That was correct."

"Right," said the boss. "It is true there were a few problems with the Cultural Revolution …"

"Ha! Not just a few. Too many people died," I said.

"Right, but you can't blame him alone."

"Who else? Lin Biao?"

"Right."

"But it's like a company," I persisted. "A company needs to have a boss, right?"

"Right."

"The basic corporate culture, the basic approach, the basic atmosphere, it all starts with the boss. If there's a problem with the boss, then the whole company has a problem. If Mao had handled things differently, then Lin Biao and Jiang Qing wouldn't have had an opportunity to create so much trouble."

"There were decision-making problems," the boss agreed. "He was getting old, that was the main thing. He wasn't as sharp as he had been."

"But there were already problems in 1957 and 1958," I added. "That wasn't a problem of old age. That was his arrogance."

"1957 and 1958 – the years of natural disasters and the anti-Rightist Movement," said the boss.

"The Great Leap Forward," I added. "All those campaigns. He was more formidable than any emperor, but Deng Xiaoping was amazing because while he held complete power in those years after 1979, he used it for the good of China and the world, not just for himself. And after him? Jiang was so-so as a leader. What's your view of Zhao Ziyang?" I asked. Zhao was chosen as Party boss in the 1980s, was arrested in 1989, and died while still under house arrest in 2005.

"We definitely liked Zhao Ziyang," said the boss. "And also Hu Yaobang."

"That was Deng's error," I said. "He let Li Peng and Jiang Zemin take control, so that during the 1990s there was no progress in terms of the system. But there was progress in other ways."

"Great progress," said the boss.

"For instance," I said, "when I first arrived in China, I lived in Beijing and as a foreigner I was only able to travel freely within a radius of twenty kilometres from Tiananmen Square. If I wanted to go further, I first had to apply for permission from the Foreign Ministry."

"Otherwise you couldn't go anywhere."

"But now I am walking from Shanghai to Tibet. One of the reasons I am doing it is to demonstrate that China is now genuinely open."

"What is your view on China's position in the world today?" asked the boss.

"Better and better," I said. "But I would say China is somewhat irresponsible in terms of some of its foreign policy decisions. They just blindly think about resources and energy. They are willing to do deals with Iran, Sudan – any crappy government – without concern for the consequences. That's not good. But if China is truly to be a mature member of the world community, then it has to consider issues from a global perspective, not only from China's perspective."

"On this question, my view is that while the Chinese often say the Americans are bad in this way or that way, in my heart I don't see America as bad," the boss said. "Why not? People call them the police of the Pacific, taking charge in everything. But with some issues, someone has to take charge, right? You can't just ignore the problems, otherwise the whole world would be in a mess."

"Right," I said. "Someone has to handle issues."

"When we were fighting the Japanese, the Americans helped us. It was basically the Americans that pushed the Japanese out of China. Without the Americans, we would never have been rid of them. In fact, at that time, the fight against the Japanese was basically the Nationalists. The Communists had nothing but rice and rifles, they fought as guerillas."

"Right, the Japanese were not pushed out. The war ended because of the American atomic bomb."

"Right," he said. "Hiroshima."

"In 1945, the Japanese armies in China were not retreating, they were still advancing," I added.

"Yes," he agreed. "If it hadn't been for the American atomic bomb, they would not have given up. And the Americans suffered greatly during the war too."

"Amazing," I said. "Here we are on the banks of this river discussing these big issues."

"Have another piece of watermelon to take with you," he said.

"Boss, what is your surname?" I asked.

"My surname is Zheng, same as Zheng Chenggong," he said. Zheng

Chenggong had been the leader of the Ming dynasty holdouts who fled to Taiwan in the 17th century in the face of the Manchu invasion.

He said he had a son studying at Fudan University in Shanghai so I gave him one of my name cards and told him to contact me when he went to see his son.

"Dinner on me," I said.

"Really?"

"Of course!"

CHAPTER 9

HARVEST TIME

Out on the wide plain that occupies most of Hubei Province it was harvest time. This is the centre of central China, the rich flat lands through which the Yangtze River flows. The area is almost totally bare – probably because over the centuries just about every tree has been chopped down for firewood. There are occasional efforts visible along the roads to plant new lines of trees, but it is obviously a recent development as they aren't tall enough to even cast a cool shadow on the road.

I walked through the harsh sunlight and watched the peasants cutting rice and wheat and picking cotton. Nowhere did I see a machine in the fields and over the next eighty kilometres I saw only two old clapped-out threshing machines being used to process rice stalks. All the hard work was still done basically by hand, as it had been forever. The grain was cut using long poles to which homemade blades had been lashed. The stalks were then tied up into bundles and humped to the roads and spread out for cars, trucks and people to trample, breaking the grain free. The cursing drivers were forced to drive over the grain and then, after a suitable amount of time, the straw was shaken, forked and lifted off, leaving millions of grains scattered over the road. These were swept up into piles and then winnowed. Such a lovely old English word and one I'd never had a chance to use; but the agricultural process here was as it was in the European Middle Ages and in the school books I had read as a boy.

I spent half an hour with a group of farmers, shaking and lifting the straw to separate the grain, using a simple pitchfork made from a forked branch stripped of bark. The farmers thought it was hilarious watching my clumsy efforts, but I enjoyed the task immensely.

The feel of the farmers out in the middle of 'Chinese nowhere' is usually pretty sleepy, but in this period – late August through to early October – they were awake, active, and engaged. This is the season they had been waiting for, after the long months of ploughing, planting and sitting around wondering how the harvest would turn out. The crops now needed a lot of work done quickly, with the reward of a big return: Grain bagged and stacked in the ceiling storerooms for the winter or sold to private traders in the nearest town for cash.

Later in the afternoon, I came upon a farmer with a pile of grain in front of him. He was using a shovel to throw the grain up into the air. The grain seeds fell into a neat pile close by and the wind carried off the chaff, leaves and other stuff mixed in with the seeds. It looked pretty easy. "Can I have a go?" I asked. He nodded and, as some barefoot village children watched, I took up the wooden shovel, as light as a feather, dug into the pile and slung the stuff up into the air.

"No, no, no!" he cried. "You have to wait for the wind! And you have to aim at that pile!"

I tried one more time, but he grabbed the shovel off me in disgust.

"Like this," he said.

I watched him closely for a while. The grain went up maybe three or four metres into the air and up there, beyond our heads, the wind flow was different. It can be calm where our heads are, but breezy a couple of metres above. A world so close, and yet so unknown to me.

Apart from the slight mess I had made, the grain pile was almost pure, and the road beyond was sprinkled with the bits and pieces that the wind had carried away.

He asked me my name; I asked his.

"So do you have a religion?" Mr. Liu asked me.

"No."

"But what religion do most people in England follow?"

"Christianity is the most common religion in England," I replied. "How about here?"

"We have a lot of Christians. Also Buddhists."

"Are they government-approved Christian churches or underground?"

"Oh, all approved," he said.

"Are you a Christian?" I asked.

Liu lightly wafted some leaves off the grain by waving the shovel just over the top of the pile. "No. I don't believe in any religion." He wafted some more. "But I have a conscience, which I think is enough." I nodded.

Another farmer walked up to us, his eyes red and glassy with alcohol, and as he approached I took some photographs of Mr. Liu in his tattered and patched shirt, slinging grain into the air.

"What are you doing?" the newcomer demanded.

"I'm taking some photographs."

"Why?"

"Because your home district is beautiful."

He gave off a confrontational vibe, said something to Mr. Liu and then to the children, then walked off.

"He thinks you shouldn't take photographs of us, because he thinks the scene is backward."

"It doesn't look backward to me," I said. "It looks traditional and interesting. What's your view?"

Mr. Liu shrugged. "I don't see it as a big deal."

I took some more photos.

I was walking towards the town of Sanlifan, on Highway 318, and on the way met up with a man named Zhu Wenhua (Culture Zhu). I said:

"How old are you?" although I already had a pretty good idea from his name. "Forty years old," he replied. Precisely; the Cultural Revolution began in 1966.

He was dressed in dirty, ragged shorts, was bare from the waist up, and one of his eyes was staring in the wrong direction. I asked Mr. Zhu if he was a farmer.

"No. I dig iron-sand. Sand that's sold to the iron plants. They use it to make pig iron."

The road was sloping gently downwards and beyond us was a long, long bridge over a wide, wide river flat. On the other side of the bridge was the town of Sanlifan.

"England is much better than here," he said.

"In what way and how do you know?" I asked.

"No corruption like there is here," he said.

"There's corruption everywhere," I said. "What's the situation here?"

"They want to stop us ordinary people from mining the sand because they've sold the concession to big companies. I've been fined more than ten thousand RMB and detained for several months."

"But you still do it?"

"What else am I going to do?"

We arrived at the bridge and he pointed to a little boat in a pond in the middle of the dry, sandy riverbed. What was left of the river was on the other side of the flats, closer to the town, a couple of hundred metres away. "That's my boat," he said, making it obvious that it wouldn't be difficult for the authorities to catch him in the act. Beyond, in the distance, was a huge industrial sand-mining craft.

I invited Culture Zhu to dine with me that evening but he took a rain check, saying he had another appointment: the busy social whirl of sand diggers in rural Hubei.

I walked on into the town and spent a few minutes watching some children playing billiards on a table set up on the pavement. A man in black slacks and a black leisure shirt walked over and it turned out he was Public Security Officer Chen. He asked me who I was, what I was doing and invited me to accompany him to the police station in his official car. I declined, saying I was just walking along the road, but I added that he was welcome to join me for a stroll.

"You're from England and England is a place with the rule of law, just like here," he said sternly.

"Absolutely," I replied. "Come on, let's keep walking. No time to waste."

He was unsure of how to handle this. People were supposed to just get into the police car when he told them to.

"So what are you doing here?" he asked, falling into step beside me.

"Just walking through. Having a look. This place is really beautiful. Actually, I am walking from Shanghai to Tibet."

He tried to make me stop again, but hesitated to physically restrain me. He asked for my passport, and I showed it to him without handing it over. I knew he wanted to hold it hostage, so I offered him my name card in its place, which he refused. I was the first foreigner that Officer Chen had ever met and he had no idea how to manage this situation.

Before too long he dropped back, made a call on his mobile, and disappeared. Fifteen minutes later, on the outskirts of town, a police car was cruising up just as I was saying goodbye to two young men on a motor scooter with whom I'd been chatting. I walked on, but instead of following me, the police car stopped at the scooter. Officer Chen and a man in a white shirt stepped out of the vehicle and started questioning the two young men. I walked back to them as I didn't want anyone to be in trouble because of me.

"Hello, officer," I said. "Let me introduce you. This is Xiao Li, a computer technician and very smart. His friend is Xiao Xu."

Total puzzlement. "How long have you known them?" asked the man in the white shirt, who turned out to be Officer Chen's commander, Officer Zhang. The latter had been drinking, but there was nothing wrong with that. It was a sleepy Saturday afternoon, after all.

"I just met them," I said breezily. "Xiao Li here also speaks some English. He would make a good official." I offered Officer Zhang my name card and he took it from me.

"Thank you," he said. "I also offered one to Officer Chen earlier, but he declined." I grinned at Chen, who looked sheepish and then took the re-offered card.

"So you're walking to Shanghai," Officer Chen said, pointing west.

"Officer Chen," I said, "that's the way to Tibet. Shanghai's that way," and pointed in the other direction.

I left the policemen talking to the two boys and walked out of town, back into the countryside. Another half hour went by and then three police cars passed me and stopped up ahead. Out stepped Officers Chen and Zhang, plus a senior police official in uniform and a lady in her thirties with shortish, fashionably dyed hair.

The senior officer led the delegation towards me, saluted and said: "Good afternoon, here is my ID card." With that he handed me a credit card sized piece of plastic with the police logo, his photo and his name.

"Officer Tu," I said. "Good afternoon."

"May I see your passport?" he asked.

"Will you immediately give it back to me?"

"No problem," he said politely.

I gave him my passport. He examined it briefly then handed it to the lady, who gave my document the full treatment. The other man pulled out a small digital video recorder and started filming the scene.

"Please stop that, I haven't given you permission to film," I said, pushing my luck a little, but he put it down.

One of them said something that indicated the lady could speak English. She must be the designated person in the local government to deal with English-related issues.

"Your Chinese is very good," she said.

"Thank you. I'm sure your English is good too."

But she stuck to Chinese as she asked me questions about what I was doing walking through their district. Later, someone told me the police had told him they were suspicious of me because, unbeknownst to me, the area contained several military bases (smart move, guys.) But I stuck to the truth, which was that I was walking from Shanghai to Tibet.

The lady continued to examine the passport, trying to find some clue to back up my statement or find another explanation for my presence.

"I think it's like this," I said gently. "Things are changing. The 21st century is here."

She nodded, head still down in my passport and its multitude of visa stamps. "The world is turning," she murmured.

I gave Officer Tu a name card.

"You have a Chinese name," he said.

"Sure!" I said. "And I would imagine the lady has an English name?"

"Yes, I do," she said. But she didn't tell me what it was.

"You could also have an English name, if you like, Officer Tu," I said.

"Why?"

"Because English is now the international language."

"Chinese is becoming very popular too," he said.

"Definitely," I agreed vigorously. "Many foreigners are learning your language and taking Chinese names."

The lady finally looked up from the passport.

"So it doesn't appear I'm committing any crimes, right?" I said with a smile.

She smiled back.

"Could you give me your name?" I asked, "Just in case I run into any problems along the way."

She wrote out her name and mobile number on a card. I invited her and Officer Tu and Officers Chen and Zhang to dinner, but they all politely indicated that they would not be available (the social life of Sanlifan is clearly totally frenetic). She handed me my passport, we all said goodbye, they drove off and I continued my walk.

The end of the harvest season was drawing close, but, sadly, it was not a very good harvest due to the dry weather. Already, there were tinges of brown visible in the fields and the ponds and streams were low-to-disappearing-to-gone, making me wonder if overuse of water upstream was a part of the problem. However, there was still a lot of cotton action as the last of the picked crop was being dried and packed in bags. In turn, the roads were filled with trucks and three-wheel putt-putts carting the bags of cotton to town to sell to small traders. "It ends up in England, where you come from!" said one cotton trader, beaming.

But for most of the farmers, the peak of activity had passed and I saw many in doorways playing cards or mahjong in the balmy late autumn weather.

I was walking towards the town of Xinzhou, the main town in central-eastern Hubei. The road was long and straight, the country flat and featureless. There were denuded cotton fields and some late rice. I passed a cemetery with a sign stating 'No firecrackers' surrounded, of course, by the detritus of many spent firecrackers. The peasants need to mark the passing of their people with noise and if they can't do it in the cemetery then they light the crackers right outside the gate.

It was about noon when a group of children passed me on bikes, each with a red neckerchief indicating they were members of the 'Young Pioneers,' the Communist Party's equivalent of the Boy Scouts. The youths asked me where I was going and I returned the question. "We're going to school," they responded.

"What time does school start?" I asked.

"At 11.30."

"You're late. Pay the fine!" I said.

One of the boys laughed. "We'll fine you!" he shot back.

They turned off the road towards their school, but before they left I gave them a couple of name cards and told them to give them to their teachers. "Tell them I would love to come to the school and meet them," I said, but I didn't receive a phone call.

Xinzhou was a booming little town, but my main memory of it was the chaos outside a primary school gate. School had just finished, the students were streaming out, and the entrance was a cluttered mess of taxis, motorcycles for hire and private cars, all with drivers waiting to pick up children. This was a vastly different scene compared to the country school I had passed a few kilometres back. While Xinzhou was expanding quickly, the nearby country hadn't yet given up its quiet ways. Still, I did see a cow on the main street and there remained a few little country touches along the roadside.

I continued to head west along a shaded back street and noticed quite a number of small medical clinics along the way. In each one I could see people sitting quietly and hooked up to intravenous drips.

I passed a donkey grazing on some grass under a sign that stated: 'Warmly welcome the victorious holding of the third Xinzhou Party deputies meeting!' I thought: third? And then the town ended and I was presented with a long bridge over a wide river, no doubt the original reason for Xinzhou's location, but now an unused waterway except for some sand diggers in the distance. I presumed all the rivers in this region had once been used for transport, at least to some extent, but the low water levels and the growth of the road system meant they'd become irrelevant. I could see only two sampans on the water, both moored and neglected.

Over the bridge, I was back in the countryside. Cotton and more cotton had been laid out on the road to bake. The country lane I had chosen was an old thoroughfare, straight as a die and lined with trees and farmhouses. I stopped at a small store and sat beside a friendly tabby cat that started licking the sweat off my fingers. I talked to the people sitting around enjoying the sunshine, including one man who turned out to be a 'doctor' whose clinic was next door. I asked him about the intravenous glucose drip situation.

"I administer probably a dozen or so a day," he said. How much for one? "One note (yizhang)." I looked puzzled. "Ten RMB," he explained. Ah. Up to the early 1990s, the ten RMB note had been the largest denomination in the country. So I did some quick math and guessed he was doing turnover in terms of drips alone of around three thousand RMB a month. Plus other medicines and services. Not a bad little business.

"For what ailments do you prescribe a drip?" I asked.

"All sort of things," he said with a shrug. "Colds… "

I went with him to the clinic, which consisted of two rooms, one with a desk, the other with two bed spaces and drip stands. An old man was lying on one bed with a drip attached to his arm.

"So you're taking a drip," I said as I shot some photos in the gloom of the room.

"Yes," he said, his eyes gleaming slightly.

"What's the problem?"

"I have a cold."

Ah.

Basically, it seemed to me, the drip treatments were a money-making scam by country doctors and the peasants were completely convinced that if they were feeling even a little out of sorts a pick-me-up intravenous drip would solve the problem.

I came upon a man sitting on a motorcycle and we chatted for a few minutes when I noticed he had a character tattooed onto each of his wrists: Hong (red) on one and ping (peace) on the other. I asked what it meant.

"It's the name of my wife," he said. I walked on and as the man drove by, I stopped him. "Did she ask you to do the tattoo, or was it voluntary?"

"It was voluntary," he said with a smile.

A little further along the lane, I entered a village bustling with the cotton harvest. Guys were loading trucks and heaving bags and racing off to market. Directing operations was a powerful, thickset man astride a motorcycle. He took one look at me and decided he wanted to have a conversation. He was Ren Xueqiao (Snow Bridge Ren), the local village party cadre.

"How did your parents choose your name?" I asked him.

"I don't know."

"Were you born in winter?"

"Yes."

I asked about the harvest, and he said it was not great. I gave him my mobile number and suggested we have lunch the following day.

Further along the road was another clinic. Sitting by the door were two young women with their children passively sitting on their laps with intravenous drip needles stuck into their bodies. One child had a needle inserted in a wrist while the other had a needle stuck in the forehead.

I asked one mother what the problem was, but received the same old answer: a cold.

"Does the child regularly have intravenous drips?" I asked.

"Not so often, but this is the second day in a row."

"Why stick the needle in the forehead?" I asked.

"It's less likely to fall out if the child moves about," she said.

I wanted to whisper to these mothers that all children suffer from colds, that it's okay and they shouldn't give them drips because it is bad in many ways (I was thinking of possible infection, needle dependency, increased passivity), but I didn't feel it was my place to do so. Instead, I asked some pretty direct questions and asked them to justify their approach to child-rearing, which seemed to be 'when in doubt, stick in a needle'.

I passed through Liji, another town by another apparently unused river, and rejoined Highway 318. At the corner of the highway, as at many intersections in rural China, there was a clump of motorcycles and three-wheelers – the local equivalent of taxis – waiting to ferry people arriving on the little minibuses that ply the routes between the towns. I said "ni hao," and the drivers gathered around. One in wraparound sunglasses said in English: "Hello."

"Hello," I said.

"Good morning," he said, also in English.

"Good morning," I replied, intrigued.

"Police," he said in English with a wicked smile on his face. That stopped me.

"Uh, police?"

"Police!" he hissed. "Jingcha!"

The others laughed. Ah, a joke. "Please sir, don't arrest me!" I pleaded.

One of his friends had a military police helmet as his motorcycle helmet. He pointed at my camera and asked me to take his photo. I did and then pointed to his helmet. "Can I borrow that?" He handed it over and I put it on, then handed the camera to him, and asked him to take the photo. Several drivers clustered around to be in the shot and a slightly crazy woman, who couldn't talk but grunted a lot, busily tidied up my shirt and patted my pockets straight before the shutter clicked.

A driver asked where I was from, so I said England, and another driver, with a useless left hand, said: "Blair."

"Right, but not for much longer," I replied.

"You can vote," he said. I nodded. The implication was clear: we can't. Who said ordinary Chinese people are apolitical?

The countryside was turning bleak, even in the rich autumn. There were virtually no trees, and I decided there was a strong connection between trees and civilization.

I trudged briskly over the bridge in Liji and spotted a little restaurant on the side of the road with the sign 'Xinhua Restaurant'. I was taking a photograph of the sign when several men came up and asked me what I was doing.

"I am taking a photo of the Xinhua Restaurant. Is it related to Xinhua News Agency?" I asked.

"No," they said.

"There's a big difference between the Xinhua Restaurant and Xinhua News Agency," I said, and paused. They waited for the punchline, bless them. "The Xinhua Restaurant makes money."

They looked at each other for a moment and then laughed.

CHAPTER 10

MR. REN

As I walked into the village of Gantang, my mobile rang and it was the party cadre I had met the previous day, Snow Bridge Ren. I invited him over for a chat and he agreed to come. So I walked up and down the short strip of buildings that is Gantang, looking for somewhere to sit and have a drink with him. There were no tea houses and no restaurants, so I stopped off at a fruit stall on the north side of the road and started talking to a fat, jolly guy who introduced himself as the local butcher. "If you want pigs killed and cut up, I'm the person for the job," he told me.

There was a shop front there, although it was not clear what happened inside. I asked if there was a table and some stools and these were brought out, but it was too hot in the sun, so I arranged for everything to be moved over to the south side of the road, in the shade. It was great; we had a table and lots of chairs under a tree, about a dozen people sitting around chatting, and I bought a dozen or so bottles of mineral water to lubricate things. I asked them about Gantang, when a young boy came up and stared intently into my face, fascinated by my blue-grey eyes.

"Ni hao," I said. He ignored me, concentrating on my eyes. I was determined to make him acknowledge my existence beyond the colour of my irises. "Ni hao? Can you talk? Did you hear me?"

"Answer him," someone else said to him.

"Ni hao," said the boy, off-hand. "Wow, there are all sorts of colours there," he said, turning to someone else.

I asked his age (seven years old) and asked him to write out his name, which he did. I gave him my name card. There was a little girl looking at me steadily, so I also asked her age. She crooked her finger in the Chinese way of saying nine. "Nine," she said. She was smart and patient. I gave her my name card as well.

The conversation with the group continued, and it was extremely pleasant sitting on the little stools around the little table by the side of the road in Gantang. I kept one stool vacant and one bottle of water waiting for my friend, the village party secretary. After a while, my mobile rang and it was Comrade Ren announcing his arrival. I looked around, saw him a hundred yards down the road, and waved to him to join us. Instead he disappeared into a shop. I waited a few minutes, but there was no sign of him, so I stood up and walked over to the shop. He was inside choosing a drink, and as soon as I saw him, I realized the problem: he was an official, and felt uncomfortable with the ordinary people unless it was clear – as it was in his own village – that he was the boss. Sigh. The Communist Party's myth of itself is so far from the reality.

We sat outside the store, the two of us, and the two children came over to join us, but the other people stayed at the original table or drifted back to their lives.

The seated store manager joined in the conversation, but he was a certified idiot. Mr. Ren the cadre was a little better. He had come because I was a foreigner, someone from England, and he wished to address this English person on the state of global politics from the Party's perspective, as he had absorbed it from meetings and documents that had filtered down to his little village.

"I tell you, I only came over because you are disabled," he said as an opening. "You understand?"

"Really? Yes, it's true I have a little problem with my leg."

"Where are you from in England?"

"Manchester, in the north of England."

"Is your country scared of Germany?" brayed the store manager, who was listening in.

"No," I said.

"I wanted to discuss a fairly political topic with you," said the official, "So please give me your thoughts with no sugar coating."

"Okay."

"It's like this. The US has been the dominant world power and the United States and Britain are basically like one big family, with a really good relationship."

"That's right, there is a good relationship."

"Right, a really good relationship. Whatever action the US is planning, it always pulls the UK in. Look at the war in the Middle East, you see that? They're partners. Now, let's address a question, the question of Iran, and its nuclear facilities."

"And nuclear weapons?"

"No, they're not working on nuclear weapons. Not now. What they are doing is nuclear (power) facilities and nuclear materials."

"Really? I don't know."

"Listen, why does the US meddle in Iran's nuclear projects? Do you have any idea?"

"I have no idea."

"It is a fine example of the powerful bullying the vulnerable."

"So the US is bullying Iran, is that how you see it?"

"The US is not only bullying Iran. The US is this mammoth economy that is ... really, really rich!" He shifted on his seat. "We don't have too much time. I would like to make a suggestion to you."

"Okay, go ahead," I said.

"You are welcome to visit China," he declaimed. "Wherever you go, you are an international friend."

"I appreciate that, thank you."

"We talk straight with our friends no matter where they come from.

Although, of course, there may be certain political or sensitive subjects that should be avoided."

"Ask away," I said. "Any sensitive question is fine."

"Okay, here's one. Do you have British or Chinese citizenship?"

"British."

"Do you have a lot of friends in China?"

"Yes, I do. You can never make enough friends, right?"

"Life isn't easy when you are away from home. Have you been away from your home country for more than a year?"

"Yes."

"Our country is in a developing stage."

"Okay. But what about your sensitive question? I'm disappointed you haven't asked it yet."

"Here's the question: once a country becomes powerful, other countries begin to take a different view of that country. Some issues cannot be decided by you or by him. If your country is relatively small, then he (the powerful country) can use economic sanctions or military means (against the smaller countries). Have you seen this?"

"Yes."

"The Western world's attitude to the Communist Party ..."

"How many years is China behind the West?" asked the shop-keeper insistently.

"There's no precise answer to that question," I said.

"Make an estimate. Twenty to thirty years? Fifty years?"

"I have no estimate. The two places are completely different. In some ways, China is more advanced than England," I said.

"No way!" the shopkeeper shouted dismissively.

"Have you been to England?"

"The West always seems to have a negative view of communist parties," Cadre Ren said.

"Yes, the West has a negative view of communist parties," I agreed.

"Right, that's the way it has always been, that is clear. In the time of Mao, there were two camps in the world, and our side was led by the

Soviet Union. Later that camp broke up, but communist parties are not what they say they are. They still operate on behalf of the working masses, for the people. Basically, the policy of our country is 'serve the people'."

"But there's no transparency," I pointed out. "You can never see what they are doing, so there is corruption."

"Transparency … It's true that there is a deficiency of transparency in some areas compared to the West."

"So that leads to corruption, which is a problem, right?"

"Yes, that is a problem I have to admit."

"So how to solve that problem?"

"This is not a problem that can be resolved overnight, I think."

"How about with a multi-party system?" I suggested, more to goad him than as a serious suggestion.

"There are many problems that have not been resolved," he replied. "China's corrupt officials are very numerous."

"Yes, because there's no way to effect proper supervision."

"That's the way it is for a corrupt official. If you are discovered, if someone accuses you, then you are exposed. But if no one comes forward, then they are safe. Imagine how much money those corrupt top officials in China have taken for themselves!"

"So would a multi-party system be better?" I asked.

"Not exactly."

"So which would you advocate? A one-party system or a multi-party system? If it was your choice."

"I would definitely choose the single-party system," he said. "But it must be democratic. You can't go without democracy."

"That's good," I said. "Are you a party member?"

"Yes, I am a party member," said Ren.

I smiled, telling him: "In fact, I guessed." The shopkeeper cackled.

"I'm a party member and I must heed the opinions of the party and the people. In terms of other parties participating in government …"

"Are you corrupt?" I asked him straight out.

He looked around, a little flustered. "Me, corrupt?" He had never before been asked this question. "No… well… I'm not in a position to be."

"Not in a position to be? You mean you just don't have the opportunity?"

"I don't have that situation," he said (meiyou zhege tiaojian).

The shopkeeper howled in delight. "So it's not that you don't want to be corrupt, ha-ha-ha!!!" he shouted.

"You can't say that it's not that I don't want to be corrupt," Cadre Ren scolded him. "Let me tell you, this ruling party here in China, it's not every official that is corrupt. I'll give you an example, listen. In Xinzhou there is a finance official who made a comment, let's see if you understand it. He said: 'I can have a meal, or receive a packet of cigarettes, but other than that, nothing. Why? I've got an annual salary from the state of several tens of thousands. If I was corrupt and lost that rice bowl, then I would have nothing.' What do you say to that? That's the way people are. For people who want to be corrupt, no amount is ever enough. When he's got 100 million, he wants another billion, when he's got a billion, he wants ten billion. As the old Chinese saying goes 'The human heart is never satisfied.' Do you also have a lot of corrupt officials in England?"

"Not as many as there are in China."

"It has to do with the system," he said.

"Exactly," I replied. "It absolutely has to do with the system. A one-party system means there's no one who can oversee them. So they're not afraid. You (plural) are not afraid."

"You are missing the key point of this problem."

"Really?"

"Corruption is not the result of our one-party system. But it is true that there are not many communist countries left in the world."

"Why is that?"

"Tell me your view," he said.

"I have no idea. You are a communist party member. Why have other countries decided to abandon communism? Why have they thrown away their communist parties?"

"Because communism doesn't work well, ha-ha-ha-ha!" squealed the shopkeeper.

Soon after this, Cadre Ren announced his departure. We shook hands and he returned to the little village where he ruled supreme.

The group down the street had broken up. The butcher and I moved the table back across the street and the owner of the shop who had lent me the table refused to accept any money in return.

Back on the road, I began to pass posts by the side of the road inscribed with the words: 'Defense Communications Optical Fiber Network'. The People's Liberation Army had dug a trench alongside Highway 318 and laid a cable to link their facilities in Hubei into the national defence network, then put signs every couple of hundred metres to let everyone know. Great! Plug in here!

I am in a position to state categorically that the Hubei plain is huge and boringly flat, and I walked quickly. One day, I watched two PLA air force biplanes doing training passes above me for a while; I photographed a blacksmith at work – he shouted at me when he saw me taking pictures, but his assistant grinned in delight – then I passed through the town of Liuzhi, meaning six fingers, and of course I had only one question. I went into a shop and bought a bottle of water, put up my hand and asked it.

"I have five fingers," I said. "Why is your town called Six Fingers?"

"That's the name of the town," said one man.

"I know that. But what is the derivation of the name?"

An older man with an abacus sitting towards the back looked up. "There used to be someone living here who had six fingers on her hand," he said. "An extra finger beyond the little finger. That's where the name comes from." I thanked him and carried on.

CHAPTER 11

HORSE COUNTRY

I finally arrived in the town of Huangpi, directly north of Wuhan in the middle of the plain. Up until the late 19th century, it had been a major financial centre, but was now of little consequence compared with the bulk of Wuhan about thirty kilometres to the south. I only skirted the northern edge of the town, however, and continued westwards along a road that I soon realized was reserved for military establishments, many of them air force. I decided to take fewer photographs as I passed by as there were sentries on several of the gates and there was no point in risking a misunderstanding.

Soon the military compounds yielded to rice fields again, some containing late rice crops, ripe but not yet harvested. There was a light drizzle, which faded gradually, leaving just a grey, overcast day. There was almost no one along the way to talk to, and the countryside was nondescript, so I concentrated on putting some kilometres behind me.

I came to the village of Songdian, a drab line of dwellings fronting onto the main street and, as I walked along, I was suddenly aware of a disturbance on the other side of the road. There was a man dragging a human being along the road as if he or she was a rag doll. He was angry;

the rag doll was limp. He was almost running as he pulled the load along, perhaps thirty metres, and it happened so quickly I barely noticed any details, but I believe it was a woman, not a child. He threw her inside a door and slammed it shut, then walked back onto the street, muttering. He looked like just any guy I would meet on the road, and I was shocked by the suddenness, the violence and the implications of what I had just seen.

Was it a domestic quarrel? No. The woman would have been kicking and screaming. A mentally impaired person who had escaped from the house and had to be thrown back inside to avoid embarrassment to all? That seemed more likely. But this man really, really wanted this person off the street.

I wasn't sure what to do, as a stranger – and foreigner – in a small village who had witnessed such a distressing and violent incident. I stopped and looked at the door and at the man for a little while. A woman, who had also seen the extraordinary event, walked past, but she seemed oblivious. Meanwhile, I was just an outsider passing through. I felt powerless.

From that point, I walked straight through and out of Songdian and tried hard not to make eye contact with anyone else in the town. The sense of evil was compounded by the ordinariness of the guy and of the house into which the person had been thrown, and it made me suspicious of everyone in the vicinity.

A little further west, I walked through a tunnel under the main Beijing-Guangzhou railway line, which in some ways is a 'meridian' with the line dividing China vertically in two. There was a steady stream of freight trains passing in both directions above me and, as I stood under the bridge, a thought occurred to me: I had been at this exact spot once before in my life.

In March 1979, I had been chosen to be the third of three Reuters correspondents in Beijing. My wife and I travelled from London to Hong Kong and then, to enter China, we walked across the border bridge at Lo Wu, where we were met by a young official in a smart, light grey Mao suit. He took us to a room that, with its antimacassar-covered sofas, had the feel of the Cultural Revolution. We then boarded a train for Beijing and spent the next two days quarantined in a sleeper compartment with occasional stops at gloomy stations where the masses in blue Mao jackets (workers) and green jackets (soldiers) scurried in herds along the platforms. It was an alien world; a world with no colour or free will. We spent the time in the compartment learning Mandarin and looking out of the window at the fields and houses and great splashes of yellow rapeseed, gaining a blurred sense of Chinese rural timelessness. At some point on that trip, we passed over the underpass in which I was now standing.

The country lane linked to the main highway between Wuhan and my next objective, the town of Xiaogan. I turned right and hiked onwards. It was a long and featureless road, relieved for a while by four eight-year-old girls who wanted to talk to me. Their leader, named Ms Li, was extremely smart and asked lots of good questions.

"What do you think of Chinese people?" she asked.

"They are people, just like people everywhere," I replied. "What do you think of Chinese people?"

"Good!" she said.

"Are there any people in your village who are not good?" I asked, thinking of the man in Songdian.

"Everyone is good in our village; they all help each other," she said.

I crossed a bridge over the main north-south freeway, the Beijing-Zhuhai expressway, and found that one of the lanes heading north was closed due to a traffic accident being handled by police. "Too many new drivers on the roads," said a man standing on the bridge.

"True," I said. "But five years from now, when awareness of freeway driving and its inherent dangers has taken hold, as it has in Europe and the United States, it will be better."

That's me, always the optimist.

I walked on into the booming little town of Xiaogan, the name of which means something like Filial Feelings. I passed by the temple and garden of the man named Dong Yong, whose filial piety had given rise to the town's name. As I walked, a man approached me from behind with his jacket bunched up and held above his head to shield himself from the sun. In his late fifties, he had greying, spiky hair, and he said he was a calligrapher. We started a conversation, which was pretty tedious until he delivered this line: "I am Jiang Zemin's younger brother."

"Jiang Zemin's what?"

"Younger brother. But he won't acknowledge me."

I studied his face. No resemblance to the former party chief. No big glasses.

"I have sent letters to the Central Committee, but they say Jiang Zemin is too busy to answer me himself."

"Where were you born?" I asked.

"In Yichang. Look." He pulled out his state-issued identity card, which gave his birth date as 1947. That seemed much too young for him to be Jiang's brother. But his surname was definitely Jiang.

"You're really his younger brother?" I asked.

"Absolutely! Fifth generation removed of course. But the ancestral relationship goes back much less than one hundred years."

Ah. The concept of extended families: Chinese people often refer to a cousin as being a brother or sister, particularly in these post-population control days of single-child families. Even so, referring to a distant cousin as a big brother was surely stretching the idea.

"Well, Mr. Jiang is retired now, and his friends are all being removed," I said. "Do you intend to continue to try to contact him?"

"No, I've given up. But you must come to my home and see some of my calligraphy," he said.

"Next time, definitely," I said, and waved goodbye.

Then I made a navigation error. The map indicated that I could head southwest and link up with a road going through to the next town to the west, Yingcheng. So I turned left at a busy intersection and headed south, which I usually hate doing because there is no westward benefit. I was looking for a road that would take me towards what looked on the map to be a fairly big waterway lying between Xiaogan and the road to Yingcheng. There will be a bridge there somewhere for sure, I thought.

The city faded gradually, idyllic rural Hubei returned, and the road became a track which then turned into a path. An hour or two later, I was standing on a huge levee, twenty metres high, gazing out at the Shun river and its expansive floodplain and realized I had been wrong. There was no bridge across to the other side, so I was forced to return to the aforementioned busy intersection.

The highway west out of Xiaogan led me through the early autumn countryside. All the farm work had been completed except for some late rice that was waiting, increasingly golden, in the fields. It was the October National Holiday period, and people were sitting in doorways playing mahjong or cards, but the highway was tedious and I longed to return to the country lanes.

An opportunity soon presented itself in the form of a turn-off to the village of Shahe, and I walked for the rest of the day due west along a little lane flanked mostly by wide cotton fields.

I spent half an hour humming blues tunes and stumbling through one field to catch a closer look at the cotton plants. I marvelled at the strange disconnect between the hard, angular stalks and branches and the soft woolliness of the cotton bud in its pod, waiting to be blown away to carry the seeds inside to some new location… but more likely to be made into a padded bedspread or a shirt for sale in England.

The picked cotton was laid out in swathes along the lane for a day or so, then swept up and placed in bags to be sent to market. Up ahead was the town of Geputan, and I came upon a little bridge over a stream that seemed to go in the right direction. The structure was very narrow, the surface uneven, and there were no railings to hold on to, but I hobbled across, my heart beating hard, and found a woman on the other side.

"Is this the way to Geputan?" I asked. She nodded tentatively, but when I looked back I saw a dozen or so children galloping over the bridge after me screaming in delight "Wrong way! Wrong way!"

Damn. I steeled myself and walked back over the bridge trying to apply the advice I remembered from somewhere about not looking down. This didn't work at all, and I found I had to look down at the bridge to keep going.

Once back on the original lane, the children followed me for a while and I asked them about their brothers and sisters. They all had siblings and one boy even had four elder sisters – so much for birth control. The children walked with me most of the way to Geputan and on the way I took a photo of a river.

"Why are you taking a picture?" one boy asked. "What is there that's worth photographing here? The river is filthy."

It was. I asked him where the pollution came from, and he said there was a big factory upstream that was dumping chemicals in the water. "They don't care," he said.

I walked into Geputan and took yet another wrong turn, walking too far south along a road leading nowhere, and had to retrace my steps before finally crossing the still-wide Shun River thirty kilometres upstream from where I had first seen the waterway.

Suddenly, and unexpectedly, I found myself in horse country. Not the wild horses of Marlboro ads, or the coddled horses of children's riding schools, but working horses. There were hundreds of them, each pulling carts of all sizes. The roads had plenty of trucks too, but the horses were clearly a key part of the local transport infrastructure.

I watched a man as he urged a horse up a muddy slope, pulling a heavy cart loaded with bags of grain. The horse tried with all its might, but the wheels stalled on stony outcrops, and the man beat it unmercifully with a whip. The horse knew every time the whip was coming and flinched off to the side. It occasionally tried to seek refuge in some bushes, but clearly understood that it had to haul the cart up the hill if the torture was to stop.

"Hey!" I shouted, and walked towards the asshole still beating the crap out of the horse. "I have a suggestion. Why not offload one or two bags and put them back on later?"

The man shook his head firmly, totally rejecting this piece of advice, and continued to fight the horse. The fact was that he was crazy; it was the only explanation. Otherwise why spend probably an hour beating and shouting at a horse just to travel up one small incline?

I walked away, leaving him to it. There was nothing I could do to help the horse, or to change the man's mind. But the whinnies of the horse followed for a while and the cruel image stayed with me for the rest of the day, although tempered by many other encounters with reasonably content horses and their more sensible owners. The horses were not all that healthy, but they weren't being abused, and they plodded patiently along the roads pulling their loads and, on several occasions, I saw them grazing by the sides of the roads while their masters enjoyed a smoke.

The air quality started to worsen markedly and when I saw smokestacks over on the right, I realized I was passing a petrochemicals plant – the factory that the boy had earlier said was polluting the water.

The air was disgusting and the town near the gates of the huge factory was absolutely filthy. The people on the streets were a different, tougher breed, and it was with pleasure that I saw the plant fading into the distance behind me with the air quality improving with every step. The wind was thankfully blowing from the west.

CHAPTER 12

THE MAN WHO LOST HIS LIFE

I hate cold weather and consider global warming to be a bonus: here it was, late October, and central China was still warm, verging on hot. It was truly a pleasure; maybe offset 'slightly' by the loss of the polar icecaps.

The fields were still green, because the cold of winter had not yet come to drain them of their colour. But the land had finished its work for the year; even the late rice had been harvested and just about every field was lying fallow, mulling and murmuring as it prepared for hibernation and the rebirth to follow.

I passed a house, and a middle-aged woman called to me and beckoned. I said hello and kept going, but she was insistent and came out towards me, so I stopped to chat.

"You're from Xinjiang," she said.

"No, from England."

"From England! Oh. Would you like to, um, play with a girl?"

"Play with a girl?"

"Right." She nodded back towards the entrance of the house. "Come in and see."

"How many girls do you have?"

"Just one."

"Is she pretty?"

"No, she's not. She's a housewife (she actually said 'saozi', which means the wife of one's elder brother). Would you like to play?"

This was hardly an inviting prospect, and I didn't want to go in, but I did want to know a little more about the business.

"How much?" I asked.

She sized me up and then displayed her five fingers. "Fifty RMB," she said tentatively. "But what money would you use to pay? Dollars or pounds sterling?"

"I have renminbi," I assured her. "How much do you usually make in a day?"

"Not much." She laughed nervously. "Enough to play some mahjong, that's all. Maybe fifty a day." In other words, only one customer a day. It was a lonely stretch of road. "You would use a condom?" she asked.

"What do you say?" I asked.

"Yes, you must," she replied. I had recently passed a slogan on a wall saying: 'Mosquito and bug bites do not transmit AIDS'.

I was not interested in seeing the woman inside, so I walked on into the town of Zaoshi. 'Zao' is a word that is used most commonly to mean soap, although the dictionary also gives it the meaning of black. But what the connection was, I didn't know, and no one I asked could tell me, usually adding "it's just a place name." I doubt the soap link, though, as Zaoshi was certainly no cleaner than any of the other little towns in Hubei that I saw.

I began to notice quite a number of black caterpillars crawling about on the ground, only a couple of inches in length but fast on their suckers. I spied one striking off boldly across the asphalt road, heading from one slab of fields to another. I stood and watched as it wiggled quickly towards the centre line. Two bicycles passed, missing the caterpillar by inches, and I breathed more easily. Then a bus came past and squashed it flat.

How sad.

I walked on and soon came upon another caterpillar starting out on the same death-defying trek across the road. I stood quietly and watched, hoping that the small creature would achieve its goal. For some reason, I wanted it to realize its dream: Good grief; talk about transference.

The caterpillar gamely wiggled along and was about halfway across the near lane when a truck roared past, missing the caterpillar by inches, but the draught of its passing blew it along the road a couple of metres. It righted itself and resumed its trek in exactly the same direction, confirming for me that it was sentient, brave and determined to cross the road. But why did the caterpillar cross the road? (It wanted to follow the duck?)

Whatever the motivation, caterpillar number two undulated briskly along and made it to the halfway mark just as a minibus slightly out of its lane squelched it into non-existence.

This was becoming depressing.

Another caterpillar: This little fellow made it close to halfway and then had its back chopped in half by a passing wheel. Amazingly, the front half kept going, just like Arnold Schwarzenegger in Terminator One. But this plucky semi-caterpillar was consigned to oblivion just over the median strip by a bus coming in the other direction.

I continued along the road and watched as several other kamikaze caterpillars made a break for it across the tarmac. All killed. I wasn't sure how this could be. A car has only two tire tracks, neither particularly wide. How come all the caterpillars were being blown away in this Hubei version of Russian roulette? Surely the odds should be better? There weren't all that many vehicles on this stretch of road.

I stopped with a heavy heart and continued my death watch as another caterpillar started out northwards across the road (I almost always walked on the south side of the road, facing oncoming traffic). This grub was blown about by a passing car, but made it safely across the south lane and started its way across the north lane.

A three-wheeler truck came along, bringing with it a third more risk in that there were three tire tracks threatening the caterpillar's existence.

But it passed safely and – hooray! – the caterpillar made it safely to the other side. My faith in the principle that 'anything is possible if you try hard enough to find a way' was vindicated.

I took a victory photo of the plucky caterpillar and was then amazed to see it turn just before the edge of the asphalt and start to wend its way back across the road again.

I gave up. If the damn thing was crossing the road just to play chicken with the passing traffic, then I was not going to stand around rooting for the creepy-crawly any longer. I had better things to do.

Walking through central Hubei, the roads were straight, the country was flat and I was covering ground at a satisfying pace. By this time I was fitter and had found I could walk twice as far in a day as I could the year before, when I was walking across southern Anhui. The towns were now no sooner in prospect than gone.

My right leg, warped since childhood, still appeared to be up to the challenge of the project. While my right knee was certainly a problem compared with other people's knees, it wasn't worsening – as far as I could tell – and it had got me this far, so I presumed the exercise (fifteen and sometimes twenty kilometres of walking in a day) was strengthening the joint. There appeared to be no reason why it wouldn't see me the rest of the way. If it failed, there was always the possibility of a fake knee: 'Exoskeletons' or 'Segways'. I would find a way. Meanwhile, my biggest physical problems were blisters when I wore new shoes and stiffness in my body, which made it difficult to crouch down to capture a different angled shot with the camera.

I was walking past a couple of men when I noticed that one of them, a man wearing a colourful but filthy Hawaiian-type shirt, was holding a book. Books are rare in rural China and I couldn't remember seeing any other individual, even a child, holding a book anywhere on my walk across China. The man looked up and greeted me, so I stopped and we talked for a minute.

It was a short exchange. He asked where I was from; I gave him my name and mobile number, which he asked me to write on his book. He said his name was Zhou Yuxi, and then I was off again. But then he came after me and, as we walked along together for several kilometres, I learned his story. Or part of it.

He was born in Wuhan in 1941, his father was a KMT official and his mother a doctor who had been educated in an English Christian missionary school. He was the eldest of three boys and his father had made the fateful decision not to go to Taiwan when the Communists took the mainland in 1949. He was executed and the family endured a living hell in the years that followed. In the late 1950s, Mr. Zhou was forcibly moved out of Wuhan to a village near the town of Zaoshi, close to where we were walking. He had spent more than forty years living here, well over half of his life. He was now sixty-seven years old. He'd never married. He lived alone. His two younger brothers lived in Wuhan, but he had little contact with them. He lived in a place distant from where he was born and had no relations among his neighbours. The people in the village had never accepted him as one of their own, always seeing him as an outsider. He had a degree of education, which inevitably set him apart from the farmers. He read books.

He lived on a pension from the state of one hundred and thirty-eight RMB per month, plus occasional gigs washing dishes and wiping tables in a local restaurant. "At my age, I have no bargaining power in terms of the fee," he said. His very way of talking was different from that of the farmers.

Mr. Zhou appeared to be overwhelmed at meeting me. "I have waited decades for this," he said.

Apart from his colourful but dirty shirt, his trousers were equally filthy and his fingernails were dirt-filled. He had no more than half of his full quota of teeth. His body was thin, his hair crew-cut and greying, and his huge and watery eyes constantly glanced over at me. His breathing was somewhat asthmatic, but he talked non-stop for at least an hour as we walked along.

I asked him to show me the book he was holding. It was called 'Health and Long Life'. The cover was gone and the pages were scruffy; the book not setting a good example.

"Why are you reading this book?" I asked.

"I have always been very healthy, until these past two months, and I want to learn more about living healthily," he replied. "I don't smoke or drink or gamble; I avoid all those bad habits."

I asked about his living situation, and he told me he had just bought a house; for the first time in his life, he had a place to call home. It cost him five thousand RMB and came with electricity and water.

"You are welcome to visit. It would be my honour. Oh, I am getting quite emotional. It is like being visited by a god," he said. "I never imagined that I would be able to meet an English person. I have admired England and English culture all my life. So many great men: Newton, Watt, Shakespeare, Darwin. I read the novel Robinson Crusoe when I was young. I read it in Chinese of course. We weren't allowed to learn or to speak English, so all I can say is 'hello'. Russian was the only acceptable foreign language in those days. But, anyway, I read Robinson Crusoe. I would be delighted to be your Man Friday."

His use of language, his choice of words, was that of an educated man. It was a miracle that he'd managed to preserve that sense of an educated outlook through all the lonely decades in this isolated village. The farmers could be wise and were extremely knowledgeable about their own speciality – farming – but they didn't have a global cultural awareness. Widespread literacy was a luxury that dated from only the past two decades and awareness of the outside world really dated only from the arrival of television in rural areas in the 1990s. Mr. Zhou, on the other hand, had read books, listened to short-wave radio, read newspapers, and appeared to have kept up a lively awareness through the decades. He was surely one of the few people in that stretch of Hubei Province who had ever heard of Robinson Crusoe.

"I have had such a hard life, but I should not complain," he said. "If my father had decided to go to Taiwan, who knows where I would have ended up… But he decided to stay and the communists killed him. I was persecuted for so many years, because of my complicated background and because I once said at a meeting that 'nongmin shenghuo ku' – the peasants' life is hard."

"Why did you never marry? Because of your complicated background?"

"Exactly! No family would accept me. As a result, I have no relatives and no one to look after me. No descendants. To have no descendants is truly a terrible fate. But I have kept myself active. I read a lot and I sing. I have a good voice for singing. But the songs I sing are foreign songs." He hummed a couple of melodies that I recognized as classical favourites but could not name. "But Marx talked of the proletariat (in Chinese, this is the class without assets). I am truly a member of the proletariat. The total value of everything I have would be less than ten thousand RMB."

Plus, the farmers had a precious commodity that he, as an outsider, did not have: Land.

"I don't even have a television set," he continued. "I have a very old radio and, when the reception is good, I can listen to the BBC and Voice of America. I heard about a radio that can be hand-cranked, so that it doesn't need electricity. That would be such a good thing. I wanted to write to the United States to ask about it, but if the letter was discovered, it could cause me a lot of trouble, so I didn't write."

It probably wouldn't be a problem today, but in the 1960s and 1970s such a letter could have landed Mr. Zhou in a struggle with officials and jail. That he was still cautious today was understandable.

I asked him about his name.

"My name originally was not this name. The name my parents chose for me had the same sounds but other, more complex characters. I will write them for you when I send you a letter. But the peasants here could not read them. So I had to choose homonyms in their place, simple characters with the same sounds."

He returned to his theme of a life wasted.

"I have been struggled and criticized; my life has been ruined by the

Communist Party. I have nothing and I have no hope. Or rather, I had no hope until I met you. Ah, the chance of it all! If I hadn't decided to go for a walk, if I hadn't been standing there by the road, I would never have met you! This is the most important thing that has happened to me in my life! I have met one foreigner before. I went to Wuhan once a few years ago and attended a concert. There was an American there, and I went up and introduced myself. He was huge, really tall and fat, and when we shook hands his hand completely enveloped mine. His name was Thomas, but he couldn't speak Chinese and all I can say in English is hello, so we couldn't talk. It is truly a great honour to meet you. May I write to you?"

"Of course." It was embarrassing and overwhelming for me, too, to be lionized by this intelligent old man. But it was also a great pleasure to provide him with a link through to the world he had been dreaming of for so long.

During this long conversation, he asked me almost no questions about myself, but discussed his own situation, volunteered information and views, and answered all my questions fluidly. It was as if I had opened a floodgate in his brain. "Finally, someone to talk to!"

As we walked, I occasionally stopped to watch a caterpillar fail to cross the road alive.

"Are you a biologist?" he asked.

I shook my head. "No, I just hope that at least one of them can make it to the other side. It seems to be a metaphor for life."

He stared at me for a moment.

"You are such a romantic," he said.

CHAPTER 13

THE SPECIAL FARMS

I saw a sign for Yichang city that announced it was two hundred and forty-eight kilometres away, but I was hoping the actual distance for me would be less as I planned to leave the main road and take a shortcut through Shayang to Dangyang. I was anxious to reach Yichang, the gateway to the Gorges, and began to resent roads that veered off towards the southwest or northwest.

The western stretches of the Hubei plain were a pleasure to walk through: I shielded my eyes from the brilliant sunshine and blue sky as I stopped to look at trees that stood stark and bare against the low horizon. The freezing cold air numbed my hands, but I set a brisk pace that helped to keep me warm.

Cotton and oranges. Those were the cash crops spread around me in the wide, flat country east of Shayang, the largest town in the region. Vast, undivided cotton fields stretched out on either side of the road – an economy of scale approach that is the very opposite of the small paddy fields, where each is assigned to a family. The word 'farm' in Chinese (nong-chang) suggests something large-scale and separate from family agriculture. But the flatness of the country and the cotton definitely made farms a sensible way to use the land.

In the midst of this winter scene, I saw a large group of people walking along a track in the fields that, based on previous experience, must have been a funeral procession.

Just outside a petrol station on a corner of the highway, I came upon an accident. There was a large blue truck with its windscreen smashed, and a crowd of people gathered around the front, with a police car just arriving.

I walked a little closer and saw a three-wheeler farm vehicle tangled up under the front of the truck with a man dead beside it. Another truck had slammed into the side of the blue truck and another man, also dead, was lying under its wheels. Many of the truck drivers on these little roads are hardly paying attention much of the time; they pass each other around corners at ridiculous speeds. The combination of these maniacal truck drivers and the farmers leading their lives in the same space but at a completely different pace was a recipe for disaster.

I did not linger, and took no photos. I have seen over a dozen dead bodies on roads across China. Blood on the highway is altogether too final and the situation is almost always treated by all present with too much of a collective shrug, even taking into account the cultural differences. But how should one react in these situations? I really didn't know.

I was about twenty or thirty kilometres east of Shayang city, and entered a small town called Wusan Farm, which means Five-Three Farm. I asked several people the meaning of this rather terse and categorized name. No one knew.

I walked along the town's broad boulevard with its city-like sidewalk, which led into the centre of Five-Three Farm town. Two boys came towards me and, as always, I said hello. One of the boys said something in reply that I didn't quite catch. He repeated the words and I assumed I had misheard due to the local accent, but he said it one more time and the words were unmistakable.

"Give me some money."

I looked at him in shock. He was only eleven or twelve, was dressed warmly in a good jacket and was playing with several coins in his right hand.

"Give you some money?" I responded indignantly. "You must be joking!"

In all the hundreds of kilometres I had walked across China to this point, in all the conversations I'd had with children – some of them as poor as it is possible to get in China – I had never had a child ask me for money. The only adult who had ever asked me was the deaf-mute I had met in south-central Anhui.

"Do you know what you are saying?" I asked him. "Are you a beggar?"

He grinned slyly and stepped back a couple of paces. "You want to be a beggar?" I asked. He jumped on his friend's bike, which was respectable and not a cheap children's model, and cycled away.

I walked on, and met some other children who were quite normal, which somewhat restored my faith in Five-Three Farm, but I still felt uneasy with the people and the feeling of the town.

Then a conversation with a man on the road clarified the situation.

"This is where all the people sentenced to Reform Through Labour (laodong gaizao) are sent from all over Hubei," he said. "Shayang is famous for it."

So that was it. I was walking through prison farms. That crowd of people I saw in the fields must have been prisoners. And the boy asking for money – that also made more sense now.

Further on, closer to Shayang, I saw a gang of about sixty men walking along a path beside the road. At the front was a man holding a small red flag, while at the rear was a man in uniform. It was obviously a chain gang, although there appeared to be no chains, and the prison officer behind the column was not holding a shotgun. So it wasn't a complete Chinese re-run of that classic Paul Newman film 'Cool Hand Luke', which is about a prison farm set in cotton country not dissimilar from western Hubei. The prison officers – there was another following fifty metres further behind the gang – appeared smart in their uniforms and bored by their jobs.

Security seemed extremely lax, but if this entire area consisted of prison farms, as appeared to be the case, then escape would be a pretty difficult feat, even though we were all on a public highway. No bus driver would pick up anyone who looked like they were on the run.

I stopped to take some photographs of the prison gang, and they noticed that I was a foreigner. "Hello!" several of them shouted in English and I shouted "Hello!" back and waved and smiled at them. I half expected the prison guards to object to this, but they continued to trudge along after their charges, hunched up in their fur-lined black jackets without comment.

Once I was told about the prison farms, I began to notice road signs that referred to the 'prison region' and I realized that the plain to the east of Shayang was a massive prison farm system stretching over hundreds of square kilometres. I found many articles on the Internet about people incarcerated in the massive Shayang system, a key link in China's Gulag chain. But I was still walking along a public highway, so I continued to snap photos of the bare fields and the farmers, and when I came upon a building which had a sign outside announcing that it was the 'Shayang Re-Education Through Labour Centre, Number 1 Sub-Centre', I naturally took a photograph of it too.

Mistake.

A man rushed out of a little guard room at the building's entrance, jumped onto a bike, and cycled toward me shouting: "No photographs!" I stopped and waited for him to catch up to me.

"What are you doing? Who are you? No photographs!" he shouted.

"This is a provincial highway," I said. "Why not?"

He ignored me and made a call on his mobile, which resulted in four groups of police arriving over the next thirty minutes, each group higher ranking than the last until the real decision makers arrived. I knew they were the most senior officers because they were not in uniform. They put me in a police car and off we went to a police station. I was so disappointed. I wanted to be taken into the Re-Education Through Labour Centre, but it was not to be.

The 'apprehension' was the same process I had been through before with the people's constabulary in other places, but this time it was a little more serious. We sat in a small room with the standard wooden desk and tired sofa and they asked me what I was doing in the area. I said I was walking from Shanghai to Tibet and they said *uh-huh*. The problem for them, as you will see if you do a web search, was that the Shayang prison system is quite well known for various human rights related reasons. They were worried, I guess, that I was there to gather information for some international human rights organization. Of course, all I was doing was walking along the road taking photos of water buffalo. To confuse the issue further, I threw the 'charity card' onto the table as well (I had recently founded a small charity called the China Reading Project, which donates story books to schools in rural China, with the aim of encouraging children to read, and I said my walk was aimed at raising money for the charity).

The officials made calls, they discussed this explanation and they pored over my passport. They asked to see the shots in my digital camera, and they stood in silence as I showed them photos of trees and fields and water buffalo. And then they saw the offending image of the front of a prison.

"Delete it," the main policeman said.

"But it's a building right next to a highway," I said.

"Delete it."

"No problem," I said. "But my suggestion is that if there are any buildings along the highway that you don't want photographed, put a wall up in front of them."

I deleted the image (although I confess I later undeleted it).

"You may continue your walk," he said. "But don't take any photos until you have passed Shayang. And stay on the road."

They drove me back to where I had been picked up and I walked on through the bright winter's day. I put away my Canon SLR camera, but still took some photos with a smaller camera. I did also leave the road a couple of times and walked along the convict paths, trying to put myself into their mindsets.

The kilometres passed quickly as the dead straight stretches of road fell behind. I finally came to the massive bridge that spanned the Han River, which courses from north to south over the Hubei plain before heading east for the Yangtze River, which it joins at Wuhan.

I crossed the bridge slowly, enjoying the wide watery vistas of the river channel, and then came to the tollbooth that marks the start of Shayang town. Just beyond was a small group of people waiting for me. Word of my walk had preceded me, as sometimes happened.

"Welcome!" they said, shaking my hand and smiling broadly. "Welcome to Shayang!"

CHAPTER 14

THE CASINO OPERATOR

The country lane wound its way through rolling hills before deteriorating into a rutted muddy mess, which lasted for several kilometres. I was walking on the border between the Shayang and Dangyang counties, so the issue may have been that neither government could be bothered to fix up the road. This was a very peaceful part of the country and there were almost no farmhouses, with the calm broken only by small three-wheeler farm vehicles overloaded with straw that chugged by every ten minutes or so.

The weather was chilly but dry. I found that I was wandering through a countryside that was steeped in stillness, which is very rare in China. All I heard were sounds of relaxed domesticity emerging from the farmhouses I passed: the tinkling of rice bowls, gentle talking and laughter. There was no need to shout or strain to hear in the rich quiet of this country.

I passed a courtyard in which three girls were playing, and said hello.

"It's a foreigner!" one of the girls exclaimed.

"You're Chinese!" I replied in mock surprise.

I kept walking, and after a few minutes or so, the girls ran up behind me, and one of them asked in English: "What is your name?"

Her surname was Xiao and she said she was twelve years old, but she looked more like sixteen and was precocious enough to be in her late teens. The other two girls, who she introduced as her elder sisters, said nothing and just stared wide-eyed. I gave them all name cards, and walked with them for a way. They raced off home and appeared again five minutes later, running hard.

"I have a present for you!" Ms. Xiao said breathlessly, and handed me a bag of melon seeds.

It was the first of several gifts I received in this region. As soon as I had reached the vaguely hilly country, the reception became warmer and people became more hospitable than on the plains. I wondered why.

My next 'visitor' was a man on a bicycle. Mr. Zhang, aged fifty, was a teacher of Chinese literature at the local high school and a part-time life insurance salesman. He invited me to visit the school, which was a couple of kilometres up ahead and close to where my country lane connected with the main road to Dangyang.

He cycled on ahead, and I walked through a pine forest and emerged back onto the highway, coming up from the south and heading towards Dangyang city. The highway headed generally northwest through the town of Harong, which is noted for garlic and the trilling way in which its residents speak, their accent sounding a bit like Russian.

This is also the region in which most of the action in the classical Chinese book 'The Romance of the Three Kingdoms' takes place. The book, written in the 16th century, is considered to be about eighty percent historically accurate. It involves stories of the wars and machinations between the three kingdoms that emerged from the collapse of the Han Empire, around the years 220 to 280 AD.

This period of instability generated huge upheavals in Chinese culture and society, and the events have fuelled story-telling ever since. It is a part of Chinese history about which I knew almost nothing, but I felt, unfairly, that it should mean that there would be an extra depth to the people I met and the things I saw. I was disappointed; the mud on my boots was the same as that which had dirtied the boots of the soldiers of that era, 1700 years ago, but around me there was no sign of the history and events that had taken place there.

I was told that there was a tomb in the area that belonged to the warrior Guan Yu from the Three Kingdoms period. The Lord Guan, Guan Gong, was such a formidable fighter and general that he was promoted to the post of God of War, and as such he is still honoured in millions of little red shrines in restaurants and homes across the Chinese world, not to mention in police stations in Hong Kong. Sprouting a lush beard, he wears a big headdress and carries a massive halberd that allegedly weighed over forty kilograms. He sometimes shares shrine space with a statue of Guan Yin, the feminine Buddha. I am reliably informed that they are just good friends. I didn't visit the tomb, because I was told that it probably wasn't Guan's, and I was eager to move on to the Three Gorges. It was enough to imagine Guan Gong striding along the road with me, just as he appears in Peking operas.

I reached the school and teacher Zhang greeted me warmly, but the school itself was virtually deserted and the headmaster was not answering his mobile phone. I asked if we could visit the library, but it was locked. I asked how many students there were. Teacher Zhang said the number was dramatically fewer than even a few years ago; at its height, this high school had fourteen hundred students, but this year there were only seven hundred. Why?

"The birth control policies, and the shift of people to the coastal regions," he explained.

I asked if the school would be interested in taking books from the China Reading Project.

"Fine for me, but I think the headmaster wouldn't be very happy about it."

"So could we just give books to your class?" I asked.

He seemed reluctant. I left.

A man passed me on a motorcycle, did a double-take when he saw me, then swung back round to check me out. His name was Yang Feng, and he pushed his bike along beside me for a while as we talked. Yang Feng said he had a small business that traded in construction materials.

"This is Guan Gong's home," he said.

"I know."

"There is a brand of baijiu liquor made near here that has his name, but the company forgot to register the name, so a baijiu manufacturer in Hunan registered it and stole the market away from them," he said. It was clearly something that really hurt his pride, but hey, that's the way business works in China, and it was interesting to see a Chinese company being hit by piratical intellectual property rights practices.

I asked him about life in the Harong area, and he volunteered a view that dovetailed with my sense of disappointment in that I could feel no sense of historical depth in a place with such rich history.

Chinese culture, he told me, had been thoroughly trashed in the past few decades, and anything of value had been discarded.

"All that is left," he declared, "is baijiu and gambling."

A sad summation, and surely not wholly accurate, but I knew what he meant. He offered me a lift to the next town, and then invited me to his home, but I declined both, saying it was very kind of him to offer.

"All Chinese people are kind," he said.

He invited me to meet his grandfather, a man in his eighties who had been a KMT military officer and had attended peace talks between the KMT and the Communist Party rebels in the late 1940s. After the Communist victory, his grandfather was purged and persecuted and later rehabilitated. Yang Feng asked me if he could join me on the walk the next day. "It would be my honour," I replied.

A light drizzle fell as I walked through Dangyang the next morning, a town which plays a central role in many battles of the Three Kingdoms period. True to his word, Yang Feng, who was wearing a suit and tie, arrived as I was sitting on a plastic stool on the street outside a little restaurant next to the local high school. I had given my card to the gatekeeper of the school and asked him to give the card to the headmaster, but he didn't call me.

It was cold, and I was drinking hot water, which was provided free by the ladies in the restaurant. They absolutely refused to accept even a couple of yuan in return. Yang Feng sat down on a stool next to me and immediately suggested we go instead to a karaoke joint called Beijing Spring. I said: "No, let's drink hot water at this stall with the ladies instead."

Yang was uncomfortable, but handled it well. He gave me a jade pendant carved as a dragon in recognition of my birth sign, and also a painting he had made just for me and inscribed with my name. It was, as he admitted upfront, as good as a child could do. But as I told him, it was valuable, because he had put the time into painting it for me.

"All Chinese people are kind," he said again.

"Even 'Re-education Through Labour' convicts?" I asked, and the ladies collapsed in gales of laughter.

But I was puzzled – Yang was definitely not your standard peasant, and he was talking about how he planned to buy a car.

We left the ladies and he walked with me through the slush for a few hours. And as we talked, I finally put together a clearer view of this small trader in construction materials. While that was definitely part of his portfolio, he also dabbled in other things, including running a small casino in a village near Dangyang.

"Gambling," he said. "It is ripping this society apart. Everyone is doing it, and the gamblers who lose have to sell their houses to pay their debts, while the guys who run the gambling are driving around in luxury cars."

"What is the main gambling method?" I asked.

"Mark Six."

Now, that was interesting. Mark Six was a lottery run by the Hong Kong Jockey Club, where six balls marked with a number are pulled out of a churn several times a week. Guess the number sequence closely enough and you get a prize. I remember back in the 1990s, when working for the Reuters news agency, my colleagues and I were amazed to find that the top accessed page on the Reuters system in Taiwan was the page showing the Hong Kong Mark Six results. It was being used by gambling syndicates in Taiwan and now, fifteen years later, I found the same deal at work in darkest Hubei. Amazing.

In China's major cities, the state-run lotteries are the only legal gambling outlet but in Dangyang, the state lotteries are virtually ignored. Anyone interested in gambling – and that is a fairly large proportion of any Chinese population – is playing other underground games. Gambling on football is very big nationwide, particularly on the English Premier League games.

"Are you doing Mark Six?" I asked.

"No, that is controlled by the big syndicates," he said. "I just do casino evenings."

As I walked southwest from Dangyang through rolling countryside, everyone was preparing for the Lunar New Year. There were fireworks on sale everywhere, and there were masses of pigs on the move, headed for the slaughterhouse. Overall, however, rural life continued unchanged: the water buffalo were resting or munching the hay stored up from the previous harvest and the fields were quietly waiting, like the buffalo, for the hard work to begin after the Lunar New Year had passed.

I walked through the little towns and villages along Hubei's Provincial Highway 107. Traffic was relatively heavy, with a lot of people and goods moving around ahead of the New Year break. It was the pigs I felt for most; they are expressive animals that put up patiently with the indignities and discomfort of being squashed together inside the trucks taking them to the slaughterhouses. I really do think the world would be a better place if people stopped eating animals. The damage caused to the environment by the mass production of animal flesh, with the chemicals and the excrement that get poured into watercourses, along with the sight of the pigs crammed like subway riders into two-tier trucks on country roads in rural China, make me happy to be a fishy vegetarian. Fish are sentient creatures too, you can argue, but they appear to be on a different level of awareness from pigs or buffalo. The animals look at me and I know they know I am here. The buffalo, particularly, seem like gentle creatures, like small animals trapped inside a large body.

I passed a slogan daubed on a wall: 'Sternly attack underground Mark Six', then sat for a while with a restaurant owner named Mr. Zhou. He was the youngest of five children, while he himself had only one child. He said that many couples in the countryside today don't want to have even one child.

"Medical treatment and welfare are now good enough that people don't worry so much about having children to look after them when they are old," he said. "Also, some guys decide not to get married at all, saying it's just too much of a hassle and unnecessary. I don't really understand it myself."

We were seated on little bamboo chairs on a concrete space in front of his restaurant.

"Do you like this place?" he asked me.

"It's OK. It seems very quiet."

"But relatively poor."

"Really? It doesn't seem so poor," I said. "I've seen much poorer than this."

"Right. In the mountains. But they are building roads to open those areas up."

"How's business?" I asked.

"Pretty good."

"Are most of your customers locals or people passing through?"

"We get both. How old are you?" he asked.

"Fifty-four," I said. "How about you?"

"You look just thirty-something! I'm just over forty."

"Where are you from?" asked his wife.

"I was born in England, and I now live in Shanghai."

"What are you doing here?"

"I am walking from Shanghai to Tibet."

"You're kidding. When did you start?"

"I started in 2004."

"2004? So how long have you been walking?"

"What year is it?" I asked.

"Ha! He doesn't know what year it is!" she exclaimed, missing the point. "It's 2007."

"Then three years," I said. "It's a warm winter this year, right?"

"Yes."

"Is that good for the crops?"

"Not so good," Mr. Zhou said. "The pests die when the temperature falls. But it's the result of global warming."

"Were you born here?"

"Yes."

"How were the winters when you were small?"

"It used to be very cold when I was a child. It has been getting warmer since 1997."

He said he had a nineteen-year-old son who was studying at a college in Shandong.

"What about after graduation?" I asked. "Will he come back here or look for work outside?"

"Find a job outside."

"What about you? Have you ever worked outside?"

"I'm a farmer! I don't have much schooling. I only went to primary school. I have three brothers and a sister. Plus my father died early and we were brought up by our mother."

"It's not easy to raise five children," I said.

"I'm the youngest. In those days, only a well-off family could afford to send all their children to school."

"I went to college but I didn't graduate," I replied. "Whereas my daughter is a university graduate. So, things get better from one generation to the next."

"England is a good country with a very developed society," he observed.

"China is experiencing much faster development than England," I countered.

"The current leaders led by Hu Jintao are doing a good job for us farmers. For instance they abolished the agricultural taxes."

"The farmers must feel happy about that," I said.

"Yes. People are leading a better life than before and social order is better. You know, education is really important. As our ancestors said: 'A man becomes well-behaved through education'. That's correct, isn't it? A few years ago, in my time, children would laze around all day, and steal things and fight. Now my son, who goes to school, never uses swear words and never wastes time."

"That's good. So what is the biggest problem here?"

"We don't have any big problems here."

"No big problems? That's great!"

"The country's system is being reformed. Medical reform, for instance. For instance, if you're sick and have to stay in hospital, you can claim back the costs," he said.

"You have medical insurance coverage?"

"Yes. I bought medical cover for the entire family. Myself, my wife and my son. We pay three thousand RMB a year."

"That's expensive," I said.

"I think paying three thousand RMB for medical coverage is okay," he replied. "We just have to be a little more careful on spending each day so we can afford it."

I drank some more tea with them, and then moved on, walking through the gloom of a rural winter's day, everything grey, slow and muffled, to Wangdian (King's Inn) and then to the town of Yaqueling (Magpie Ridge). On the outskirts of Yaqueling, there was a paper-making factory with a chimney stack that was belching black smoke into the sky and spurting out a steady flow of filthy water. A huge sign that ran along the entire factory wall read: 'Protect the environment, love life'.

As I carried on towards the town, a man rode up to me on a motorcycle and stopped. His name was Mr. Yang, he was well-dressed, and told me he worked in the paper factory.

"I saw you taking photos of the factory," he said.

"That factory is dirty," I said.

"We're doing renovations now," he replied sheepishly.

The road into town was blocked by a police checkpoint, and the policeman told me the main road was impassable because so many people were in town doing pre-New Year shopping. I walked into town and it was indeed packed. The streets were lined with stalls selling bright red and gold couplets to paste on either side of the doors – 'Good fortune and wealth, streaming in from all quarters', was the general drift of the brightly-coloured messages. Chinese people have a strong belief in the mystical power of the written word, and these New Year strips are still pasted up on farmhouse doors and often stay in place throughout the year, becoming more and more tattered but still casting off a power to protect the family inside.

I came across a huge compound on a hillside. It was surrounded by a high brick wall and contained many small brick huts set well apart from each other and connected by paths. All were empty, and some were blackened as if burned. There were no trees or other vegetation around the huts. It looked like a retirement village gone wrong. Was it a village? But why the wall? And where were the people?

I came upon two guys having a smoke next to their motorcycles and I asked about this place above us.

"It's a fireworks factory," said one. "The huts are separated to reduce the risk when there is an explosion."

Ah. It was now empty because production for the Lunar New Year had been completed and all the workers had gone home (many of them with all their fingers).

On the other side of town, I left the highway and struck off north, planning to walk along quieter roads north of Yichang city, now only twenty-five kilometres to the west. The map showed a road going round the north of Yichang that connected back up to the highway, which led to the Yangtze Gorges. I had been waiting for this for months, and the anticipation of finally stepping off the Hubei plain and entering the first gorge was making me eager to keep pushing on. But just before leaving Yaqueling, I saw a shoemaker sitting under a tree, dressed in many layers of clothing, reading a book. Not only that, but he was making annotations in the book with a stub of a pencil.

I walked over and asked him which book he was reading. He invited me to sit down and started to tell me its story. It was about a man named Xue Dingshan, a fictional character from the Tang dynasty of the seventh and eighth centuries, who is often featured in Chinese opera. The shoemaker told the story with great earnestness and in rich detail and clearly intended to go on for hours. I understood only some of what he said for his accent was thick, but he was a lovely old man, and I asked him if he ever told stories for the children in the area. He shook his head.

"They don't want to hear them," he said.

"Because of television?" I asked.

He nodded.

"Well, I'd like to hear them." And with that, I made myself comfortable and sat with him until he had finished.

CHAPTER 15

MILLION DOLLAR ROCKS

I was walking into the town of Xiaoxita, which on the map is a separate entity, but in reality is already a part of the expanding city of Yichang. Yichang sits just to the east of the Yangtze Gorges and has for centuries made its living off the river trade, mainly with oranges and some rock farming on the side. Rock farming? More on that later.

Even though this was Chinese New Year's day, the day was dull and lacking any festive atmosphere, marked only by sporadic gunfire-like rackets of firecrackers. I asked a few people I met about that, and heard a variety of answers. "Things aren't what they used to be," was the most common reply, with "Everyone is inside eating and gambling," a close number two.

The farmhouses in the country to the east of Yichang looked prosperous. There were various three-storey designs that looked solid, decorated with baroque pillars and stucco attachments, and painted in shockingly bright colours – purples and oranges which seemed totally out of place in this rolling rural scene. The farmers here clearly had something to prove, and wanted to flaunt their wealth, which came mostly from the orange trees planted everywhere, including in front of every doorway. There were also huge piles of rotting oranges at many points along the roadside; the ability of mankind to overproduce everything has extended even to the orange groves of Yichang.

The area was also notable for the generally dire state of the environment. Large amounts of rubbish were scattered along the road edge, and the watercourses were filthy. I passed a substantial alcoholic beverages factory that had a clean compound, but the river beside it was a sewer filled with the industrial effluent by-products of its baijiu manufacturing process. Virtually all the vegetation in the river was dead.

It was the piles of old clothing in discarded piles that I found particularly surprising. I wondered if it was related to the new year tradition of buying new clothes, or whether it indicated that these people had enough money to afford new clothes and hadn't yet seen that throwing rubbish right outside their own doors meant they were living amid a growing refuse heap.

The country at the western end of the Hubei plain was bleak – the grass was brown and I was not seeking out conversations as I strode on purposefully for the mountains. I was heading into a new county, Yiling County. Yi is a word that means barbarian or outsider, and Ling means tombs. The tombs referred to are for a tribe that has disappeared. The encroachment of the Han people into this and other regions south of the Yellow River valley of north China that originally gave birth to Chinese culture inevitably involved the retreat, dilution and destruction of local tribes. Shadows of these earlier groups still exist in various parts of south and central China. This particular tribe in the Yangtze Gorges checked out early and all that was left was the place name.

While there was little sign of festive good spirits, the doors of the farmhouses were invariably flanked by "spring couplets", with phrases like "May the five good fortunes come to our door, and ten thousand undertakings all be successful."

Then a bus passed me that was not the usual country minibus, but a town bus in red livery stopping at regular bus stops, and before I knew it I was in Yichang city.

I walked through the northern reaches of the city, past restaurants and convenience stores and a shop selling sex aids. And after having navigated my way successfully across half of China, I got lost in the middle of it.

The Google Earth satellite images I was using for navigation at this point showed a path heading in the right direction through the city, and took me through a tunnel under a freeway which led into an amphitheatre of terraced vegetable gardens, ringed by old and decrepit apartment blocks. I made my way up a filthy path swarming with midges and reached the top to be met by a man who looked at me with a puzzled expression. "There is no way out this way," he said. "You have to go back."

It was a perfect fortress within a city. The only entry point was an easily defended tunnel. I retreated, climbed up another hillside through an apartment block estate and crossed the freeway via a bridge that took me through a series of other housing estates, forcing me to walk southwards and then eastwards. For a while, I was getting closer to Shanghai with every step. Eventually the housing estates released me onto a road that curved round to a bridge over the Yellow Cypress River, which marks the western edge of Yichang city.

Having crossed the bridge, the road headed quickly upwards, flanked by a forest. To the left was the Yangtze River, my first view of it from my path since Tongling in Anhui province, and then it hit me – I had done it! I was now entering the Yangtze Gorges. I had walked all the way from Shanghai to the centre of China, the point at which the Yangtze River emerges from the mountain barrier separating the Sichuan basin from the central China plain. I felt pretty pleased with myself. I had had enough of the plains, and I had the Three Gorges Dam and the long Gorges region ahead of me. I would now be shadowing the Yangtze for another four degrees of longitude, up to the river town of Wanzhou at which point I would strike off across Sichuan away from the river.

There were almost no water craft visible, presumably because of Chinese New Year. Above me were enormous electricity transmission lines that I assumed were feeding power from the Three Gorges Dam. The air directly under the wires sizzled with the voltage.

The first section of the road heading into the Gorges featured a few largely deserted tourist spots. There was the White Horse Cave and a small gorge that featured pumping disco music, a bungee jump, a restaurant stapled to the vertical rock face of the mini-gorge and a swaying bridge for the tourists. A few touts tried to tempt me into the trap, but I could not be distracted from my mission and before long, I was back in quiet, rural China. The road veered far away from the river and downshifted to third rate. The farmhouses were basic and poor, the stone-built rice terraces weathered but sturdy.

It was similar to the Dabie Mountains, but already, just in from the entrance to the Gorges, the scale was clearly much larger. In just a few hours of walking, I had transitioned from the central China plain with a height above sea level of fifty metres to a height of more than five hundred metres, and in some places the rice terraces were spectacularly precipitous. It was quiet except for the occasional report of firecrackers far away, followed by impressive echoes stretching far back into the mountain valleys. The return on investment on a firecracker bought and lit in the mountains is spectacularly louder, more far-reaching and longer lasting compared to those in the plains, where all you get is a dull thud.

Suddenly, people were being more hospitable towards me, but it may have just seemed that way because I was more open to conversations now my race to the Gorges was over. An old man I saw walking off the terraces invited me into his home, and I sat for a while in a stuffy little sun-filled room with his entire family, all of us huddled around a stove, chatting. When I left, I was loaded down with peanuts, melon seeds and sweets that they insisted I take with me.

It was a relatively warm day, but the locals were still dressed for the middle of winter and they all asked why I was only wearing a shirt and no jacket. I think they were just subconsciously operating on the basis of what the temperature should have been at Chinese New Year, rather than what it actually was. The weather was the result of two factors: Chinese New Year was late this year and global warming.

I passed a few patches of ground by the road on which there were strangely shaped rocks. They come in all forms – angular, asymmetrical – but all have shapes that somehow remind the viewer of something else. These rocks have been traditional courtyard ornaments for rich Chinese people for centuries; they range in size from minuscule to massive (fifty tonnes and more), and can cost into the millions of US dollars. Viewing them is like lying on one's back on a summer's day and deciding what cloud formations look like – lions on guard, Buddhas with radioactive hearts, or whatever your imagination directs.

I saw the first peach blossoms of the year, and there were whole hillsides of terraced fields that had been abandoned, as part of the policy expressed in many signs along the road urging the farmers to 'Return the Fields to Nature'.

I walked down into a little village and found the strange rocks standing in front of all the houses. All for sale, and no fear on the part of the vendors about them being stolen – they were far too heavy to cart away in the dead of night.

Four people were playing mahjong outside one open doorway, and a woman invited me to play. I declined, saying I played too slowly, but I sat and watched for a while. I asked about the rocks and the lady immediately became business-like. "You want to buy rocks?" she asked.

I was now high up in the mountains and the crags and deep valleys were breathtakingly beautiful, the subject of countless classical Chinese paintings. I saw an impressive number of rocks, both massive and miniature, lined up outside a small house, and a man was there to greet customers. I sat and chatted with him in the sun, surrounded by these grotesquely shaped rocks.

"Who are your clients?" I asked.

"Our clients usually come from park bureaus or real estate developers," he said. "They need rocks like these for all sorts of gardens and flower terraces."

"Mostly from the coastal regions?"

"Basically now from all over the country: Inner Mongolia, Qinghai, Beijing, Shanghai, Guangzhou, Shenzhen, Shantou, Wuhan.

Everywhere."

"And they all come to buy your rocks?"

"Right."

"Interesting. How do you determine the quality of a rock? What are the key factors?"

"The key factor is that the rock has a natural shape, with no scars or traces of having been damaged, and that it looks good. With some rocks, it is a matter of choosing a good name."

"A good name! What is considered to be a good name?" I asked.

"Well, this one for instance is called Jiang Xia Gu Zhai (Old House in the River Gorge). The one over there is called Huang Shan Zhi Feng (Huang Shan Mountain Summit), while that one is called San Xia Da Ba (the Three Gorges Dam). It really does look like the real Three Gorges Dam."

"So how do you decide on the price?"

"The value of a rock comes from its shape. It is not based on the costs of getting the rock here."

"What is the highest price you have ever heard of?"

"The best rocks, with really unusual shapes, sell for several million each, some for tens of millions," he said.

"Wow."

"They are bought by rock collectors. But for that price they are going to be the very best, meaning that there is only one like it in the whole of the People's Republic of China, or maybe even the whole world."

"What kind of shape is considered good?"

"It is partly the quality of the rock itself. There are many different types of rock, some are even more valuable than jade."

"The shape of some of the rocks appears to include a 'head'," I said. "Is it that the closer the shape of a rock is to the human form, the more valuable it is?"

"No." He dismissed such a simplistic view with a shake of his head.

We walked past the rocks lined up on the other side of the road from his house.

"How about this one?" I asked, pointing to a smooth pale grey rock, around one metre square, with strange flecks of purple and red throughout. "How much would that be?"

"A few thousand," he said.

"What about this next one?" It was very similar, but the markings were at first glance not as interesting.

"That one is called Three Gorges Dam. The minimum for that one would be eighty thousand RMB. Absolute minimum."

"What is the difference?" I asked, puzzled.

"The price is determined by the appearance, and the quality of its shape. Look at the Three Gorges Dam. It actually looks like the dam." I peered at the markings, and now he mentioned it, they did look like a dam with water spilling out. Interesting.

"Is this painted on it?" I asked

"No, It's the natural shape."

"Really?"

"It has to be, to be worth money."

So the value came not so much from the rocks, but from the ability of the rock seller to see pictures in the rock faces or shapes. The image of the dam would not have been obvious unless he had mentioned it, just as my elephant-shaped cloud to you may look like nothing at all.

"So you have to be able to tell stories to do this business," I said.

"Right. You have to be able to make up stories. Even if the rocks have no value, you can talk them up and give them value."

"Who makes up the stories?"

"I think them up myself."

"So it is not the rocks that have value, but your stories," I said.

He smiled. "Yes."

"Where do you find the rocks?"

"Up in the mountains. This one weighs around fifty tonnes." He patted a huge rock that dominated the space in front of the house. "You need a special truck to get it out of the mountains. I brought this one out three years ago. At the time I priced it at two hundred and twenty thousand

RMB. But today I wouldn't sell it for less than three hundred thousand. Rich people don't mind spending a hundred thousand or a million. They have money, a good car and a good job. They just don't care."

The rock had dirt all over it, just as it had in the mountains. "Why don't you clean it?" I asked.

"Because it is the natural element that has value with a rock like this. If you wash it or polish it, then it becomes artificial."

But while some of the rocks were rough and natural, others were highly polished. He showed me one polished rock that he said was called 'Old Shanghai'. Looked at in a certain way from a certain angle, the markings looked like old buildings and alleyways.

Value, as always and with everything, is in the eye of the buyer.

"Is the rock business better or worse than it used to be?" I asked.

"Better!" he said enthusiastically. "The bigger the business gets, the easier it is to sell and the higher the prices I can get."

"And there are more rich people in China now, right?"

"Right."

"When did you begin this business?" I asked.

"In the late 1970s."

"But it must have been illegal to do private business like this in the 1970s, surely?"

"Yes, it was illegal. When I started, the county government confiscated everything. But I picked myself up and built the business back again from scratch. I've always taken a confrontational approach to the government. Whatever you say I can't do, that's what I am going to do."

I laughed at the audacity of this statement.

"You must be rich to be able to afford such a walking trip," he said to me, turning the conversation to business, as any salesman of his calibre would.

"I am not rich," I protested. "I cannot afford your rocks."

A little further along, my attention was drawn to a rock promontory that seemed to be blocking the road, while out to the right was nothing but sky. As I got close, I saw why. I had rejoined the river, which was sparkling three hundred metres below. The road doubled back on itself and headed downwards, but I first spent some time examining the rock on the corner, the face of which was covered in cultured graffiti dating back years, decades and centuries – the carvings of poems and phrases in Chinese calligraphy, some indented and some raised from the rock face with the artist having chipped away the rock from around the characters.

'The spring waters of the river flow towards the east', said one, a clichéd line from a Chairman Mao poem. 'The clouds and rain wrapped in passion, a thousand mountains intoxicated', read another, which was more interesting. Clouds and rain are a Chinese metaphor for sex. Maybe the calligrapher brought a friend to visit the rock.

The road ran sharply down towards the Yangtze River, with a high cliff face on the right and the bluest of China blue skies above. It was a magical late winter day, the only drawback being a slight haze, which made it difficult to make out much of the river except for the glint of the sunlight on the currents. "It is clearest just after it has rained," one man told me. "You must come back."

The cliff above me, about five hundred metres straight up, was dominated by a rock outcrop that looked like a head, which watched me as I descended, the road winding back and forth.

I passed a ladder leading up to a terrace with a house behind, and a sign that said 'water refills'. An old woman with a weather-beaten face and a smile that transcended hardship was sitting outside with her family and waved to me to come up, so I did and sat with them for a while.

"This is my mother," said one man. "She has nine children and she is seventy-four years old." He was very proud of her, and quite rightly so. She brought me some tea, so I had the water refill that was promised on the sign.

Feeling replenished, I met a man further down the road who asked me if I had a torch. "You'll need one for the tunnels ahead," he said.

"Tunnels?"

"Three tunnels."

And tunnels there were. Each one around half a kilometre in length, pitch black, hacked through the rock. A regular stream of cars and motorcycles came through as I walked in the blackness, and their headlights plus my PDA served as my torches. It was a little unsettling walking through the absolute darkness under tons of rock, and I sang loudly to check the acoustics of the tunnel, and to keep fear at bay. The song I sang was one I had been listening to earlier that day, a tune by David Bowie and Pat Metheny called 'This Is Not America'.

The last of the tunnels opened out right on top of the river, which was still deserted. The water glistened even more brightly for being viewed in contrast to the tunnel blackness.

I walked along the river for several kilometres, conscious that at this point, just below the Three Gorges Dam, it was at the same levels as it had always been, as were the shape and depth of the valley. I passed through a little town built at the mouth of a tributary, with a bridge from the early 1970s featuring slogans such as 'Long Live the Great Leader Chairman Mao'.

There is a place from where the cut-out shape of the mountain ridge on the southern side is said to look like Chairman Mao lying embalmed in his Beijing mausoleum, and there were a bunch of people at the spot trying to make out the shape through the mist. It was vaguely visible, and the pavilion built at the viewing point also featured a massive bust of Mao next to which lay a pile of discarded peanut shells. The ridge did look like Mao's corpse lying in state. But enough of Chairman Mao, for god's sake. The real China was doing all it could to move on, and it seemed silly to stand there trying to make out his fake likeness in the mountains. I pressed on, the Three Gorges Dam now only a few kilometres up ahead.

CHAPTER 16

THE DAM

There is a four-lane highway running from Yichang city west to the Three Gorges Dam, built to move leaders and honoured guests quickly to and from China's biggest showcase infrastructure project. There are military guards on every entrance and exit.

I walked along the modest local road which tracks that barbed-wire enclosed highway on the northern side of the Yangtze River just inside the easternmost of the Gorges, the Yichang Gorge. There were only a few boats and barges on the river, but there were plenty of trucks on the local road, shifting goods unloaded from boats above the dam a few kilometres ahead.

The road turned away from the river and passed through a tunnel under the official highway, then doubled back into a village. There was a shop front featuring tourist signs – 'See the Dam!' – with several young girls milling around outside, presumably waiting to take on the role of tour guides, and maybe more. A man in a black tracksuit came over to me.

"You want a tour of the dam?"

"No, thank you, I am just walking through."

"There is a guard post up ahead," he said. "I have a car with a permit that can take you through."

"We'll see," I said. I walked on towards the river, and came to a gate with a sentry box beside it, and the Gorges highway beyond, which is now the only way of getting to the dam. I said hello to the guard, who was distant and unforthcoming, as was required of him. But I got out of him that I could walk through onto the highway, but cars could not pass without a permit, which had to be obtained in Yichang.

I asked the man in the tracksuit if I could walk across the dam. I had to somehow cross the river to the south side to get to the next town, called Maoping.

"No, it is impossible."

"So how do I get across to the other side?"

"There is a bridge below the dam, but you cannot walk across that either. It is not allowed. You will have to ride in my car," he said.

"I'll deal with that problem when I get to it," I replied, and started off through the gate and onto the empty highway. I arranged for the driver to follow me in his car, just in case.

The dam was now only five kilometres ahead. Along the highway were several large office buildings, headquarters of government departments, banks and state enterprise corporations – each one representing a large and lucrative construction contract, and in scale far beyond the needs of the area. They were prominently displayed signs of the cash that had been funnelled through the Three Gorges Dam construction project, which had begun in 1993.

It was raining, misty and miserable. I trudged along and came to a turn-off to the left, beyond which I could see the white pillars of a massive bridge. I walked towards it, shielded from the rain by a purple-flowered umbrella, which I had bought in a local shop for a few RMB. The driver Mr. Wang hung back in his Ford Transit van, convinced that he would have to take me across.

There was a sentry post at the edge of the bridge, and the guard was wearing a steel helmet and white gloves.

"Ni hao," I said, and gave him my most winning smile as I made to continue walking past him. He shook his gloved hand at me vigorously.

"Stop!" he said. "You cannot walk across."

I stopped, and from a little booth beside the raised dais of the sentry post, there emerged a young officer in a smart military uniform, putting on a military peaked cap as he came out. He looked no more than twenty-five years old.

"You cannot walk over the bridge," he said, apologetically. "You must take a car."

"But I have walked here all the way from Shanghai, and I am from England and I am walking to Tibet and it is a charity walk for the poor children in Anhui province." I linked all the possibly useful lines together, added a smile and tried to look as non-threatening as possible. It is just little me, said my body language. And the purple-flowered umbrella helped.

"Are you sure you can't take a car across, and then resume your walk on the other side?" he asked.

"I am afraid not," I said with a broader smile. Phrasing the question in that way meant it would be okay. "I cannot cross any way other than walking. Otherwise my whole journey from Shanghai has been wasted."

"All right, then," he said.

"Thank you!" I exclaimed, gave him a name card and walked triumphantly across the bridge.

The genius of China is its flexibility. Nothing is allowed, but everything is possible.

So I strode triumphantly across the Yangtze River from the north bank to the south, singing in the rain as I went. It was the first time I had crossed the river since the city of Tongling in southern Anhui province more than a year before. I would now be on the south side of the river for a fair way, up to the town of Badong in the heart of the Yangtze Gorges region.

I peered west from the bridge, looking for the dam, but the brown mist was so thick that nothing could be seen except the vague shapes of man-made channel dividers carving up the river. The Xiling Bridge is just over a kilometre in length and it was completed in 1997, around the same time as the Tongling bridge. I realized that even ten years earlier, the idea of walking from Shanghai to Tibet by a relatively direct route would have been a non-starter because the bridges that are required in order to make the journey possible didn't exist.

On reaching the southern bank, I walked along the river promenade. The rain cleared, the mist lifted a little, a long, low barrier topped by cranes became visible and there it was: the Three Gorges Dam. It was impossible to get a sense of scale, but the assumption had to be that it was huge. It faded into the mist with electricity transmission lines stretching away in all directions.

Mr. Wang and his van were still following me and I stopped and chatted with him about the dam.

"You were born in this area?" I asked.

"Yes, back there." He pointed back to where I had met him.

"What impact has the dam had on the life of people around here?"

"Neither good nor bad really," he said. "Although for people with good connections, it has provided an opportunity to make a lot of money."

"Is it safe?"

"Safe? Oh, yes. It won't collapse. But the danger is war."

"War?"

"Right. If there is a war, this dam will definitely be a target."

This dam had been with me in a sense since I first came to live in Mainland China in the late 1970s. Chairman Mao, with all his god-like arrogance, believed he had the right to remake China, destroy the past, and replace a culture that had flourished over thousands of years with his own vision. Amongst other things, he wanted to tame the Yangtze, just as he wanted to tame the Chinese people.

In fact, the construction of a dam across the Yangtze had been discussed at least as far back as 1919 when the first president of republican China, Sun Yat-sen, proposed the project with the aim of controlling the annual floods downstream. But it wasn't until 1979, the year I moved to Beijing, that the State Council finally approved the project and serious planning began. In 1981, the Gezhouba Dam at Yichang – outside the Gorges and a sort of trial run for the real thing – was completed. In the 1980s, there was a relatively lively debate about the Three Gorges Dam in terms of environmental impact and construction safety. It was really the first topic in the history of communist China in which a relatively free and open public discussion of the pros and cons of a policy proposal was allowed. Some delegates to the National People's Congress famously voted against the project in the late 1980s, but Premier Li Peng was behind it and he prevailed, with the go-ahead being given in 1992.

His replacement as premier, Zhu Rongji, is said to have had a meeting in the mid-1990s with the heads of the state construction companies building the dam, and told them bluntly that if the quality of the construction was found to be wanting, they would be executed. It was the only way to stop these guys from playing their usual games of doing substandard construction, skimming off public funds for their private use.

By 2003, the dam construction work was basically completed, and the reservoir behind the dam began to fill up and back into and submerge the watercourse, the side valleys, the villages and terraced fields to the west. Hundreds of thousands of people were resettled as part of the project, mostly moved from their ancestral farmhouses to new apartment blocks and houses in the main county towns.

The dam is the largest in the world. It is about one hundred and fifty metres in height and 2.3 kilometres in length. There are power generators on the north and south sides of the dam with floodgates in the middle to discharge the excess waters and recreate the river eastwards.

As I walked along towards the dam, the density of electricity power lines above me increased. The electricity generators on the northern end of the dam started producing power in 2005, and the dam's total production capacity is now 84.68TWh of electricity, which is approximately a hell of a lot, providing power to cities as far away as Shanghai. My laptop, it occurred to me, was usually powered by the electricity that was tingling through the air above me now.

The dam was getting closer and now looked more imposing. I came to an intersection; the road ahead went straight into the dam construction area.

"Don't go down there," warned Mr. Wang, still keeping up with me. "You will be detained by the military police and that will waste time."

"It would," I said.

Mr. Wang said security was tight because a foreign spy had been arrested in the dam area in 1998 taking photographs. He had no details on nationality, but if true, it was a pretty useless waste of a spy, given the visibility of the project and the ease of taking satellite photographs.

A turnoff to the left headed up the hill to the side of the dam. The road was lined with little farmhouses and terraced fields, as they had been forever, now looking out over one of the world's largest construction projects. I passed a courtyard with an open gate, and a view out over the dam. I was still below the top, but it was impressive from the higher elevation, and I was closer than I expected to be, given all I had heard of security.

The road curved up to the right, around the southern end of the dam, and a man carrying some postcards came up to me and said: "Do you want to go to the dam?"

"Yes! How much?"

"Twenty RMB."

Good deal. I followed him along a track off the road, and we came out at a point level with the top of the dam, looking along its length with the southern generating plant, not yet commissioned, directly below us.

My guide, Mr. Tan, gave me a quick run-down of the statistics relating to the dam, and I asked: "How is security?"

"Pretty poor. Full of loopholes. But if it wasn't, I wouldn't be able to make a living."

I asked Mr. Tan about the environmental impact of the dam, and he said: "It's terrible."

"In what way?" I asked, expecting to hear about silting, landslides and extinct Yangtze dolphins.

"When the water spills out of the floodgates in the summer, the roar of the water makes the windows of our houses shudder," he said.

Hmm, that sounded less than desperate.

Mr. Tan said he and his family used to live in the valley below. The land was 'bought' by the government from the local farmers. Mr. Tan said his family of seven received a total of two thousand five hundred RMB for their land. He made a living as a workman on the dam construction for some years after his fields were taken, but when the main construction work was completed he became a tour guide, hawking postcards and leading tourists into supposedly closed parts of the project.

We walked back to the road and around the hill to the back of the dam. There was a road to the top of the dam just one hundred metres away but it had a sentry box.

"They just set up the guard post a couple of months ago," Mr. Tan sighed. "Before that, I could take people out onto the dam."

The reservoir was now below us and beyond it, through the mist, I could make out the vague shapes of the new Maoping town with tall apartment blocks perched on the hillside above the new water level. Part of the old town below the water level was still there, but it sat protected by a huge secondary coffer dam. I walked across the top of this coffer dam, and looked down at the old Maoping valley, looking just as if there was no dam cutting it in half.

I glanced at my global positioning unit and saw I was at one hundred and eighty-five metres above sea level. The reservoir itself looked benign, and children and couples were sitting on the rocks below the road, chatting peacefully. The sense of danger, negativity and impending environmental disaster that one got when reading about the dam in the Western media was entirely absent. The Yangtze dolphins had gone, due to human activity up and down the river over the past few decades, and there were dredgers under the shadow of the dam battling with silt. But the bottom line is that China was probably always going to build the dam and the ultimate consequences were always going to be unknown.

As I walked up the slope towards the town, an old man with big tinted glasses and lively liver spots approached me and asked where I was from. Mr. Gong said he was seventy-five years old and was a "migrant" – that is, someone who had been uprooted and relocated due to the dam project.

"What is your profession?" I asked.

"I am a farmer," he said.

"Where are your fields?"

He smiled. "Underwater," he replied.

The dam had always been a key objective in my walk westwards from Shanghai, and with that now behind me, I was presented with new and unfamiliar territory: the Yangtze Gorges region.

I had been through the Gorges once before, travelling downstream on a boat from Chongqing to Yichang. At that point, in the year 2000, the Gorges were deeper than they are today, but their shape and feel were the same, and they were cloaked in the same misty haze I experienced during the first few days of my walk upstream. Maoping has been almost totally reconstructed with Three Gorges Dam money, and there were even a couple of hotels that claimed four-star status. But they still had no coffee.

I had dinner in Maoping with a local guy and we discussed the dam and its impact. That led to a discussion of the balance of power between the Communist Party and the Chinese people, and the extent to which the people can influence events in today's China. He was optimistic and gave an interesting example from his own world.

"In about 1997, when construction of the Three Gorges Dam was in full swing, Maoping was full of workers and construction companies and it was messy with lots of karaoke bars and gambling and prostitutes. It was pretty wild. The police chief of Yichang city one day decided to crack down. He sent all his police in several dozen buses and raided all the brothels and karaoke bars and casinos in the dam zone and arrested everyone they could get their hands on. Over the next few days, a huge sum of money was withdrawn from the local banks in the dam construction area – something like five hundred million RMB. The banks were just cleaned out of money, leaving the whole project unable to pay salaries or any other payments. What happened was that many of the people caught up in the sweep were the bosses and managers of the private construction companies involved in the dam project, and the bosses of these companies just pulled all their money out of the banks all at once. There was nothing the authorities could do. Everyone was released unconditionally."

The road out of Maoping along the edge of the reservoir came to an intersection, and I wasn't sure of which way to go, so I asked a girl walking in the same direction if this was the right road to Badong. She nodded and we walked along together for a while. She told me she was going to school, which happened to be on the same road, so I asked if she could introduce me to her headmaster. She agreed we would try to find him.

"How many students are there in your school?" I asked.

"About eight thousand," she said.

"That's huge!" I exclaimed.

I asked her about her life as we walked. Her name was Xiang Fangqiong, she was seventeen and she had a naïve openness and a full figure, a combination which spells trouble for many girls. She told me almost nothing about her parents – her mother worked the fields, and her father was away all the time working somewhere else, she was not sure doing what or where. She didn't enjoy school. "I want to stop studying," she said. I tried to argue against this line, but looking at her, I realized there was little chance she would make it through to graduation. She was most animated when she talked about her boyfriend.

"What is it about him that you like?" I asked.

"I don't know, but I just do," she said. "So I have decided to give everything to him."

"How long have you known him?"

"About a month."

Uh-huh.

We arrived at the school, the Zigui County Vocational Education Centre. It was massive and pretty modern with maybe six or seven white multi-storey buildings. Some were dormitories, some were classrooms, but there were no elevators in any of them. We went to the headmaster's office, on the sixth floor of one of the buildings, but he was not in. So I wrote out a note in Chinese introducing myself, saying I was passing through and would like to meet him. Then Ms. Xiang's English teacher appeared. Mr. Tan's English really was very good, but he treated me with caution and suspicion. I explained that I was walking through town, and he took the note with some hesitation. "I will pass it on, but I don't know if he will believe you," he said.

"Believe what? That I exist?"

Sigh. The conservatism of petty bureaucrats. Do nothing and you are safe. I invited Mr. Tan to dinner, but he said he was busy. So I said goodbye to both him and Ms. Xiang and left the premises.

That evening, I had dinner with Ms. Xiang and her boyfriend. The boy was twenty-three, thin as a rake, with longish hair covering his ears and twinkling eyes. I asked him to write out his name. He could hardly do it. I asked him about his work. He said he was a photographer who specialized in wedding photos but then, moments later, he said he was unemployed. He had nowhere to stay that night, so after dinner, we went to a local doss house, where he had to borrow the girl's ID card to register. While he signed in, I stood outside with the girl.

"What do you think of him?" she asked.

"Well, he cannot hold down a job, he's a drifter and I would guess he has a girlfriend in some other city." No point not being frank.

"I told him that if he wanted to have another girlfriend, he had to tell me first," she said.

"Do you sleep with him?" I asked.

"No, I am still young," she said haughtily.

"Well, when it happens, remember to use a condom. You're okay as long as you are not pregnant," I said.

"Wow, you foreigners are so open!" she said, looking at me with wide eyes.

Sigh.

I passed the main river passenger terminal, a large and new building, and then a fruit warehouse where the local oranges were waxed and shined to give them a higher resale value. For much of the way, I could see the river out on the right – or rather, what had once been the river, and was now a lake. The waters were now broader but quiet, lacking the eddies and pretty imperfections of a flowing body of water.

I also saw the Line. The Line ruled the world of the Yangtze River Gorges. It marked the 175 metres above sea level contour, which is the highest water mark chosen for the Three Gorges reservoir when fully filled. In preparation for this, officials, engineers and workers had gone round the whole Gorges area during the main project years and destroyed, moved, razed and scoured everything under the Line. This involved houses and fields of course, but also vegetation. Above the Line was a lively green; below the Line was a dead brown.

Close to Maoping, there were ferry wharves and repair yards for the huge flat-bottomed boats that diesel-chug up and down the waterway. The calmer reservoir waters had made life much easier for anyone operating on the river.

The people I spoke to gave me a feeling for the river as a separate social and economic entity. I met a man from Yueyang in Hunan province, and another from Jingzhou in Hubei, both cities hundreds of kilometres away to the east, but tied to the Gorges region by the river. I passed a wharf where trucks were being loaded and unloaded with cargo heading up or downstream. Lined up on the other side of the road were massage and 'take a rest' joints, there to service the drivers.

The next village, Yinxingtuo (Silver Apricot Tributary), was a faded semi-Potemkin settlement. Various signs indicated that the village had been reconstructed in the late 1990s, and faded photos on a signboard showed that a variety of Chinese leaders visited in 1998. The absence of any subsequent photos indicated that once the propaganda advantage had been gained in terms of the relocation of farming families to "dream" villages, no one of note had been back.

All the houses for this group of refugees from below the Line were two-storey and of identical design, covered in white tiles with windows and doors all painted yellow. On a notice board there was a detailed listing of presumably all residents in the village, giving the name, registration number, gender, profession (mostly "other") and employment skills (mostly "none"). Another notice said that six hundred households comprising two thousand one hundred and sixty four people had been moved from below the Line, with one thousand four hundred and thirty-eight settling in new homes in the area and the rest being sent to other parts of China. Diplomats and reporters from a dozen countries had visited the village, it said. Now, the village was messy and ugly and surviving not on the tourism referred to in the notice board, but on rather pathetic rows of tea bushes and orange trees.

The river-reservoir was about a kilometre across at this point, and the old submerged farms had been replaced by floating farms – fish farms. Just about every inlet now had a steel grid on its surface with fish swimming in cages below, eating turbo-charged fish food, effluent from upriver and perhaps the occasional natural morsel floating by. The steep hillsides around me were covered in tea bushes, the same standard green tea I drank at houses along the way, invited in by farmers.

The people I passed were often carrying things in elegant fluted wicker basket backpacks which are everywhere in the Gorges, and nowhere to be seen anywhere else. Even more brilliant is a wooden stand used by people carrying heavy loads in the baskets. I passed a man standing by the road with a massive pile of firewood on his back, and I was very impressed by his strength and the nonchalant way he bore the load. But walking past him, I saw the firewood was supported by a wooden leg, which took all the weight off his back.

I passed a man who was selling piglets. He had a dozen of them divided between two cages on either side of his motorcycle. The piglets were lying squashed higgledy-piggledy but peacefully on top of each other, unsure of what was happening but going with it. I chatted with the seller for a while, and as I was taking photos of the cute pigs, he suddenly gave one of the cages an almighty kick, which set the piglets flying into a prison cage squealing frenzy.

"Hey!" I shouted in alarm.

"Get them moving to give you something to photograph," he said with a grin.

"No! They are animals too, you know," I said. "Just like you."

It came out not quite as I meant it, and the atmosphere went suddenly chilly.

"He called you an animal," said one of his mates quietly.

I said goodbye.

CHAPTER 17

THE GORGES

The road I was walking on was designated Provincial Highway 334. Once upon a time, before the waters rose, it would have been a steep drop of more than one hundred metres from the road to the river. These days it almost skirted the river channel in many places, while at other times it headed off into side valleys, curving round over a bridge and then making its way back to the riverside. After making my way through one of these side valleys, I suddenly broke out of the regular countryside and into the real Gorges. There was a sheer cliff face in front of me several hundred metres in height and then a straight drop to the water far below.

The Yangtze Gorges are unique in their magnificence: the river demands adjectives such as 'mighty', and the cliffs that silently watch over it are daunting and formidable. The lonely farmhouses perched high up on the precipitous slopes of the Gorges speak to the proud independence of spirit.

A steady flow of large boats passed by in both directions and at any given moment, there were probably two or three boats visible: ferries and huge flat-bottomed cargo boats carrying mostly containers or coal. It was a very different scene from a century ago when the river was lower and laced with whirlpools, rocks and rapids. The boats back then were tiny – sampans and wupans (boats made of either three or five boards), and in order to get upstream the boats had to be hauled by trackers who lived and sometimes died in harness struggling up the paths and over the rocks against the flow of the river.

Edwin Dingle, in his book *Across China on Foot* published in 1910, gives an illuminating description of the scene:

> On shore, far ahead, I can see the trackers – struggling forms of men and women, touching each other, grasping each other, wrestling furiously and mightily, straining on all fours, now gripping a boulder to aid them forward, now to the right, now to the left, always fighting for one more inch, and engaged in a task which to one seeing it for the first time looks as if it were quite beyond human effort. Fagged and famished beings are these trackers, whose life day after day, week in week out, is harder than that of the average costermonger's donkey. They throw up their hands in a dumb frenzy of protest and futile appeal to the presiding deity; and here on the river, depending entirely upon those men on the shore, slowly, inch by inch, the little craft, feeling her own weakness, forges ahead against the leaping current in the gapway in the reef.

Today, that drama has gone from the Gorges, and so has the suffering and the deaths. Only somewhat muted, the natural glory of the Gorges is still there.

I passed a blackened slope with slides stretching down to the water, and next to it a house that had four storeys, three of which were below the level of the road, cutting into the side of the cliff. A truck was parked outside, and the driver beckoned me into the house where three women and two men were just sitting down to lunch. I joined them, and we sat and ate next to a television that was showing infomercials from Tianjin Satellite

Television, while outside lay the truly magnificent Xiling Gorge.

"This is a poor meal compared to what people eat in England," declared Mr. Zhang, who ran a small coal trading business.

Actually it was quite a spread: two meat dishes, one beancurd, and two green vegetables with rice all round, all cooked lightly and cleanly with minimum intrusion by extra ingredients – I don't think there was even MSG, a flavour enhancer which is prevalent in Chinese cooking in the cities. In terms of nutrition, dietary balance, quality of food and cooking, this was far superior to the average plate of baked beans, sausage and chips. A bottle of beer was opened in my honour.

"This is better than what most people eat in England," I said.

"But this is just ordinary food," Mr. Zhang said in surprise.

I asked him about his business, and he told me that the driver, Mr. Tan (a common surname in the Gorges, it would appear) carried raw coal from deep in the mountains out to this house by the river, after which it was delivered by the long rickety chutes down to barges that carried the coal down to Wuhan. Mr. Zhang declined to say how much money he made: "It's just a small business," he said.

"What do you think about the river and the dam?" I asked.

"The main impact is that it controls the flooding downstream, and it makes water transport easier. Apart from that, it has had almost no effect on our lives," he said.

Some of the people I met along the road said they used to live down below; others said they had always lived where they were today. I sat for a very pleasant half hour with a farmer who was gazing out over his steep terraces of corn and vegetables to a stunning Gorges vista.

"I was born here, and I have been here all my life, except for a few years in the time of Mao Zedong, when I was a worker in Dangyang," he told me. "Building roads, that kind of thing."

He looked so content, and also robust; the older people in the Gorges region seemed much more healthy than the average Chinese. Was it natural selection in terms of the tracker times of old? The hardy life of climbing up and down the hills? A cleaner approach to food preparation?

Something in the air? All of the above?

The gorge below me was the Xiling Gorge, approximately eighty kilometres in length, and, as the most easterly of the main Gorges, it had shrunk the most as the waters rose. The shoals and rocks that used to be such death traps were now well submerged. On the northern bank of the river opposite me, I could see farmhouses perched on impossibly steep mountain sides and a road being built through from the west along the cliff face to link even these remote houses into the 21st century.

The road I was on had been cut into the cliffs on the south side of the river, with tunnels at various points that linked tiny communities along the way. Walking through the tunnels was pretty scary – there were no lights and no ventilation, and I felt rather strongly that asphyxiation in the pitch darkness of a tunnel in the Yangtze Gorges would not be a good way to die. I handled the shorter tunnels by the light of the occasional passing car and my PDA set to full brightness, but there was one tunnel that felt really, really long as I entered it. I saw a woman and her twelve-year-old son walking in just ahead of me.

"Do you have a torch?" I called out.

"No," she replied.

"How long does it take to walk through?" I asked.

"About forty-five minutes," the woman shouted. Good grief. That would make it over two kilometres in length.

"How do you handle the tunnel without a torch?"

"We walk when a car passes through, then stop when the car has gone and wait until another one comes," she said.

I thought about how that would feel; standing there alone in a tunnel deep under the peaks in total darkness, breathing stale, particle-filled air, and waiting for who knows how long before the next car came along. When a vehicle approached, it filled the tunnel with a breathtaking rumble that rose quickly to an ear-splitting roar; the reality of the little three-wheeled truck that came trundling past did not quite match up to expectations.

I got a car to drive slowly behind us, lighting the way with its headlights.

Then, just before we emerged into the light on the other side, I stopped in the tunnel, waited for the car to leave, and gave a quick shout, as loud and powerful as I could, and listened with great satisfaction as it echoed far back down the tunnel.

"When was this road and tunnel built?" I asked the woman.

"Maybe fifteen years ago," she said.

"How did you get out before that?" I asked.

"Walked over the hills," she said, pointing up at the steep slopes above. Phenomenal feats seemed to be the norm for the people of the Gorges.

Back in the blessed daylight, I was confronted with a massive sign saying "The Hometown of Qu Yuan". Qu Yuan was an official who committed suicide in the third century BC – more than two thousand three hundred years ago – to protest again corruption in the imperial court.

Qu Yuan's alleged 'hometown' was not much. There were several houses by the road that followed the Xiling Gorge above the river that looked fairly new and I spotted a small shop that had a few people sitting around inside. I went in to buy a bottle of water as an excuse to ask about the famous man.

"So this was where Qu Yuan was born?" I enquired.

They looked at me, thought about it a bit, then shook their heads. "Up in the mountains," one of them said.

Qu Yuan is said to have committed suicide by throwing himself into the river. Presumably he was not able to swim, or else he had weighed himself down with weights. In any event, he died and he was so respected for his fatal act of protest that even today people in the Chinese-inhabited parts of the world mark that day, the fifth day of the fifth month with dragon boat races. The paddling of the dragon boats marks the way in which the people of the town beat the water to chase away the fish to try and stop Qu Yuan's body from being eaten. Rice dumplings wrapped in leaves are also eaten on that day, harking back to food thrown into the waters by the people to distract the fish, again in an effort to keep Mr. Qu's body intact.

The steep mountainsides above me on the left and across the stretch of water were awe-inspiring and high up there, far from my world, were the lonely farmhouses. The colours of this section of the gorge on this particular day were sharp and satisfyingly coordinated: blue sky, rocky grey and shrubby green walls, and the rich brown chocolate fondue of the river.

There was steady traffic out on the 'water road', as one person I spoke to called the river. I passed some purple flowers and spent a couple of minutes photographing a besotted butterfly, while a ferry glided below through the frame. I passed a pile of cathode ray tubes nestling in the undergrowth. Cathode ray tubes in the middle of the Gorges? I know – total disconnect, but welcome to 21st-century China.

The river widened for a while and the cliffs became less precipitous, and then the Gorge closed in again. The day was hot and the sun was beating down mercilessly. Anywhere with even a little space was planted with orange trees and corn; one a long-term investment, the other incredibly short. Corn grows very fast.

I came upon more tunnels dug through the cliffs above the river, long and dark with air heavily laden with particles my lungs did not wish to experience. I am not naturally claustrophobic, but a few more of these tunnels could definitely change my mind on the subject.

My daughter Jennifer, who accompanied me on this particular stretch of my journey, quite rightly decided not to walk through the tunnels with me – it was my decision to walk every step of the way from Shanghai after all. As I usually walk alone, it was a pleasure to introduce her to the stunning vistas of this beautiful part of China. We came upon many interesting local sidelights together: Chinese medicinal herbs and ingredients laid out by the roadside to dry in the sun; a disgusting cement factory surrounded by vegetation, where every leaf was covered with a thick film of creamy cement dust; a huge pile of old shoes. We came upon the self-styled "orange town" of Guojiaba, which is a little settlement at the western edge of the narrowest part of the Xiling Gorge that was newly built in the past few years after the old town sunk beneath the waters. Being half-English and half-Chinese, Jennifer was perused with interest by all the people we passed; not your normal country girl by any means.

As we stopped for dinner in Guojiaba, I decided to have a haircut. An attendant from the restaurant-hotel took me up the street and into a simple storefront hair salon with a few chairs and mirrors and decorated with faded photos of Chinese singers with impossibly sophisticated hairstyles. The lady of the salon was in her early thirties, wearing white jeans and a pink T-shirt with shoulder-length hair fashionably tinted brown at the edges. She was pummelling the shoulders of an older gentleman, and her eyes sparkled as I entered.

"How do you do?" she said in understandable English.

"I am well, thank you," I replied with a smile. That was a bit too advanced for her, but never mind.

I sat down and her young male assistant gave me a dry shampoo.

The lady continued pummelling the man's shoulders as she was talking to me. Her surname was Jiang and she was thirty-four years old. The salon was hers, she said, and she made a profit of two or three thousand RMB a month. A haircut cost ten RMB.

"How old are you?" she asked in English, practising a phrase she said she had learned in high school, but had never had a chance to use.

"You are the first foreigner we have ever had in here," she added in Chinese, and started to cut away at my hair.

"How is foreign hair compared to Chinese hair?" I asked.

"It curls at the ends. I have never seen that before," she said. "What do you think of China?"

"It changes fast. How about Guojiaba?"

"It hasn't changed much," she said.

Well, maybe not in the past year or so; the town in its current location did not exist ten years ago. All the towns in the lower gorges were flooded by the rising waters of the Three Gorges Dam in the early and middle portions of the first decade of the 21st century. The old Guojiaba disappeared underwater and its inhabitants moved up the hill to the new town that had no old buildings or history, but brand new multi-storey structures.

"I have an eleven-year-old son who is well-behaved and smart," Ms. Jiang said proudly.

"Where would you guess he will be and what will he be doing in ten years' time?" I asked.

"Hmm, probably studying or working. But not here."

Another client sat down next to me, a policeman. He looked at me with interest, and as the assistant gave him a close military crew cut, he made a call on his mobile phone.

Ms. Jiang finished my haircut, which was not half bad, and I suggested we take a photo together to commemorate the occasion. Just then, in walked two more policemen wearing sky-blue short-sleeved shirts, epaulettes and a silver number pinned over the heart. They pulled out their ID cards to show me.

"We are policemen," said one.

"I know," I replied. "Could you take a photo for me please?"

I offered my camera to the one who had spoken, and he held it for a moment, uncertain of what to do, then passed it to his colleague, who took the photo. Ms. Jiang was no longer sparkling.

"Could you come to the police station for a chat?" said the taller of the two policemen, whose name was Li.

"I am just about to have dinner," I replied. "Why don't you come and join me for a chat?" I gave Ms. Jiang ten RMB, bade her a quick farewell and walked out of the salon.

"Where are you staying?" called Officer Li after me.

"Yangguang Hotel," I said. I got back to the hotel in thirty seconds, went to the little reception counter and told the lady manager to register me quickly. I had not been registered when I arrived, and it was already dark outside. The rule is that foreigners must register with either the police or a hotel when they overnight in a town, and while many small hotels don't care, and on principle I prefer not to register, in this particular case, it would not be good for either myself or for the hotel's manager, a full-figured lady in a flouncy and revealing dress, who looked like she had a history.

I told her we were about to be visited by representatives of the people's constabulary, and we cooperated to quickly get me into the registration book. I then sat down in the entrance area, on one of those hard wooden Chinese sofas that prove that at least in terms of furniture, ancient China had little to contribute to the modern world. I ordered some beancurd, vegetables, rice and a beer, and before long, the officers arrived and sat down opposite me.

"Please have some dinner with me," I said, pointing at the food on the low table between us.

"I have eaten," one responded curtly.

"Have some beer then."

"We are on duty."

"Then a cup of tea."

They took the tea, asked all the usual questions and in response I gave all the usual answers about walking to Tibet. They didn't push for more information, and it was clear we were all waiting for someone else to arrive so I bided time by asking Officer Li some questions in return.

"How is the law and order situation in Guojiaba?"

"Pretty good. But you need to take care of your possessions, and keep your door locked at night," he said.

"Any big cases recently?"

"We had a murder in May. A man killed his wife. He wasn't right in the head."

Officer Li was twenty-seven years old, exactly half my age, and he was born near Yichang. He had been posted to Goujiaba two years ago.

"How long will you be here?"

"I don't know. I guess I will be moved at some point."

"How much notice do they give you before a move?"

"Sometimes just a day," he replied.

I was getting on pretty well with Officer Li as we were joined by two other uniformed officers and one in plain clothes. Officer Li pointed to him. "He is our leader," he said.

"He is in plain clothes so of course he is the leader," I replied. The two new uniformed cops showed me their IDs. Mr. Plain Clothes did not, but he did most of the talking.

"Do you have your passport with you?" he asked. I handed it to him, and he passed it on to one of the other policemen, who examined it for a full ten minutes, wrote out copious information from it in English letters and then asked me: "What country are you from?"

Meanwhile, Mr. Plain Clothes asked me a number of questions and told me that his concern was for my safety, and to ensure that I was not doing anything improper.

"I am just walking through, and I stopped for a haircut," I said. "I will be leaving tomorrow morning to continue my walk."

"How early?"

"Very early."

"Which way will you go?"

"West."

"Do you have a map?"

"I don't need one. I just keep going west."

"Well, the road is blocked to the west of here; it is being repaired. So I would advise you not to go. Around twenty kilometres of road are being rebuilt. So you need to consider carefully how you will proceed. Best to take a ferry along to Shazhenxi. That is the next town along the river. Also, after all the rains recently, there is a danger of landslides, so you must be careful."

He was slightly obnoxious and overbearing and was clearly trying very hard to think of ways to get me to leave the territory for which he was responsible. However, it is a mark of China's progress that a policeman in such a town no longer has the power or the need to summarily order a foreigner to leave. I agreed to everything he said, and so he went and spent some time berating the hotel manager for not having informed the police the minute I appeared.

When I started out the next morning I saw that there were indeed places along the road that were being repaved with concrete but traffic was still moving, albeit with some delays. The day was bright and clean after two weeks of flood-making rains, but the air still felt soggy. Much of the mature corn along the way looked rotten after having been waterlogged and battered by the rains, but the orange trees and tea bushes were in good shape.

The road tended southwest, away from the Yangtze River and here, away from the main body of the brown river, the waters were green. Two or three people said they had seen me on the roads to the east on previous outings, and asked where my daughter was.

Almost all the houses were newly-built three (and sometimes four) storey brick structures, paid for with the relocation allowances distributed to ensure the success of the Three Gorges Dam project. My impression was that a fair proportion of the hundreds of thousands of people relocated in the project were only moved a few dozen metres up the hill. The little bays below had been valleys just a few years ago.

The Yangtze Gorges region is serious orange-growing country, but it was not always this way: the farmers told me how all the land had been forced into grain production from the 1950s onwards through to the 1980s on the orders of Chairman Mao. Grain self-sufficiency at the expense of all other agricultural production was one of Mao's paranoid and disastrously destructive responses to the fear of invasion first by the Nationalist Chinese, then the Americans, and then the Soviets. The land in the Gorges is mostly mountainous, and unsuited to growing any grain except for little patches of corn, but it was a political requirement, and all of China had to comply. In the early 1980s, the communes that had brought Chinese agriculture to its knees were abolished and the land was returned to the farming families. In the eastern Gorges region, they immediately started planting oranges again.

The Gorges oranges were small by Western supermarket standards, but very tasty. They were sold by the farmers at around two RMB per kilo to traders who shipped them out for sale across China. They were also dried and sold for traditional Chinese medicinal purposes, and the ground in many places I passed was covered in small wizened oranges drying in the sun. I was told the dried medicinal version was sold to wholesalers for twice the rate of fresh oranges.

Yellow butterflies played around me but eluded my camera as the road wound up into the mountains south of the river while the bay below – a submerged tributary valley – receded and the tributary finally showed itself. It was the Tongzhuang River, and on this day it was running full and fast with rainwater.

I came upon a truck equipped with two decks of cages filled with pigs on their way to market. The way the men were poking the pigs to get them to re-arrange themselves was appalling. I chatted with them for a while, hiding my feelings about the poor bloody pigs – they really were bloody.

Pigs across China had been slaughtered by the millions over the previous weeks to stop the spread of a highly infectious disease, and pork was off the menu in just about all restaurants, including those in the Gorges region towns. The pig man told me he had bought the pigs locally and was taking them east to Hunan province for sale.

"Is that legal?" I asked.

"Legal!" he exclaimed, outraged, and whipped out a piece of paper with a red chop on it. "Chinese people only do business that is legal."

I rolled my eyes. "Chinese people only do business that is legal," I repeated. "Let me think about that. Are there any exceptions? Hmm," I grinned, and a couple of his friends grinned with me.

I met a man smoking a huge homemade joint-like cigarette made out of tobacco that he had grown himself. He was one of a team of around ten road-builders whom I stopped and chatted with for a while. They told me that their team could lay between one hundred and fifty and two hundred metres of one lane of road per day. The process was simple: girders about thirty centimetres high are placed along either side of the lane; concrete is dumped between the tramlines, smoothed out, then left to dry. No preparation work is done on the road surface – the new concrete slab is just plumped down on top of the existing old asphalt surface. How long could something done this way last? One sign said the contract called for the road surface to last twenty years, but it seemed unlikely to me.

The mountainsides were covered in orange groves and were heavily populated by cicadas that were screeching in full force amidst the July heat. The temperature out on the road must have been well over forty degrees Celsius, and I bought a small towel, soaked it with water from a hose and put it over my head to keep my brain from overheating.

The river valley I was walking up was truly spectacular, with views down to the racing river and views up to farmhouses perched on the steep hillsides. Thanks to the recent rains, everything was a vibrant green.

I passed an old farmhouse with a faded political slogan: 'Love the Motherland, Love Collectivism, Love Socialism'. That was then, but now, while the people still love the Motherland, no one ever loved collectivism, and as for the third… well, no one even knows what that means any more.

The old houses in this region had doors but no windows and so while I admired the simple and environmentally compatible design of the old buildings, I could understand why people were happy to move into the more modern ugly brick and concrete houses that at least allowed daylight to penetrate.

Towards the top of the valley, I entered a town named Wenhua, which means 'culture'. I had wondered about the name ever since I first saw it on maps, and then on the front of minibuses. Why would a town be called Culture? As I walked through it, I passed a large building dating from the early 1970s – grey brick decorated with a large faded revolutionary red star, a relic of the Cultural Revolution. Is that where the name came from?

The main street of Wenhua – actually the only street – ran parallel to the river, and as I came up to a rice wholesale shopfront, a lady outside smiled at me and gestured eagerly for me to stop and take a rest with her and her husband. I felt relieved by the opportunity to take a break from the oppressive heat.

Her name was Madame Han and she invited me to sit inside the cool high-ceilinged storeroom, piled high with bags of rice; but wanting to be near the action, I chose to sit near the entrance where Madame Han and her bearded husband Mr. Xiong (bear) managed the business from behind a desk equipped with an electric fan and an abacus. This was the biggest rice wholesale operation in the valley, they said, and business was good – rice is not grown in this district but the people of this district eat it as their staple, and so they must buy it. The rice sold in this shop was grown on the Hubei plain and bought from Wuhan. On hearing this, I thought to myself that I might have seen some of the rice stacked inside the store growing in the paddy fields I had passed during my walk across Hubei, and it made me feel nostalgic. I liked the mountains, but there is nothing in the world to match the green of mid-life paddy rice. I also missed water buffalo, which are in charge of ploughing – I had not seen an example of the delightful species since leaving the paddy fields.

But back to Culture: "Where did the town get its name?" I asked Madame Han.

"We like culture, so it's called Culture," she said with a smile.

"The town's name is old," she added. "And, no, it has nothing to do with the Cultural Revolution." But no one could tell me what its derivation was. I mentioned the old building with the red star to her. "That used to be a grain store," she said, "But it's used as a dormitory now because grain isn't grown here any more."

Madame Han and her husband were both born in 1953 and had both been Red Guards. "But we didn't rebel (zaofan)," she added hastily, referring to the essentially criminal destruction that many Red Guards engaged in, in the name of Chairman Mao.

"This whole area was a commune then, and there was no private enterprise. Everything was state-owned," she said.

"Do you have state-owned in your country?" asked a man listening on the side.

"Basically no. It is capitalist, just like Culture town is now."

"No!" he protested. "We are socialist!"

"Socialist? Is this socialism?" I pointed to the rice store we were sitting outside of, and over at the little Culture Supermarket across the road which had turned its lights off to save electricity. "Socialism means everyone is equally poor, and Madame Han looks quite prosperous."

After some earnest discussion on this point, the five or six listeners decided with some surprise that indeed socialism is collectivism and private enterprise is not.

I asked Mr. Bear about his shop hours. "We are open basically all the time. From 6am through to 9pm." His hand played easily with the abacus, and he looked very relaxed behind the desk.

"Seven days a week?"

He nodded. "That's capitalism," he said, and smiled.

I walked to the end of the main street where some youths were playing pool on a country pool table under an awning, the river running noisily along below us. The rules of the game allowed them to stop any time to take calls on their mobiles, presumably from their girlfriends. After watching them for a while, hoping for an invitation to play, I gave up and left. But a minute later, one of the boys ran after me and gave me a bottle of iced tea. What a nice gesture.

CHAPTER 18

HOW GREEN IS THEIR VALLEY

On my walk, the rule was always that I start from exactly the last place that I stopped – to the millimetre – and getting to and from that point can take some effort.

On this particular weekend, for example, I flew at noon from Shanghai to Yichang city where a car picked me up and drove me for two hours to the ferry terminal in the town of Guojiaba in the Yangtze Gorges, where we found the last car ferry going up-river had already left. So we stayed overnight in Guojiaba and got up at 5am to line up at the ferry ramp so that we could be sure of getting a place. The ferry – actually a barge pushed by a tug boat – left at 6.30am and cruised over the completely submerged location of the former county seat of Zigui, on up the Yangtze for an hour and a half, then hung a left into a valley and up to a ferry ramp near the town of Shazhenxi. We then drove through the mountains for an hour south past the town of Lianghe (two rivers), then east towards the town of Wenhua. But the road was blocked by a big brick and concrete barrier with a thin passage in the centre just wide enough for a motorcycle to pass through. The road was closed to four-wheeled vehicles for repairs. So I did a deal with a passing motorcyclist, paying him ten RMB to take me the final eight kilometres to the starting point of the walk, a petrol station just west of Wenhua, which I finally reached at 9.30am, twenty-one hours after leaving Shanghai.

It was raining, and the mountainous landscape was drenched in the rich hues of nature. The contrast between the dark green old leaves and the brighter new leaves on the expanses of orange trees that covered the red clay hillsides was quite a sight. The point on the mountain road at which I started the walk was around two hundred and eighty metres above sea level, while the ridge at the top of the valley, at the point where the road was blocked, was just over six hundred metres. The uphill trudge was wet, but seeing the valley magnificently shrouded in mist made it worth it. I was still tracking the Tongzhuang River and I could hear it below on the left, catching occasional glimpses of it. Above and below on the steep hillsides were the ghostly presences of old farmhouses, some with deep red mud-covered façades, that blended seamlessly and satisfyingly into the landscape.

Every inch of usable land was under cultivation, and the list of products in this rich region was long. Oranges were the main cash crop, but along the road, I also saw corn, green vegetables, potatoes, tea, rice, peanuts, melons, pumpkins and squash. I saw bright red chili peppers growing, and puzzled over a plant covered in what looked like dozens of tiny green peppers. I broke one open and inside were lots of white seeds; I had just opened sesame.

The mountains were composed of dramatically angled slabs that rose from the west and pointed up, angling east. I saw caves with squared entrances at some points far below in the face of a cliff and well above the river. Was this where the ancient people of the Gorges region had stored the remains of their ancestors before the Han arrived?

At the top of the ridge was the barrier, and just beyond it was a little house outside of which sat a woman shucking corn cobs. Inside the house were people scraping corn off more cobs into baskets. I joined them.

De-corning cobs is not hard, but I was taught a technique which streamlines the process: grasp the cob firmly in your left hand, and in your right hand hold a hard, already denuded cob. Scrape the corn off starting at the thick end, create a thin trench up the cob, then just peel off row after row down the length of the cob.

After repeating this action for half an hour my hands were tired but my eyes were full of the deep rich yellows of the raw corn, which was stuffed into bags and sold for seventy RMB each, after which it would be processed into all sorts of food (probably including the cornflakes I eat most mornings in Shanghai).

The rain began to ease as I strolled downhill. A small van stopped and three boys peered out at me curiously and invited me to sit in the van with them and rest for a while. I clambered in and learned that they were all local boys who had graduated from a local high school the previous year. The driver, Xiao Wang (Little Wang), made his living driving the minivan, while Xiao Tan said he had spent time making shoe parts in a factory in the coastal city of Wenzhou. He planned to return to Wenzhou in six months' time to look for a similar factory job, and in the meantime was enjoying just hanging out at home. The third boy, Xiao Mei, said he planned to follow Xiao Tan to Wenzhou. I asked them about their school, and they said it was just down the hill in Lianghe town.

"Can I visit?" I asked.

"Sure!" said Xiao Wang. "I can arrange that." He made a call on his mobile and then said: "It's okay. Let's go."

I followed them down the hill and after a few minutes I was at the gates of the One Pen (Yizhibi) High School, where I was met by an English teacher named Mr. Zhou.

"Why is the school called One Pen?" I asked in English. He did not understand. "Do you speak English?" He sort of grinned at me. He didn't. So I switched to Chinese and asked the question again. "Only one pen in this school?" I asked.

"No! One pen for every student!"

He led me to a small office in the main school building and introduced me to an assistant headmaster. I asked if I could speak to one of their English classes, and while that was being arranged, I asked why the school was open on a Saturday.

"We hold classes ten days in a row, then four days off," was the reply.

"Why is that?"

"Many of the children come from villages far away. They stay in the school dormitories during school days and return to their farms for four days."

I was led to a staff room and spent some time looking through the students' English exercise books.

"Myself," one page was headlined. "My name is Wang Ming. I am 14 years old. I like is cat and dog. I was born in 1992. I have is long hair three for the people in my family. I don't like red. I living is Yue Min Shan. I like every sport. Because is exercise."

The grammar was not great, but it was wonderful to see them trying to figure it out.

"Good afternoon!" I declared as I strode onto the dais. There were about 40 students in the classroom, all aged fourteen or fifteen. I talked to them in a mixture of English and Chinese, told them who I was, and what I was doing there and then tried to lead them into a conversation. It was tough. In a Chinese class, the children are not encouraged to speak out, and it was a good half an hour before they were brave enough to call out responses to my questions.

"Do you read English books?" I asked them.

"Yes," they said collectively.

"Novels and stories?" They shook their heads.

"Why not?" They laughed. "Read stories in English," I said. "If you read a story, you will want to know what happens next, and so slowly you forget you are reading English and end up just reading a story. I used the same trick when I was learning Chinese."

"You live in a beautiful place," I continued. "I don't know if you aware of that. I first arrived in China in 1979, long before you were born. It was a completely different place from today. China today is a place of light, a place of hope and potential. And because of you and the fact you are all studying hard, China will grow strong and be friendly with the rest of the world. You can be a bridge of friendship between China and the outside world, which is also what I want to be." I left some name cards on the front desk, and told them all to call me if they ever visited Shanghai in the future. "Yes!" they all said in unison.

The class bell rang, announcing the end of class and as I was leaving one of the teachers invited me to dinner. I accepted, of course, but as it was still a couple of hours away from dinnertime, I walked into town with Mr. Zhou the English teacher and the school driver, Mr. Tan. We passed a sign saying 'Prevent AIDS'.

"Is there any AIDS around here?" I asked.

"No," Mr. Zhou said quickly.

"Yes there is," said Mr. Tan. "There's one guy." Mr. Zhou glared at him.

"How did he get infected?"

"Blood transfusion," Mr. Tan replied.

We passed a restaurant called Yulong (prosperity) and arranged to meet for dinner there in ninety minutes. I continued alone to the end of the main street and turned right to cross a bridge over one of Two Rivers' two rivers where I came upon a small crowd of people looking out at something happening on an expanse of concrete by the river about fifty metres from the bridge.

I had to speak to several small groups of people before I finally figured out what was going on: a cook, in his late twenties and a native of Chongqing to the west, had hanged himself in the restaurant kitchen where he worked. The issue had been unrequited love; he was mad for a girl who ignored him. According to local custom, I was informed, when someone dies at home their body stays there until burial; when death occurs away from home then the body needs to be placed out in the open air. This man had died the day before and his relatives had arrived and demanded that his body and all his belongings be placed together in the open air and so there they were, mourning their loss as a couple of hundred people gawked at them from the bridge. I snapped a photo of the scene and walked on, but before I had left the bridge, I heard a short call from behind: "Excuse me! Wait a moment!" Two young policemen were hurrying towards me.

"May I see your documents?" asked one.

"Of course. But may I see yours first?"

He and his friend patted their pockets. "I don't have it, do you?" one said to the other.

"Oh well, next time then," I smiled and walked off up the hill. A few minutes later, a car pulled up in front of me and out jumped the two people's constables and a people's detective who had an ID card hanging from his neck that read 'Hu Xingnong' (develop agriculture Hu). He spent a lot of time looking at the visa in my passport, then looked at the passport photo and said: "Does this belong to a colleague of yours?"

"No, that's me."

"It looks different."

Well, apart from how awful passport photos always are, I'd been on the road in the rain and sun all day and my hair was looking pretty wild. Still, to suggest that the person in the photo might not be me was a bit of a stretch and after a while, he let me go.

Mr. Zhou, the English teacher, called to say the headmaster would be coming to dinner to meet me, and at 5.30pm, I was back at the restaurant waiting for the school delegation. I sat in the lobby and chatted with a cute five-year-old girl who gave me a delicious lemon ice stick and flicked between Chinese pop songs on her hi-tech MP3 player that had a speaker and a touch screen.

After twenty minutes of waiting, there was still no sign of the English teacher or the headmaster – I called Mr. Zhou's cell phone, but there was no answer. Then Detective Hu arrived with a man named Mr. Wu, who introduced himself as the mayor of Lianghe. They sat down next to me and the detective said the family of the deceased cook had seen me take a photograph and wanted me to delete it. I deleted it.

We chatted about the incident. Detective Hu said the relatives were divided as to what to do with the body – they could either take it to Chongqing for burial or bury it here in Lianghe, but both options involved buying land, which was difficult and expensive.

"What about cremation?" I asked.

"No cremation in this region," he said. "Everyone is buried."

"A waste of land," I said. He agreed and I invited them to join me for a drink after my school dinner.

"Ah," said the mayor, a little flustered. "Something came up at the school and they won't be able to come to dinner, but why don't we have dinner together!" It was highly spurious, and I had been looking forward to meeting the headmaster, but there was nothing I could do about it and we went upstairs. By the time we ordered the food, there were thirteen people sitting round the table – all either police or officials, plus the son of the local police chief. I felt I was well protected from whatever dangerous influences might have been present in the little mountain town of Lianghe.

I was surprised to discover that Detective Hu was the ranking person present – even the mayor and the police chief deferred to him. He had come from the county seat at Maoping to investigate the suicide, and I asked him what kind of issues he generally dealt with.

"The full range," he said. "But this is a pretty quiet area. It's mostly petty theft. Motorcycles." Earlier in the day, I had seen several posters pasted onto farmhouse walls warning of severe penalties for gambling, so I asked him about that.

"No gambling here," he lied. "Only mahjong for a few RMB."

Police Chief Ma reported proudly that not one single crime had been committed in Lianghe since the beginning of the year.

For them, this dinner was a wonderful opportunity to drink baijiu, and they began some rather intense mutual toasting. They all got drunk, and Detective Hu told me he was delighted to have me as a friend. I asked how many other foreigners they had seen in this region and Detective Hu told me about an Indian merchant who had visited Maoping in 2005, and the police chief mentioned a Westerner who had cycled through the town the year before, so compared to many of the areas of Anhui and Hubei, quite a lot of foreigners passed this way. It reminded me of the old story about an Englishman a century or so ago, who goes for a horse ride north of Beijing and passes through a remote village where he comes upon a couple of old men and asks them if there had ever been foreigners in the village before. "Oh yes," said one of the old men. "We have had foreigners here before. Genghis Khan came through here, for instance."

The dinner ended around 8.30pm and Detective Hu insisted on personally escorting me to the front desk to have me registered, then took me to my room on the third floor to make sure I was safe and snug.

I started out early the next morning, and the sun was still low in the sky as I passed the town's coal-fired power station. Given all the coal produced in the Gorges, it made sense for it to be used as a source of power. Further downstream, I learned that the little area was called 'the place with lots of fish'. "But with the power plant, there are not many fish any more," one man told me.

This river flows north from Lianghe towards the Yangtze, through a valley that really was one of the most beautiful and spectacular places I have seen. The landscape was painted with broad, sweeping brushstrokes of oranges, and corn that both complemented and contrasted wonderfully with the bright blue sky. I was also treated to the sight of "Sky-facing Peppers" (chaotianjiao) which grow erect and point to the sky, rather than dangling limply like normal chili peppers, and I knew without having to ask what special medicinal properties are attributed to them.

Terraces filled with different crops stretched all the way down to the river, while the tall angular Gorge cliffs watched from above. The farmhouses along the valley looked old and untouched – at least for now. As I had said to Lianghe's mayor the night before, the biggest enemy of the potential of the region is development. This valley, with its cliffs and farmhouses, its stunning landscape views up to the peaks and down to the river, is something that should be preserved. It might happen, but it would take a decision by the government to restore the old farmhouses, stop the stone mining in the river and close a few small coal mines. On second thought, maybe it won't happen.

In one of the villages I passed through that day, I sat for a while with a bright-eyed lady who asked if I planned to invest in a factory in the area.

"If I do, I want you to be manager," I replied.

"But I'm already a manager. Of this house," she said, and laughed. Her two sons, aged eighteen and twenty-two, no longer lived at home. One was at university in Wuhan studying engineering and the other was at boarding school in Maoping. She told me neither would return to live in the valley.

A man joined us on the shaded porch of her home. "How is life in the valley?" I asked him and he immediately replied: "Corruption. The officials are all corrupt."

I asked the lady whether life was changing fast in the valley.

"Not here. In Lianghe, yes, and down by the Yangtze. But here… look at this house. It's an antique!" It did look pretty broken down.

"Do you like living in it?"

"What choice do I have?" But she was smiling. She was not unhappy with her life, sitting by the road and chatting with her neighbours as she watched the world go by.

I continued my stroll through this wonderful valley and noticed some small white flowers by the roadside with butterflies jumping frenetically from flower to flower, drinking in the nectar hurriedly. A couple of them were huge, and the largest of the butterflies was a massive black creature – its wingspan was about five inches – with burnt red markings along its tail and blue and green and purple tinges in the middle.

Someone rode past on a motorcycle and stopped to say hello, and I was pleasantly surprised to see that it was the man who had given me a lift in the rain past the concrete barrier near Wenhua. Another man came out of a house holding a white vase. "Look," he said, pushing its mouth into my face. It took me a couple of seconds to realise he wasn't trying to gas me, but wanted me to see the delicate blue designs that were only visible from inside the translucent porcelain.

"How old is it?" I asked.

"Ming dynasty. I have a whole crate of them." Uh-huh.

"How much?"

"Two thousand."

"Next time."

Two of the boys from the day before came by in their van and stopped to chat. One of them, Xiao Mei, said he would walk with me the rest of the way down to Shazhenxi (sandy town stream), the formerly inland town which is now on the edge of the Yangtze River's Three Gorges Reservoir. I asked Xiao Mei what he would like to do if he could choose anything. "I would like to be a doctor," he said, but he would almost certainly end up as a factory worker in Wenzhou instead. His full name was Mei Jiangning (river peaceful), and he was born in the town of Shazhenxi.

"What impact has the Three Gorges Dam had on the valley?" I asked him.

"Temperatures have gone up," he replied, which surprised me.

And with that, we were in Shazhenxi, and I was back at the river again.

I found I was walking at a slower pace than when I left Shanghai. It was not a matter of physical capability; I was two years older than when I started the walk in 2004, but the walk had made me fitter. It was more that I found myself reluctant to go too fast, to consume too many kilometres in a day, to have this mountain experience pass too quickly. The point of the walk was the string of vignettes that I passed through, the sharp images lined up in my memory like stacked photographs.

I can remember with clarity so many moments along the way because they are all markedly different from one another and of course, worlds away from my normal life in the city. To pass through a place by car leaves almost no impression; to walk through is to enter the scene and to become a part of it, however briefly, and it was that participation that left a strong impression on me. Every corner I turned along the country roads revealed a scene I had never seen before, and the meetings with farmers and children were so random and intense that they were burned into my memory.

The town of Shazhenxi was small and quiet. I walked downhill through the town, past the vegetable market and a roadside cobbler sitting under a tree called out to me good-naturedly: "Lao wai!"

"Lao nei!" I responded. Lao wai literally means "old outsider", but the word Lao as a prefix is used more as a mark of respect than not. So it can be rendered in English as "honourable outsider", while Lao Nei, my own invention, would be the opposite – honourable insider. It usually gets a laugh.

The main street was a line of buildings constructed in the early 21st century before the old town sank beneath the rising waters. There were not many of them, and in five minutes I was out of the town and walking along a ridge towards a large orange-coloured bridge over the Qing Gan (Green Dry) River. There were lots of children wearing colourful backpacks squatting on and near the bridge; school had finished ahead of a week-long holiday and they were farm kids waiting to take a minivan or a motorcycle up into the hills. They stayed in school dormitories most of the year, and went back to the farms whenever they could.

I talked to a minivan driver for a while, a pleasant and intelligent young man named Mei Ping, and he explained to me how the business worked. The minivans cruise up and down the country roads picking up and dropping off passengers. The tiny van can hold six people apart from the driver – that is, six slim Chinese farmers who have not yet been exposed to fast food culture.

"How many vans operate in the Shazhenxi area?" I asked.

"Too many!" said Mei Ping.

"How many?"

"About sixty or seventy."

He said the drivers buy the vans new for forty thousand RMB or second-hand for around twenty-five thousand RMB. They were just about as basic as a motorized vehicle could get, but then again, that means there are fewer parts that can break down. "They have a life of ten years," Xiao Mei said. The passengers pay anything from two to ten RMB per ride, depending on the distance. From Lianghe town, where the cook had died, to Shazhenxi, was a distance of around twenty kilometres and the minivan fare was seven RMB. The drivers do not pay tax on their income.

"So how does the government take its share?" I asked.

"Through fines," Mei Ping said. "For overloading, driving too fast, whatever."

"How much are the fines?"

"That depends on your relationships," he said. "It's highest when you start out, but after a while you get to know the police, and they don't give you such a hard time."

I walked across the bridge and up into the mountains. The road took me up over eight hundred metres for long periods, with amazing views down into the valleys. This was the road to Badong, the most westerly town in Hubei province and one of the largest towns on the middle reaches of the Yangtze Gorges. It was a forty kilometre walk from Shazhenxi, essentially one day up and one day back down through rugged but reasonably well-populated mountains. I was told the road had been built – and possibly even paved – in the early 1970s, but these days it was an uneven dirt track, which suited me just fine because it meant there was little passing traffic – no more than a few motorcycles, mini-vans and the occasional coal truck. I enjoyed the quiet immensely and walked along listening to the cicadas, chatting with the occasional peasant and snapping photos of the farmhouses. A quiet country road in the middle of China: this is what I had been looking for all along.

The leaves were turning yellow and, with the blue skies, the terraced fields and the quaint old mud houses, the scene had a real charm. Autumn was in the air, but the lack of grain in this region meant there was none of the bustle which marked autumn down on the plains, where harvest time demanded a sudden surge of activity – all hands on deck to cut, collect, dry and bag the grain. Everything, aside from the falling leaves, was still.

Down below, the Qing Gan River –no longer a river since becoming part of the extended Three Gorges Reservoir – was a deep green tinged with a blue hue, as the river waters held back the brown sludge from the Yangtze.

Time and again, I asked people in the region for their opinion of the effects of the Three Gorges Dam, and I never once received a negative reply. The water was calmer. The climate was a bit warmer. The scenic spots along the river were not as spectacular because the gorges were not as deep. Okay, that is sort of negative. But pride was one of the main responses to the question; pride in China's ability to build such a thing.

There had been news reports about the negative impact of the dam and the environment of the region: silting, land slides and algae blooms. My feeling as I walked through the mountains and looking down at the river, or as I travelled by ferry boats back and forth, was that changing this stretch of the Yangtze from a river into a lake had caused some stress to the environment, and it would take time for the water, the land, the people and the algae to find a new balance. But the dam was not going to be demolished, and the waters were never going to return to their previous levels; this was how it will be, and somehow a new balance will be found.

The mountainsides along the Qing Gan River were cloaked in layer upon layer of houses, farms and terraced fields, all linked with long roads running along the entire length of the valley; on some mountainsides, there were four parallel roads reaching across the slopes at different altitudes. The mountains were upturned slabs of earth, rising gradually up to a cliff, then plunging down to the start of the next slab. The road to Badong, on the northern side of the valley, was thankfully the top tier on the mountainside.

There were some graves along the way that had been decorated with elaborate stone carvings and colourful streamers, but there were none of the small field shrines that were such a pleasant part of the rural scene in southern Anhui. Those shrines reflected an awareness of a wider context to life, and I realized that it had been hundreds of kilometres since anyone had asked me about my religious beliefs. There appeared to be vestiges of spirituality in rural Anhui that had disappeared elsewhere.

In fact, I did come upon one shrine in this region, not in the fields, but on a small rock shelf in a cliff. There was a clear water spring emerging from a cave in the cliff, and the shrine was a mess of dead incense and little red items left for whatever god called it home. The shrine was cold and deserted.

I passed some bamboo spinneys and then came upon a small hut, which turned out to be a shop so I stopped to buy some water. Sitting outside was an elderly man who gave the impression of being something other than a farmer. His name was Yin and I asked his profession.

"I am a teacher, retired," he said. "I taught Chinese."

"No wonder your Chinese is so good, then," I said and he laughed. "What school did you teach in?"

He pointed up the hill to a grey two-storey building. "That one. But it closed in 1999."

"A consequence of the birth control policy?" I asked.

"Precisely," he said.

A little further along, I came upon a coal mine. The entrance was in the cleft of the mountain, about twenty metres from the road, with a small rail track that ran from the mine entrance and across the road to a dump. Below was a place for trucks to park and load the coal, and even further below that were the plunging fields and mountainsides down to the Qing Gan River. Two miners emerged from the mine, each pushing a cart full of coal to the dump point.

I walked towards the mine entrance, but the watchman – the only person there who was not filthy with coal dust – waved me away. "Dangerous," he said. "The coal carts come out fast."

He took me to a small building nearby where we sat in the doorway and chatted. The privately-owned mine had been open for ten years, the watchman told me. The shaft went horizontally into the mountain to the coalface eight hundred metres inside. There were a dozen miners who did six-hour shifts; they dug the coal out of the seam themselves, loaded it into the carts, then pushed the carts to the dump. They got paid per full cart, and usually made between one thousand and two thousand RMB per month.

The mine owner, who was a relative of the watchman, sold the coal at the river for around one hundred and thirty RMB per tonne (each cart is about one tonne of coal). He had to pay the miners and transport costs to the river, plus taxes. Once sold, the coal was loaded into barges and taken down the river to Wuhan, Mr. Ma said.

"Is it profitable?" I asked.

"Not very, not any more." He said the mine produced about fifty tonnes of coal per day, with revenues of six thousand RMB per day. Taxes and costs were high, but the mine had made "several million" over the past decade, and the boss had a big house in Maoping that cost "more than four hundred thousand RMB," he said. It was fraction of the cost of a good apartment in Shanghai, but the mark of a rich man in the Gorges.

Later that day I visited a larger and more mechanized coal mine. As I walked into the yard in front of the mine entrance, a miner came out carrying an injured comrade on his back, while a second man, his face blackened with coal dust, hobbled along supported by another. Safety in these pits had to be a major problem and with little to hold them up, a ceiling fall could happen at any moment.

"Accidents are rare now," one man at the mine entrance said. "All the smaller pits have been closed down."

That may be the case, but you wouldn't be able to get me in one of them.

After some further effort, I made it to the top of the mountain, and stopped to take in the view. To the south of me was the Qing Gan River (green), while to the north was the Yangtze (brown). There were signs everywhere declaring that the felling of trees was prohibited. One massive mountainside had a sign on it – four square character boards spread over about a kilometre of mountain: Close the mountains and nurture the forests. I couldn't agree more. For this area, just like the Dabieshan region, there was hope that it could stay untouched simply because population levels were falling. The birth rate had dropped, the younger generation had moved away, the more remote villages were shrinking and the terraced fields in relatively tenuous locations were becoming less and less worth tending. The forest had a chance to gain back some ground in these isolated canyons.

The cicada calls followed me everywhere I went but were occasionally disrupted by a of the sound of blasting in the distance: road building. At a couple of places along the mountain road I walked under electricity transmission lines carrying power from the Three Gorges Dam to Chongqing city to the southwest. That was where my mentor, Edwin Dingle, began his walk in 1909.

I sat for a while with a wiry farmer in his seventies named Mr. Zhou, who was patiently watching his peanuts warm in the sun. I asked if I could buy some. He shook his head. "Not for sale. But take some." His wife gathered up a whole bagful for me. I asked if the peanuts were good for one's health.

"Oh yes," she said. "We eat some raw every morning."

It was a glorious late summer's day, and the air felt clean and crisp. I passed through a couple of villages sparkling in the sunlight, one called Big Bathing Pool (Da Yu Chi), and another called Determined Stand (Lizhi). The latter had a little general store with a sign on the wall saying 'Wedding and Funeral Goods – Full Sets Available', leaving only childbirth uncovered by the shop's otherwise comprehensive services.

A young boy carrying a backpack walked past me and, full of energy, he zig-zagged back and forth across the road, covering twice the distance needed to get from A to B, picking up twigs and ferns, poking things and singing to himself. I wondered if he was zigging and zagging to keep me within talking distance and I said hello. He was reticent at first, but gradually fell into conversation with me. His told me his name was Jiang and he was twelve years old, but he seemed wiser than his years. He was going back home from school for the holidays and did not have the money to take a mini-van.

He asked where I came from, and I said England. "Have you been to London?" he asked. Wow. I asked him if he had been to Yichang.

"Yes. I have been to Beijing, too. My father was working there and took me to see it."

"What did you think of Beijing?"

"Well, conditions are better there in many ways, but I prefer it here," he replied thoughtfully. "The air is cleaner, the food is better."

I asked him about his school. "Do you learn English?"

"Oh yes, we have been studying English for several years."

"Can you speak?"

"No. The lessons are like reciting the scriptures."

"But the meaning you understand?"

"Some of it."

I liked this kid.

A man on a motorcycle stopped and asked where I was going, and I said Badong. "Let me give you a lift," he said.

"No thanks, I am walking," I replied, and he drove away. "What a nice man, offering me a ride," I said to Jiang.

"It's his way of making money," he pointed out.

"True. So 'Good morning'," I said in English. "What does that mean?"

"It means good morning."

"What is your name?" I continued in English, but that was more than he knew. Oh well. He had a wisdom that already transcended language ability. He stopped again and pointed to a green lizard by the side of the road that I absolutely would have missed. He touched it with a grass stem he was holding, and the lizard posed for a photo before running off. He told me that in Badong there was a temple that I should visit.

"Are you a Buddhist?" I asked.

"No. But the Buddha's face is good to look at," he replied.

We were walking up a dusty winding road, and he stopped and pointed to a path off the road. "This is a shortcut," he said. So I followed him up a dirt embankment, through a field, and emerged five minutes later further up the road. "Thank you," I said, and I asked him what he wanted to do when he grew up.

"I want to be like you, going where I want to go, seeing interesting things."

"What about earning money?"

"Huh?"

"Money. You need money to go travelling."

"I'll work as I go along," he replied.

"Okay," I said.

"Have you ever seen cherry blossom?" he asked. "I saw a photo of cherry blossom in Japan in school. It was very beautiful."

"Cherry blossom? Yes, I've seen it."

"And the fruit tastes good, too."

"It does."

"We are harvesting melons now. White inside. Really sweet."

He said Badong was filthy. "Really bad pollution. The water is very dirty." No further need to coax him to talk, he was now chatting at full throttle.

"I want to be an archaeologist when I grow up," he suddenly said, returning to the previous topic.

"An archaeologist? Sounds great, but you have to study hard and graduate from university."

I stopped to take a photo of two old farmhouses in a pretty valley far below us. "I imagine it would be lovely living down there," I said.

"Yes, no dust."

I took a photo of a small roadside post helpfully marked 'National Defense Optical Fiber'.

"What do you read?" I asked him.

"I would like to read magazines, but they won't let us," he said. "They say they are not healthy."

"How about books?"

"Oh yes. Lots of books. I have read all the kung fu novels."

It became clear that what he had read was illustrated simplified versions of the novels, but this was significantly better than staring vacantly at a television all day. "I have to buy the books. We have three meals a day at school, but sometimes I just have two meals and save the money to buy books."

The boy eventually stopped talking and asking questions, and scuffed his way off to his home in the hills. I hope to meet him again one day.

CHAPTER 19

OVER THE RIVER

It was a misty, humid day in the Yangtze Gorges, although it was not actually raining. The road to Badong out of the mountains was a series of muddy messes, but the birds were singing and the muffling effect of the mist was pleasing to the senses.

That is, until I came upon some roadside construction. A group of workers were throwing rocks into a crusher, which roared and groaned and spat out gravel. Supervising this noxious work was a woman on the other side of the road, who, when I stopped to take a photograph of the workers, came over to see what was going on.

"What are you doing?" she asked.

She was a fairly plump woman in her late thirties, strong and self-reliant. I noticed one single Chinese character tattooed on her right forearm, and couldn't believe what it appeared to be.

"What does that say?" I asked, just to be sure.

"Hate."

"Hate?" I repeated incredulously. "Hate what?"

The answer, on reflection, was obvious: "Men."

"I hope you have better luck next time," was the only response that came to mind as I wandered off, to which she smirked and turned back to continue watching the workers.

I plunged back into silence as I walked through an area of wood and farmland, reading slogans on the walls of the farmhouses such as 'Hold to the Four Basic Principles' and 'Do a Good Job of Building a Model Anti-AIDS Base', when I came upon a young mother with her baby in a basket that she was carrying her back. The rattan baby baskets in the Yangtze Gorges region are a simple and marvellous design that allows the child to stand, sit and move around quite freely. It looked comfortable for both of them. The mother, who was smiling, had perfectly straight teeth – a rarity in China's rural areas – and a fantastic hairdo of complex ringlets, which she said had taken her an entire day to curl.

I came to a small bridge that marked the border between Zigui County, which I had been walking through since the dam, and Badong County. Each side of the bridge was marked with a stone marker dating from long ago. The farmland ended and the valley became a steep and narrow gully for the final dash north to the Yangtze River, which turned out to be almost invisible in the heavy mist below me. A ghost barge passed like a pale shadow over a sheet of grey silk. On the left was an abandoned quarry where the edge of one of the tilted slabs that make up this region had been blasted to bits and carted away. A jagged tooth of the mountain had strangely been left standing.

I headed west along the river, and as I did I thought about how I was doing this walk across China at just the right time. Ten years previously, it would not have been possible. I would have been constantly stopped by police and told to go back to Shanghai because the shift in the psychology of inland China from closed to open had not yet taken place. Ten years from now, much of the territory I passed through would no longer be the terra incognita it still is today; although it was unlikely that these regions would be overrun by foreigners, I anticipate the urban middle class Chinese will be cruising the small roads across the country in their new cars, with all the villages along the way being forced to adapt to outsiders.

As I was pondering this, walking down a quiet country road by the river, the mountainside about a hundred metres ahead of me on the left suddenly exploded.

I have never been in a war zone (unless you count central Beijing on the night of June 3-4, 1989) and I have never experienced an artillery barrage, but the shock of the unexpected explosions might be similar. In spite of having just passed an abandoned quarry, it took me a second to realize what was going on. The ground shook with blast after blast; clouds of dust rose into the air, and the air vibrated like a drum skin as the sound waves punched holes in the mist. There must have been twenty or thirty explosions in all, and a large section of the mountainside collapsed. There were workmen below, and as soon as the charges were spent, they moved forward to start digging at the rocky rubble, fodder for some factory or construction site.

I passed a hut with an old man and woman who were looking out of the door and, like me, were startled by the blasts.

"So loud!" I said.

"Yes," the old man replied and scrunched up his face.

"What is it for?" I asked.

"For the cement factory."

A little further along, there was a police poster stuck to a wall, "Concerning the collection of illegal explosive materials, guns ammunition, highly poisonous chemicals and controlled blades". In China, it is often hard to pinpoint where the line lies between legal and illegal. Either way, this mountainside was on its way to being history.

As I descended towards Badong town, I came upon the cement plant that stretched along the steep banks of the river. On the road level above the plant were huge covered pits into which the raw materials were tipped from trucks. Coal here, gravel there. The pits descended a hundred metres towards the factory, making full use of gravity; below the plant, I could imagine the sludge being sloshed into the river.

I peered down into one of the coal pits. It was quiet and very, very dark. Then a face appeared in the blackness and I saw a man crouching on the steep slope of coal with his back to me, his clothes and face all blackened by the coal dust. I took a photo. He stood up, and I shouted to him the appropriate phrase: "Tough work! (ni xinku le)". He responded by leaping up and starting to work frenetically, chopping coal slabs off the steep dunes and pushing them down a chute. The coal stream on the chute got caught twenty metres down, so he bounded down the slope, hacked at the blockage to clear it, then scampered back up and hacked away some more, watching each batch of coal slide smoothly down the chute and out of sight. I hated to think of the state of his lungs. The way he was leaping around the coal slope and silently glanced at me suggested that he was not entirely right in the head, which is probably the best way to be for this type of job.

Beyond the cement factory, I saw a river taxi – a Russian-built hydrofoil – heading down the river. These river taxis stop at about five towns between the Three Gorges Dam and Wanzhou to the west; Badong is the first stop. The trip from the dam to Badong takes seventy-five minutes and a ticket costs around one hundred RMB, which is a healthy business model. The boats carry about two hundred people each, and they always seem to be full.

I passed a series of loading dumps where coal was transferred from trucks on the road down to barges on the river. The road surface was potholed and broken, and black with layers of coal dust that had fallen off trucks over the years. The recent rains had turned it all into a black quagmire, and even the rock face along the left side of the road was stained black. The bridges along the road were in an appalling state, and I am sure that one day, one too many fully loaded coal trucks will cross one of them and the inevitable will occur. I picked up the pace.

Shortly after, I entered Badong, a bustling river town that was always above the Line and could stay exactly where it was. Despite this, there are two Badongs: the easterly old town and the new one further along to the west which was built in the mid-1990s before the waters rose to house displaced farming families.

The old town is lively but poorer than its new counterpart. There were five or six blind fortune tellers sitting on a bridge answering questions for seekers of the unknowable. Women squatted in the street with babies in their arms, encouraging them to do their business onto the sidewalk. I passed a pharmacy with the name Bai Qiu'en, the Chinese name of Norman Bethune, who was a Canadian doctor and member of the Communist Party of Canada who gained immortality, in Communist China at least, by providing medical care to the soldiers of the Chinese Red Army during its campaigns against the Japanese in the late 1930s. He died in the field in 1939 of an illness. I went into the pharmacy and asked an old lady who appeared to be in charge why they had named the shop after Bethune. She dashed to the back of the shop and hid. I asked the cashier the same question. "How would I know?" she replied. "I just started working here."

Badong was a seething mass of consumer activity. Shops opened early and closed late, and many had speaker systems blaring into the street: "Chongqing shoes, the best styles!" A little supermarket was playing Euro-disco at maximum volume. This endless noise pollution, presumably aimed at attracting customers, pushed me to walk as fast as I could in the opposite direction.

I came to a crossroads: left for Beijing Boulevard, the high road west to the new town, or right for the River Promenade. I chose the low road and passed the Galaxy Internet Bar, which shared a space with the Little Sun Kindergarten, then headed down a slope past dozens of little shops and out onto a broad road running beside the river.

The mist had cleared, the clouds were high in the sky, and the temperature was falling: it was a clear grey late autumn day in the middle reaches of the Yangtze Gorges. The land on the opposite bank of the river was a deep shade of purple, its colour heightened by the dampness; all along the road were tall ferns and grasses which were various shades of mauve.

I saw stencilled signs aimed at migrant workers, offering bus rides from Badong to Wenzhou city on the coast. Oranges were growing beside the road and of course, as always, there was the rubbish in all forms, ranging from discarded machinery to piles of old clothes and plastic detritus – this whole country needs a clean-up.

The Badong bridge came into view; its two-pillar suspension design is standard for all the major Yangtze bridges built in the 1990s. I started across the bridge and saw a depressing flyer stuck to a pillar: a missing person notice. Wu Min, a fifty-seven-year-old man, had "disappeared" while on the bridge at around 8am on June 27. "His relatives would be very grateful for anyone who contacts us with information of his whereabouts. And if Wu Min himself sees this, please come home quickly, we are so worried about you."

I was crossing the Yangtze River for the third time on my walk from Shanghai – this time for the last time. I would follow the river for another few hundred kilometres west, but the precise way to be taken on the north side of the Badong bridge towards the next river town upstream – Wushan (sorcery mountain) – was not clear. The map showed a road some way inland that headed west, but the maps were unreliable, and there was a road ahead of me that more closely followed the river, and that would have suited me better. In many places up and down the Gorges, new roads are being built right along the cliffs, about one hundred metres above the new water level. The cliff road from Badong to Wushan along the northern bank might have been completed, but no one was sure: the word from the locals on this subject was mixed, and this was not helped by the fact that the dialect here was particularly thick. Badong seemed to mark the start of a new dialect region, and my ear was not yet attuned to it.

As I stepped off the bridge and onto the northern shore, I was met by several motorcyclists waiting for fares under a sign welcoming the successful holding of the Seventeenth Communist Party Congress. They waved to me, and I asked if the road was "passable". One laughed and said: "Well, every road is passable to somewhere, right?"

Okay, good point, smart arse. I asked a minivan driver if the road was "passable to Sichuan", and he nodded. That was good enough for me. I started out along another muddy track.

I crossed a smaller bridge over a tributary channel, the water bright green in a healthy way. I walked through a village that had recently been demolished, then into a new village where a party was in progress.

The day was cold, but both sides of the street were lined with people drinking and eating snacks. One man called out "Hello!" to me in English, and I walked over to him through a mess of spent fireworks on the road and asked what the party was about.

"It's a birthday party," he said.

"Whose birthday?"

"The old man, father of the big guy," he said. "He's seventy years old."

I asked who the big guy was, and it was Mr. Zhang, aged forty, who thrust a cigarette upon me. He apparently ran a trucking operation of some scale – big for this little place, anyway. I asked him how many people were attending his father's birthday party – I estimated one hundred and fifty or so, including several rooms of revellers off the street. He shrugged and shook his head. I congratulated him on his father's birthday. I wanted to go and see the old man but he was presumably in the middle of the crush in one of the rooms, so I dodged a couple of trays of food being rushed over the road and went on my way.

CHAPTER 20

ACROSS THE LINE

It was late November and a glorious day to be walking in the Yangtze Gorges. The sun was shining, the air was warm and the birds were singing as if it were May.

I was following my walk with the Google Earth application, but most of the images of the Yangtze Gorges region dated from the late 1990s and were of low resolution. I wondered why they had not been updated. Obviously the Gorges were not going to be updated as regularly as the New York City images, but I wondered if this was part of a deal that had been done between the company that tries not to be evil and the party that can do no wrong. In any event, the result was that the Three Gorges Dam was still in an early stage of construction in the images and the current dimensions and the extent of the river/reservoir could not be clearly seen.

I was walking along the north bank of the Yangtze and wanted to head west, but the road had other ideas. It wound backwards and forwards, doubling back upon itself, staying mostly within sight and sound of the town of Badong on the other bank. At noon the ferry terminal's electric clock sounded out Big Ben chimes and 12 solid 'bongs' echoed up and down the valley.

I stopped to speak with a man named Fu who worked for China Mobile. He was optimistic, and said life in the region was much better now than it was before the dam. He told me there was greater prosperity, higher living standards and more money in the system than before. Property values in the towns along the river were rising gradually, and Fu was planning to buy an apartment in Maoping town. "This area used to be really poor but it's not any more," he said.

A woman with a thick Gorges accent in a village in Guandukou (which means 'the place for officials to cross the river') was also very positive. "The life of the people has improved, thanks to a number of changes in government policy," she said, as we sat with a group of other villagers in the sunshine. "The agricultural taxes were abolished, there is now free education for nine years, and there is medical care at a reasonable price. The employment situation is improving gradually." No one contradicted her.

The villages further up the mountain were clearly poorer than the areas closer to the river, but this also did not dampen the positive outlook. "Life is pretty good now," one fellow said, as a small wedding convoy of minivans passed us. "There are no major problems."

I went into a small general goods store in the next valley north of the Yangtze valley. "We are poor," the owner told me. But the shop was well-stocked. I asked him how things were now compared with a few years ago, and his face lit up. "Oh, much better. People have some money now."

I asked him what sells best in his store, and he said food products. "People now have money to buy food, and we sell more and more."

I sat for a while with a woman in her thirties and her three-year-old daughter. "Where is your husband?" I asked.

"I don't have one," she replied.

"Do you work?"

"No."

"How do you manage for money?"

"I get by," she said.

We were sitting in the doorway of her house in a quiet little mountain village maybe twenty kilometres from the river, and inside the open door, arranged in the traditional way, were a square table and stools facing the door with a colourful poster above. This one was a travel poster rather than Chairman Mao. The woman was well dressed with high leather boots. She hugged her daughter and said life was pretty good.

Until a few years ago, the local farmers survived almost entirely on food they had grown themselves and had virtually no money to buy extras. In contrast, rice crackers, biscuits, soft drinks, processed sausages and sweets are now the top sellers. Compared with Shanghai, of course, these people are poor. But compared to their own recent past, they were doing well and as a result, the peasants were not revolting.

I talked at some length to a man named Tan Youcai, aged sixty-four, who described himself as a retired civil servant. "I would invite you back to my home, but my wife died a few days ago," he said calmly.

I asked him how old she had been.

"Sixty."

"I am so sorry," I said. "That is much too young." He didn't respond.

I asked him about prices. "We are now in the second inflationary surge of the period of opening and liberalization," he said. "The first one was in the 1980s, but of course there is no comparison between the two. This is very mild. Pork prices are up, but other commodities have not risen by much. The real difference is that people now have money to handle higher prices."

The overall sense of the Chinese countryside was that it was peaceful – possibly the most peaceful that it had been in several hundred years. The people of the villages had the basics of life: they had readily available food, were well dressed in simple but warm clothes and even the most basic mud-brick farmhouse had satellite television. They had the time and the peace of mind to sit around in the sun playing cards for hours. There was some money, both from local activities and from remittances sent from relatives working in the coastal cities. I passed a couple of houses where the kid of the house was inside playing pop music at jet engine volumes on the stereo while his mother did the washing outside, using a washing machine, and what struck me was the Western middle-class culture feel to the scene – a young teenager monopolizing the family stereo.

I crossed a ridge and passed out of the Yangtze valley and into the valley of the Shennong Stream. It's a deep gorge with steep sides that are hundreds of metres high, with a wide cross-shaped lake that is connected by a narrow channel through to the Yangtze. Beyond the ridge, I experienced the same sense of shift in perception that I had felt several times before; the sounds, air pressure, plants, smells are unique in how they feel as a whole to each valley and there is a distinct point where that shift takes place.

This valley felt less modern and showed signs that its inhabitants led a more basic farming life. Almost immediately, I came across a farmer wearing traditional straw sandals of China's past that he had made himself; they looked so ancient that it felt like I was looking at an exhibit in a museum. I saw plenty of goats, but the young children were camera-shy and quick to bounce away.

Today, I was following a narrow and poorly maintained dirt road that stretched from Guandukou to the town of Huofeng (Fire Peak) in the middle of the mountains (about thirty kilometres to the northwest). I noticed there was a bit of traffic and managed to identify the source: two trucks had somehow managed to require a tire change at exactly the same point on the road. With mist wrapped around them, the drivers worked slowly in the mud to effect repairs while minivans full of people waited patiently on either side for the work to finish and for one of the two trucks to move on. It looked like it could take a few hours, but nobody was angry or exercised – it was just a part of the travelling experience in rural China.

My trudge over the damp dirt was rewarded when I came upon the most impressive tomb I had seen so far. Constructed of grey concrete, it was shaped like an old Chinese arch and was covered in elaborate carvings of dragons, lions and calligraphy. The written word is a powerful thing in the Chinese world and it possesses the power to ward off evil.

Upon closer inspection, the tomb told a story of two local people, both born in the year 1923 – a boy surnamed Xiang and a girl surnamed Zhao. They married at the age of twenty in 1943, and the next year Xiang left home to join the Chinese army and fight the Japanese. That meant he joined the Nationalist Chinese army, and in 1949, he went with that army to Taiwan as the Communists completed their occupation of the mainland. The couple had two children, and they and their mother stayed in the Gorges. For decades they were separated until 1986, when Mr. Xiang returned and was reunited with his wife and children. He commuted for a time between the two worlds, but in 1997, he made his choice and returned to live permanently in his old home village. He built the tomb for the two of them, with engraved inscriptions to tell their tale. The dates of death of Xiang Guocai and Zhao Shiyin were not given, meaning they were probably still alive.

I entered the town of Huofeng, which was a rather sad collection of houses and a few shops. It was so poor that Badong looked prosperous by comparison. There was a blackboard showing in detail the marriage and offspring status of couples in the town, giving the names, and birth date of the wife and the husband, the date they were married, the number of their children, birth dates and whether or not the couple was "within or outside the government policy". In all thirteen cases, they were "within". That is, they had only one child, or else two daughters. Out of the sixteen children, only four were boys.

A little further along, I could hear the sound of a brass band coming from behind a row of low shops, and soon arrived at the entrance of the local junior high school. A couple of hundred children milled around the wide open school yard, some of them marching along a portion of a running track to the beat of the band. It appeared to be some kind of rehearsal. I entered the gate and took a couple of photos. The students spotted me and some started to walk tentatively towards me. "Hi-i!"

one boy shouted. The two-tone up-down Hi! sounded Australian in its intonation and I discovered several days later that the basic language tapes being used by schools in the region were Australian. Australian English, while strange on vowel sounds, is politically neutral, so maybe we can expect in the years ahead that China's English will move in that direction. G'day comrade!

Anyway, I shouted "Hi-i!" back. I would have been the first foreigner they had ever seen in the flesh, so they were shy. They edged forward, laughing and pushing each other in embarrassment, then suddenly ran off. I turned to find an imposing man with a shaved head standing next to me.

"Can I see your papers?" he said.

"Can I see yours?" I replied.

"I am public security. I need to see your papers. Foreigners need to register, do you know that? That is the law."

"I know only a little about the law," I replied. "But may I see your papers first?"

He showed some irritation. This was the local policeman and he was used to having his way and his orders followed because he was in a minor position of authority and because he was rather large. There were a number of other people standing near us listening intently and holding their breaths.

He sighed. "I am not on duty, so I don't have my ID with me," he said.

"Never mind," I replied. "Next time."

"But you know that when you entered the country, you had to be formally registered," he said sternly.

The image of Pudong International Airport arrivals hall popped into my head. "Absolutely!" I said, saluted him with a smile, strolled out of the schoolyard and onwards out of Huofeng.

That winter saw China's biggest snowfall in decades, and the Huofeng region was effectively cut off from the world for a few weeks. I am not scared of the cold, but there was one particular section of mountain dirt road across the river from Badong town that was worrying even on a sunny dry day, with its precipitous edges, fast corners and a surface from hell. The prospect of negotiating it when it was covered with ice was not enticing. The minivan drivers were good, but for several weeks they refused to take me.

Once the weather finally began to thaw in March, the roads in the Yangtze Gorges were open again and I was back on track. I walked north from Huofeng town, up a valley through one of the east-west mountain range ribs of the Gorges region. The snow had melted but the weather was still wet and miserable and I passed large areas of shrivelled tea bushes that had been killed by the sudden cold.

I was faced with a choice between a road down into the east-west valley beyond, or a walk up the mountain – I chose the mountain. It was a shorter distance as the phoenix flies, and far more scenic, but the road up the mountain doubled back time and again, rising from around seven hundred metres to one thousand three hundred and fifty metres within the space of half a kilometre.

In spite of the icy massacre of the vegetation, there was a feeling of spring in the air: I passed a spinney of bamboo that was alive with the squealing of what sounded like thousands of tiny birds and the fields were bursting with young bright green vegetables and rapeseed plants.

The route I had selected was paved with concrete – surprising, as I had seen only dirt tracks from Badong. I veered off west along a track that one driver I spoke to described as "possibly the worst road in Hubei". It was on this road that I finally went across the line, leaving the massive Hubei province behind me.

There was no sign to indicate precisely where I crossed the line into Sichuan, so when I asked a passer-by and was told, "You're in Sichuan", I was very happy. Sichuan no longer exists here on modern maps – the eastern part of the province was carved out to become the Chongqing Municipality in 1996 – but for older people on this isolated mountainside, it remains Sichuan.

It was a clear day and the vistas down to the valley floor – seven or eight hundred metres below – were breathtaking. This was a very poor area right in the heart of the Gorges region, and there was a sense of desolation that suggested the population here was in steep decline. Many of the farmhouse walls featured stencilled signs with phone numbers to enquire about buses heading to the coastal cities. As I had seen in other valleys, there were occasional signs about AIDS. I asked about them, and it all came down to blood selling. In the 1990s especially, people would sell their blood, and the blood collection units in some parts of China reused needles that were contaminated, thereby spreading the virus through many rural regions of China. One person told me there were quite a lot of AIDS sufferers in Badong town.

I was briefly interrupted by a truck blocking the road as a group of workers broke rocks off the hill and heaved them into the back. I worked with them for a while and one man stopped me as I was pulling out a brick-sized rock, pointing out that it might dislodge a larger rock on top and crush my hand. The professionals clearly had a keen eye for these details, and rightly so. For a larger rock, about one hundred kilos in weight, the men fixed steel wire around it and then four of them would lift it using wooden slats balanced on their shoulders. As they swayed to the truck, the rock suspended between them, they sang out a chant, led by one, then answered by the other three. It was the same chant, I was told, as that used by the ancestors of these Gorges workers – the trackers who had pulled boats up the river.

Each man got five RMB for each truckload of rocks, with ten truckloads making up a day's work. So fifty RMB a day, or one thousand RMB for twenty days a month. It was not bad for the Gorges, but still a small amount compared with the two or three thousand RMB a month the workers could get if they went to work in a coal mine or in the factories on the coast.

I headed west along the slope at twelve hundred metres above sea level, but the track got worse and worse. On Google Earth, I had spotted two interesting features on the mountain range as viewed from space

– one looked like a natural amphitheatre, while the other was a huge circular dent in the mountain rib, like a bullet hole six kilometres in diameter and going from sixteen hundred metres at the rim to two hundred and fifty metres at the centre of the depression.[1] In person, the 'amphitheatre' looked like it had been created by glacial action and it was pretty impressive. Alas, the track ran out before I reached the bullet hole crater.

I walked down to the floor of the valley and then along the south-facing hillside opposite, which was dotted with only the occasional farmhouse. I met a woman walking a pig as if it was a dog, and I passed a couple of lazy and pleasant-looking dogs whom, I was told, probably had rabies.

I sat for a while with a woman whose eighteen-year-old son, crippled with a brain ailment, was confined to a wheelchair; he was unable to read and unable to utter much more than a barely intelligible mumble, but he could understand what I was saying, and answer questions in monosyllables. He sat all day, every day in his wheelchair in the doorway watching the road, and knew everyone and everything that was going on. He watched television every evening, his mother said, and particularly liked the war dramas. He had never been to school. His mother had somehow collected the money to send him to specialists in the city of Xian but was told they could do nothing for the boy. There didn't seem like there was anything more that could be done. So I told the boy I would send him some picture books, and he squeezed my hand in thanks.

---

[1] If you are interested in taking a look, the coordinates are as follows: The amphitheatre is at 110.09 East, 31.07 North; the bullet hole crater can be found at 110.06 East, 31.06 North.

CHAPTER 21

Signs of a Storm

It was the Qingming Festival – a day on which the Chinese honour their ancestors by visiting and sweeping their graves – but there was little sign of it in the Yangtze Gorges. The traditions of the past seemed to have disappeared faster here than in other regions; my walk in southern Anhui during Qingming had been a procession of streamer-covered graves and fireworks but here, the grave sites along the road were untended and forgotten.

Nature's cycle, on the other hand, could not be forgotten or suppressed and, as is tradition, the bright yellow rapeseed flowers were in full bloom, illuminating every mountain slope and spare piece of earth. In this part of the Gorges region, at the extreme eastern end of the Chongqing Municipality, the earth was mostly a vibrant purple-red colour and the vibrant palate of colour it yielded at every turn was highly satisfying to the eye.

I bumped into some children who were making their way to school. It was Sunday afternoon, and they were walking the ten kilometres or so along the dirt track to the closest town, where they would take a minivan to their school. As with the children in many of the villages I passed through, they stayed in a dormitory during the week and returned to their homes on the farms on the weekends.

"Good afternoon," one girl said in English. It was still morning, but I appreciated the effort she was making.

There were four of them: all aged fourteen, all from different families, and not one of them was an only child. I asked them about their plans for the future. They would all graduate from junior high school in two years' time but they told me there was little chance they would get into senior high school. It is not a matter of intelligence – simple farm children are just not programmed to do well in exams.

I asked them about the pink earth, and whether it was good or bad for farming. One of the boys said: "It is of average quality," and I laughed. "That's a very professional reply," I said.

They knew nothing of the past, had no idea of how long people had lived in the valley we were walking through, or where their ancestors had come from. The past disappears so quickly in a world without records and with a government determined to control the nation's history.

"Where do you think you'll be in five years' time?" I asked them. The two girls had no answer, which was in itself an answer. The two boys said they would probably be far away, the implication being that they would be migrant workers in the coastal cities, and my guess was the girls would end up going too. As always, I gave them my name card, and told them to call me when they were in Shanghai.

They walked at a relaxed pace, resting at regular intervals, and I ended up walking on ahead. The road came to a series of hairpin bends down the mountain, so I decided to short-circuit a couple of the curves by taking a path straight down through the vertical fields of vegetables and rapeseed, slipping and sliding on the rough path used by the farmers. It was not so easy in the leather-soled boots I wear, but I am pretty sure-footed, largely because I know I am so imbalanced.

I next ran into a honey gypsy and his wife. China is the world's largest producer of honey, with around forty percent of the global market, and I had met about twenty mobile honey farms on my journey so far. Their produce is mostly sold to middlemen and funnelled through to the world markets. They move regularly, to give their bees fresh pastures, but the setup is always the same: a couple dozen wooden hives ranged along the road, flanked by a tent in which the honey gypsy lives. Inside the tent is a bed and a vat full of honey. This was only the second honey production facility I had seen in the Yangtze Gorges, but this was the peak season. The pink peach blossoms were breaking out, the yellow rapeseed flowers were in full bloom, and the bees, drunk on spring, were everywhere, working hard for the global economy.

"How's business?" I asked the beekeeper's wife. "Business is good," she said as she ladled honey into a water bottle for me. "The quality of our honey is good and we sell most of our honey to traditional Chinese medicine factories." As I paid her thirty RMB for the honey, I thought of the old Hong Kong girlie bar line. In this case, it really was 'no money, no honey'. Then suddenly, one of the bees mistook me for a peach blossom and attached itself to my hair. Its buzz was deafening, and I danced around trying to brush it off.

"Stop! Stand still!" the woman shouted. "You're just making it worse." I stopped and she deftly picked the bee off my head, crushed it and let it fall onto the road. I stomped on it as well, just in case the bee had missed the point.

The Wushan region is truly remote (although my phone and wireless internet remained connected the entire time), and the language spoken in this region was special. The locals were proud that their dialect was, according to them, unintelligible to people from Chongqing or even Badong, but I thought 'unintelligible' was going a little far as even I could understand some of it. A key point was the word for 'what', which is 'shi me' in Mandarin, but 'mo ni' (maw-nee) in the local lingo, and once I got that straight, things became more manageable linguistically. But the local people are very resistant to Mandarin, and I found even some twenty-year-olds struggling to speak in anything like Mandarin; they could understand most of it, but I never heard a 'shi me' the entire time I was in the area.

Many of the farmers of this region have an interesting headdress arrangement, now unknown in China east of Badong – they wrap their heads in a piece of cloth or a scarf. One old man I saw had a Burberry-patterned scarf, but mostly they wear a piece of white cloth, or a heavy winter hat, no matter how hot the day is. It functions partly a sweatband and shades the scalp from the sun, but I was told the main reason for it was the fear among old people of catching cold.

I saw Chairman Mao posters peering out at me from most farmhouses along the way. "He was a great man," the farmers told me. Power attracts respect no matter how it is wielded.

The mountains were impressive in height and the valleys were spectacularly deep, but the hillsides were often scarred and gouged with quarries and new roads. I passed a pair of tunnel openings which would soon be part of a new freeway that would link Wushan to the next town up-river and eventually all the way through to the regional capital of Chongqing. The mountains were being destroyed in the process and while it is all very well mourning the disappearance of quaint customs, the disruption of rural calm or the loss of a hillside's virginity, a region such as this is poor, and such development forms an inevitable part of the process of escaping poverty. Balanced against this is the fact that the only future for this scenically magnificent region must be tourism, which would benefit from fewer mountain scars. I hoped they would figure out a trade-off between the two somehow, as they raced forward in their mad way, constructing and bulldozing as they went.

A man I met gave me some help in figuring out my route, and we talked for some time. In a Chinese way, he knew he had built up some credit with me and that it was possible to ask for some favour as a payback. I could feel it coming, and when he mentioned Shanghai, I was sure he would ask me to find a job for him. But I was wrong.

"My father," he said, "is a farmer, and he is immensely strong and also an expert in a special form of the martial arts. Is there any chance you could help him find a job as a bodyguard? Knives and even bullets do not harm him. He would be really good at protecting someone."

"Wow," I replied. "He sounds like one of the Boxers in the Boxer Rebellion. But they were fake. They died when they were shot."

"Well, I've seen him and it's true," insisted my new friend. I said I did not know anyone who needed a bodyguard, but would let him know if I chanced upon an opportunity for his father.

I finally came off the dirt track and found myself on a real tar road for the first time since leaving Badong. I was in the large village of Chuyang, the mostly easterly of the settlements in Chongqing municipality, which consisted of a string of houses along the Biancheng River. The river was littered with rubbish and I found the sight very depressing. Next to the bridge was the intersection of local Highway 103 and my dirt track, and I sat for a while outside one of the nearby shops with the local men. It was hot, being already twenty-nine degrees in early April. "Strange weather. It doesn't usually get this warm for at least another month," one of them said and they all agreed.

A van delivering cigarettes in bulk to the shops pulled up and an argument developed over goods that had allegedly been paid for, but not delivered. The shopkeeper next door wandered out to listen, saw me and sat down to talk to the foreigner. He was a man in his mid-thirties named Mr. Feng, and he was dressed in a natty black Nehru jacket with a tuft of dyed brown hair over his forehead. He was a mobile phone salesman, which is a cool thing to be in Chuyang.

"China is strong," he declared. I agreed. "It is one of the top nuclear weapon nations along with the US and Russia," he said. "This is true," I replied.

"Are you American?"

"No. I was born in England."

"England is okay. But not the US. The US attacks Iraq because they are weak, but they won't dare to attack China."

"Does the US want to attack China?" I asked.

"They wouldn't dare," he repeated.

As China becomes richer and more powerful, and gains in confidence, a key question is how it will interact with the rest of the world. If it is Mr. Feng's attitude that prevails, then we are in for trouble. But with luck it will be the middle class, with assets to protect and a need to feel good about their country in an international context, who will steer the course. China's future hangs on its middle classes.

I asked Mr. Feng about his business. "Everyone has a mobile phone now, even in this district, which is very poor – the poorest in China," he said. "I am selling about twenty phones a month."

I turned to the lady sitting next to me. "Do you have a mobile phone?" I asked. She shook her head.

"Well, there's at least one in every family," Mr. Feng said.

"Does your husband have a mobile phone?" I asked the lady. She shook her head. The digital revolution still has some territory left to occupy.

There were butterflies playing in the rapeseed by the road as it headed up and up through the hot spring day, skirting the river. I walked from six hundred and fifty metres above sea level down to two hundred and twenty, and then back up to twelve hundred, but the tortured winding way of the road meant that in two days and more than thirty kilometres of walking, I progressed westwards by only three minutes of longitude.

A man on a motorcycle stopped to chat with me. He made a living ferrying people up and down the road for a small amount of cash, and I had seen him four or five times during the day. I was very surprised when he told me he was not native to the Wushan region.

"I was born in the Jinmen area of Hubei province. Do you know it?" I nodded. Jinmen was a large city on the Hubei plain, just south of the route I had taken. I asked him how long he had been in the Wushan region, and he said six years.

"Why did you come?"

"Many reasons. My wife is from here. But the main thing is that I lost my land near Jinmen."

That sounded like an interesting story, so I asked for details.

"I was a farmer with fields about twenty kilometres outside Jinmen. We signed a contract for thirty years in 1998. But the land was appropriated by officials so I had to leave, and I came here. I have talked to the procuratorate officials in Jinmen and they say I have a good case, but nothing has happened."

I asked him how different the Jinmen dialect was from the Wushan dialect. "Completely different," he said. "I have been here six years and I can hardly understand it."

I walked past a series of huge birth control-themed murals, idealizing one-child families or single-daughter families in a simplistic modern socialistic style of art. Brought to you by the Chuyang Birth Control Bureau. But given the size of local families, every one with multiple children, or so it seemed, it made me optimistic about the future; if they can't stop farmers having children, then many other things would be beyond their control as well.

At about the twelve hundred and fifty metre level and about forty kilometres east of the Wushan county seat, I came upon four young boys dancing along the road waving bouquets of flowers around as if they were ecstatic bridesmaids. They were shouting and laughing, thrusting bunches of pink flowers into the air.

As I caught up with them, they were striking poses in front of a traffic mirror on a sharp curve in the road, holding the flowers high and admiring themselves. All rather camp. Then I noticed they were eating the petals; practically gobbling them up. I asked them for the name of the flower, and after some discussion they decided on Ying Shan Hong (Reflecting Mountain Red).

"Are you sure you can eat them?" I asked.

"Oh yes!" they shouted.

"They taste sour," said one. I pulled a petal off one of the bouquets and nibbled at it. It tasted more tangy than sour – a sweetish tartness that was reminiscent of berries.

We walked together for a while, but they were not really paying attention to anything except the flowers, and the eating of the petals. Before we parted, they gave me a big sprig, and I continued to nibble on the petals through the day, enjoying the taste but getting none of the buzz they seemed to be experiencing. As I passed a tollbooth later in the day, still chewing on a petal, the man in charge confirmed the name of the flower but added: "You can't eat it." Too late.

On this day, as a result of a conversation with my friend James Kynge – the author and Old-ish China Hand – I was paying particular attention to the messages that the farmhouse walls are covered with across China. James had expressed regret that during his years in China from 1984, he had not had the chance to study these rural slogans as he had always wanted. So interspersed through this section of my walk tale are all the slogans that I saw in one thirty-kilometre stretch of road in the middle of China.

"The new approach to marriage and childbirth has been accepted by ten thousand households, having fewer children brings greater happiness," said the first one I saw. "Learning creates the future, knowledge changes fate," said the next.

Past some more fields was a China Mobile ad on a house wall: "The Masses Card – use your mobile just as you would a land phone." It was good to see that the masses had survived the leap from the Cultural Revolution's political slogans through to the Consumer Revolution's commercial taglines. But really, it is all the same. Buildings in China's countryside have always been plastered with Chinese characters, regardless of whether the residents could read them or not.

Chinese characters, as previously mentioned, have a mystical power for Chinese people. The characters provided protection from evil spirits and are a plea to the gods for health, wealth and good fortune. Red vertical strips stay in place on and around the doors for much of the year, and are renewed each Chinese New Year. The Nationalist Chinese government started putting up political slogans in the 1920s and 1930s, and the communists took the process even further, leading to the wall-to-wall (as it were) political sloganeering that was such a feature of China's countryside from the 1950s through to the late 1980s that included: 'Seize politics as the key link'; 'Self-reliance'; 'Long live Chairman Mao, the communes, socialism and Marxist-Leninist-Maotsetung Thought'; 'Down with Lin Biao, Confucius, imperialists (i.e. Westerners), the Gang of Four, hegemonists (i.e. Russians), speculators, and capitalist roaders'. It makes me nostalgic just to type out the words, but in the late 1970s and early 1980s when I first travelled through China, these were the signs you saw everywhere.

The farmers don't seem to mind having these slogans on their walls, although of course they didn't have any choice when seizing politics as the key link was all the rage. These days they hopefully make a little money from China Mobile and Hai'er for providing signage space. One interesting aspect of the shift from political slogans to advertising is that ultimately, they continue to support the goals of the Communist Party, which now wants to encourage consumer spending as the key link, as well as the profitability of China Mobile.

I came to a village and was invited to have tea in the door of one of the oldest houses, a mud-brick dwelling with no windows. Inside was an image of Chairman Mao, and sitting next to me was an old fellow in his nineties, dressed in far too many clothes, as all older people are in this part of the Yangtze Gorges region. He smiled at me benignly, but did not respond to my questions. "He's deaf," his middle-aged granddaughter-in-law told me, and disappeared into the darkness of the house. I smiled back at him and walked on.

The farm terraces in this area, close to the top of the mountain range, were impressive structures, all with solid stone walls that looked very old.

'Further resolutely implement school lesson reform, raise the overall level of education' read a slogan on the wall of a building as I entered the largest town I had yet encountered in Chongqing municipality, Luoping. 'With a Green Card in hand, you are ready to travel all over China' said another, referring to a mobile phone card. 'The random chopping down of trees is strictly prohibited' warned one just out of town.

Close to the top of the ridge, I saw three men in their late twenties sitting in a doorway and said hello. They invited me to sit with them, as did everyone in this hospitable region.

"What are you doing on this road?" asked one.

"Walking," I replied. "I have walked from Shanghai."

"And where are you going?"

"Tibet, and then maybe Kashgar and Kazakhstan."

"Tibet? Don't you help the Tibetan independence people," he warned.

"That is not my problem to solve," I replied, with a smile. "The fate of Tibet is in your hands, not mine. But it is a problem that needs solving."

"Tibet is part of China," he proclaimed.

"I don't think anyone is disputing that Tibet is now a part of China," I replied. "From what I know, the people there are just asking for respect for their culture."

"China is a powerful country," he declared.

"I am sure everyone in Tibet today can feel that power," I replied.

"Which country do you come from?" he asked.

"I was born in England."

"England is a friendly country towards China," he said, as if he was in training for a job with the Information Department of the Foreign Ministry.

"Is it? Okay," I said. "That's good."

"China wants peace, but America always wants to go to war. Look at Iraq," he said.

Now, while I personally believe the US made a terrible blunder in 2002 in not focusing on finding and killing Bin Laden, and plunged itself too soon into regime change in Iraq, my instinct in random political discussions in the countryside is always to offer an alternative point of view, and to gently challenge the standard views I heard.

"Well," I said, "A key cause of the Iraq war was 9/11, and the ultimate goal of the United States in the Middle East is stable oil supplies, which China needs as much as the US does. China is now dependent on imported oil and needs a stable Middle East. So we all have to hope the US does not lose."

"Taiwan," he said, rapidly changing the subject. "That is our biggest problem."

"Taiwan," I replied, "is no longer a problem. The KMT are back in power, they have renounced independence and everyone in Taiwan just wants the status quo."

"But we must unify the motherland!"

"The Communist Party right now absolutely does not want unification with Taiwan," I said. "They also want the status quo. Unification could destabilize the mainland political situation in all sorts of ways."

"Chairman Hu and Premier Wen love the people," he said.

"They seem to be doing a pretty good job," I agreed. "China is more and more open and linked into the rest of the world, which is good. It was closed for so long."

"You are English," he said.

"Right."

"The Opium War…" he said, lapsing into the usual line of argument.

It was not an aggressive conversation, just an exchange of views on a rainy day in the mountains, and we parted by swapping names and mobile numbers.

My overall impression is that ordinary Chinese people are just beginning to think about politics again for the first time since 1989. I believe the consequences of that reawakening will be positive overall, even if we don't feel comfortable with some of the things we hear along the way.

I passed a house with a family group standing outside, including an old man who was limping. He pointed to my leg. "Your leg," he said, and then tapped his own right thigh.

"Right!" I said. "We've got the same right leg problem." It was almost identical – he had a right hip problem and his right leg was shorter than his left, just like mine. "We're twins. Let's take a photo."

The ladies of the family shrieked in delight at the sight of granddad

and a foreigner limping identically. I handed the camera to one of the
group and the old man and I hobbled into place beside each other for the
shot. I put my arm round his shoulder.

"What is your surname?" I asked.

"Jiang, as in Jiang Zemin."

"And Jiang Qing, right?"

He just looked at me mutely. Hmm, Mao's widow remains in the
doghouse.

Within view was an old farmhouse adorned with a slogan: 'If you
don't want your family to worry about you, make more phone calls'. It
was a clever line for the phone operators to use in a region in which every
family has members working in factories far away on the coast.

I passed a quarry that had hacked a gaping wound in a beautiful
hillside, with a small farmhouse cowering on the other side of the valley
looking distraught (in my fevered imagination) at the mutilation of the
land.

I stopped and chatted with a seventy-year-old farmer named Mr. Tan,
and his mother, who was in her nineties. There was something about this
region that made for longevity. I complimented her on her stylish green
head covering. She smiled and handed her pipe to her son to light. I
asked the son about life in this valley.

"Good. Things are good now," he said. "They abolished the agricultural
taxes and now we don't have to pay anything to the government."

"So what is the biggest problem now?" I asked.

"Well, it is hoodlums and tricksters," he said. "They are doing all sorts
of tricks, cheating the people in all sorts of ways, doing all sorts of bad
things. At the moment, it is a localized problem, but if it is not dealt
with, it will become a big problem. These hoodlums and tricksters are
supported by people higher up in the government or they wouldn't be
able to get away with all the things they do. They prey on the people. It
is very bad. You are a foreigner. I ask for your help to get this problem
solved."

"Me?" I said, surprised. "There's nothing I can do."

As I moved on, I passed a house with two slogans across the wall: 'When you go into the forest, it is strictly forbidden to light fires', and 'The illegal planting of poppies is strictly forbidden'.

Poppies? Are we talking opium? As in the Opium Wars? Well, well. Can't blame England for this problem any more.

I rounded a corner and found myself at the top of a deep and heavily wooded valley that stretched thirty kilometres southwest down towards Wushan on the river. I was at twelve hundred metres, and I could just make out the floor far below, cloaked in mist, nearly one thousand metres down. The face of the mountain range, the valley wall, was angled up at sixty or seventy degrees, and there was a huge fresh gash in the green wall, extending straight down hundreds of metres with a rock quarry at its peak. The mutilation of the land continues.

In the bushes by the side of the road, I saw what looked like coloured streamers flying in the breeze and immediately wondered if it was some sign of support for Tibetan monks. It was, of course, just some of China's famous red-white-blue tarpaulin material that had gotten snagged. The night before, I had had a conversation with a guy who had come from Yichang city and when the subject of Tibet came up, he said a band of Tibetans were engaging in robbery and violence in the city. Tibetans rampaging through Yichang. Whatever next? "Were they arrested?" I asked. "I don't know," he replied, "But people are feeling pretty uneasy right now. They are used to good civil order."

'To achieve prosperity, you must send your children to school' said a slogan, painted white on a grey concrete wall. 'Birth control must be resolutely implemented to escape poverty'.

The natural setting here was wonderful and full of birds. Several times during the day I stopped and listened to birds calling out close by me, and then whistled back their one phrase at them. I tried to alter the notes, to see if I could get them to mimic me. I think I may have increased the frequency with which they repeated their one phrase, but I never heard them improvise.

I was so far above sea level that while dark clouds gathered overhead, the massive valley below was filled with fluffy white clouds. I passed a little shop and sat with some children, including a six-year-old girl who looked exactly like the late Taiwan singer Teresa Teng. I pointed out the likeness and her mother strenuously disagreed. Teresa was one of Nationalist Taiwan's most potent ideological propaganda tools in the early 1980s.

I passed a suspended optical fibre cable prominently marked as being part of the National Defense communications network. I made a mental note to call MI5.

'Education and birth control – teachers are the key!' announced a sign. Then came one of several dozen 1980s new socialist China art movement murals that I saw throughout this region, all credited to the local Communist Party committees. 'With birth control, the merit comes now, the benefit comes through one thousand autumns' it said above a picture of a couple gazing at a red sun. Then came a slogan warning against marriage between close relatives, with a picture of two children playing under it.

Meanwhile, down in the valley, a grey veil had appeared that indicated rain was imminent, and the wind was picking up. I passed a huge slogan panel with absolutely nothing written on it, and breathed a sigh of relief. Today, we have no instructions for you.

The grey clouds down in the valley were moving, and the dark grey clouds in the skies above were churning like they were auditioning for a cameo appearance in the Lord of the Rings.

I saw some boys rolling a metal hoop around on the road. It was wonderful to see such a 19th-century toy, the hoop controlled by a stick with a hooked groove at the end but rolling free. It looks easy, but I gave it a try and quickly gave up. The boys proudly did tricks and turned sharp corners with the hoop, and I was very impressed.

'Mobile phones with 133 prefixes are good, the signal is everywhere' declared a China Unicom slogan. 'Eliminating polio among children is the responsibility of the entire society' affirmed a farmhouse wall nearby.

As the dark, swirling clouds had already indicated, there was a storm coming, but as I had an umbrella, I didn't mind. The first drops started to fall as I passed underneath the massive electricity transmission lines taking power from the Three Gorges Dam to Wushan. The pylon towers were gargantuan, and the transmission cables sagged loosely across 18th-century mountain farming scenes, sometimes reaching across a couple of kilometres in a single hop from pylon to pylon. The buzz of the electricity dancing in the air as I passed under the lines was an amazing demonstration of power.

I walked into the village of Sanhepu and shook my head sadly at the piles of rubbish in the gully by the side of the road. I passed another neo-socialist mural, this one showing a lone girl dancing on grass as her parents looked on. 'Break a thousand years of old feudal customs, establish an era of new approaches to marriage and child-bearing' it read, while next door, a China Mobile slogan helpfully suggested: 'Make the calls you want, relax with me wherever you go in the land of the spirits (i.e. China)'.

Then the rain really started to come down. After half an hour, my umbrella started to leak and I gave up and sat under a shelter by the side of the road. As the rain eased, I started out again, and found that the entire view below had been transformed. The rain had cleared away the mists but created whole new tiered vistas, with cloud banks at various levels above and below me and wrapped around the buttresses of the mountains, outlining and enhancing their crags and curves. I took photos of a cloud down in the valley, lying below several hundred metres of terraced fields, and then realized it was moving.

I had never seen a cloud climb a mountain before, and I was captivated. It raced up the slope, covering about five hundred metres vertically and almost two kilometres in distance in less than two minutes. Farms and fields were brightly glistening and clearly visible one minute, and the next they had been swallowed by the advancing wave, which suddenly topped the rise and enveloped me in a dense fog that made it impossible to see beyond twenty metres.

And then, just as suddenly, it retreated. The whole process, from clear valley to total fog and retreat to clarity again took only fifteen minutes, and I stood and watched the whole performance, entranced.

The scene seemed to inspire a bird close by and I whistled with him for a few minutes, then walked down to some houses at a bend in the road, one of which was a brick barn with small windowless air vents. I knew what it was – a mushroom-growing barn – because I had seen the east China equivalents on my walk through Zhejiang, although there they were made of wooden frames covered in thick black canvas.

'If you want to become rich, installing a telephone is one way to do it' advised a slogan on a wall. There was no attribution or company name tag to the slogan, which strengthened my belief that even the advertising wall daubs are partly ideological and aimed at meeting Party aims. 'If you want to become rich, quickly become a member of the credit union' recommended another big sign.

It was still drizzling lightly and I passed a couple of peasants, one male and one female, wearing hats with huge wide brims made of woven bamboo and covered with plastic sheets – very stylish and practical, leaving both hands free to carry other stuff.

The view below me of hills and valleys interlaced with mist and clouds then overlaid with electricity transmission cables was like a propaganda poster from the 1970s – traditional China going industrial.

On the slick road, following the rain, I passed hundreds of earthworms – some up to half a metre in length – wriggling their way across the road. Just as with the caterpillars in Hubei, many didn't make it, especially as their length pretty much guaranteed that some passing wheel would connect with a part of them. But unlike in Hubei, I didn't bother to spend time watching the earthworms crossing the road and rooting for them to make it. If they were not smart enough to cross diagonally to limit their exposure to oncoming vehicles, then it was clearly their own fault if they got squelched.

In the village of Liang Ping, I crossed an important line – the one hundred and ten degrees east longitude. Shanghai, where I started the walk, is near the one hundred and twenty-one degree line, so I had now traversed eleven degrees or three percent of the Earth's circumference.

'Resolutely implement the decision of the Chinese Communist Party Central Committee and State Council regarding the full scale strengthening of population and birth planning and childbirth work as a means of solving the population problem' said a long red banner. It was exhausting trying to photograph it, let alone read it.

There was a tollbooth on the road with the name Liu Jia Tang – Liu Family something or other – I did not recognize the third character. I asked the toll operators, three or four young girls, what the Tang character meant, and they discussed it for a minute or so but decided they didn't know. What a shame. China's education system could and should be so much better. Later on the Internet, I looked it up and the character Tang literally meant to drip or drool – perhaps the older members of the Liu family had to have their chins wiped regularly.

Just beyond the tollbooth, on the right, I saw a slogan written in black on a red brick building, and did a double take: 'The planting and cultivation of opium harms others and harms yourself'.

I came to a doorway, inside of which four men were sitting around a small table playing cards.

"Excuse me," I said. "I just saw a slogan on a wall about opium. Is there any opium grown around here?"

"No," one of the men said sharply, glancing at my camera. "It is the national policy to oppose drugs. None in this area." I didn't believe him, and I had a chance to ask a local girl about the matter a little later.

"Oh yes," she said. "Opium poppies are grown in the mountains, in inaccessible valleys. You can buy opium in Wushan. But there's a lot more in Yunnan than here."

I walked into the little village of Seven Stars and saw the biggest collection yet of neo-socialist China 1980s birth control murals; there were twenty-nine murals all in a row, each of them different. The local party officials had really put some effort into this art form. 'You need good seeds for a good harvest, with bearing children you must pay attention to quality birth' read one.

Further on was another slogan on a wall: 'Those with learning please teach, those without learning please learn'. It was a plea for a self-help approach to ending illiteracy, and it seemed like a good place to take a rest.

CHAPTER 22

SMOKER'S COUGH

The walk out of the mountains and into Wushan town on the river was a downhill saunter; easy and relaxed. The sun was shining so brightly that it was one of those days when the sun will boil your brain juices if you don't wear a hat. A constant stream of motorcyclists passed me going up and down the road, looking for fares, and they all stopped beside me, trying to get me to ride down to Wushan for two RMB. They could not understand why I would rather walk in the heat, but I explained about Noel Coward, and they nodded and drove away.

As I passed a tree, a big German Shepherd dog suddenly lunged at me, barking in a deep and vicious tone, and I sprang back in fright as the dog bounced backwards, the rope around its neck having reached its limit. The dog was seriously angry (as I suppose I would be if I was tied up), and I hoped suddenly and fervently that the rope and knot were strong. I walked on slowly, heart pounding and very aware of the fact that I had no idea what to do if a dog really did attack me.

I came to a concrete bridge, crossing the entrance to the so-called Little Three Gorges, which is a narrow valley and tributary of the Yangtze with high walls and narrow channels. Some of the motorcyclists tried to get

me to take a ride up into the valley, but I declined. I had seen it in all its
glory ten years earlier – pre-flood – when it had been narrower and even
deeper, and there was no point seeing it as it was now, a sunken shadow
by comparison.

So I entered Wushan, which is a large town of several hundred thousand
people, perched on the mountains above the river-lake. All the buildings
were new or newish with the old town now under the water. It was one of
the steepest towns I had ever been to, with cliff-like streets, endless steps,
and the best minivan drivers in China. They can really work the gears on
the hills as they climb up or fly down the slopes and my advice is that as a
passenger, it is best to keep your eyes closed. Unlike just about anywhere
else in China I have been, almost all the minivan taxi drivers in Wushan
are women.

I found that karaoke was big in Wushan, as was getting blindingly
drunk on baijiu and staggering around in the dark. There were also public
dancing exercises for the non-baijiu drinkers. On the main square in the
centre of town every evening, I saw hundreds of people, mostly women,
gather and arrange themselves in lines, all facing the same direction and
performing vaguely tai chi-like movements and undulations in time to
appalling and very loud Chinese disco music. They paid thirty RMB for
a year's right to join the lines any night they wanted.

I spent some time in Wushan talking with people in their late teens
and early twenties about life and the future. The girls in the Wushan
area, I was told, should be married by the age of twenty and arranged
marriages remained the norm. The men were mostly working in factories
on the coast and were back home in Wushan on a sort of break from the
pressures of being a migrant worker. One was with his girlfriend and said
he wanted to settle down back in Wushan, but could not think of a way
to make any money there. The only businesses I came across related either
to coal mining and shipment, or else to service trades – drivers, shops and
restaurants. As a result, he said he would soon return to Zhuhai, where
he had worked in a succession of factories and now worked for a logistics
company, trucking containers from the factories to the port. Another

fellow was in the same situation and planned to go back to his factory job in Zhejiang the following week. I asked how they felt about being away from home, and there was just a shrug in reply. There was really no choice.

I talked to an eighteen-year-old boy named Ouyun Dongshan, Ouyun being a Chinese surname I had never come across before. He was thin and had a cool hairstyle with strands hanging over his eyes and filthy fingernails. I asked him if he was still at school. "No," he said and hacked out a rich smoker's cough.

"So what do you do?"

"Just play around."

"Play how?"

"Video games. In the Internet bars."

"How many cigarettes do you smoke a day?"

"Twenty."

"Smoking is stupid," I said. "You shouldn't be coughing like that."

"I know. It's not good." He lit up another within ten minutes.

"So what is your plan?" I asked. "Where will you be in five years and what will you be doing?"

"I don't know," he said and shrugged, looking off into the distance. I pushed and he said: "Probably driving a minivan or else in the army. But you have to pass an exam to get in the army."

I looked at his appearance, the cigarette in his mouth, his complete lack of direction in the middle of a nation running collectively and individually to improve itself, and decided that for him, the army might be a good choice.

I found myself becoming more proactively anti-television. One intelligent-looking boy of about ten years old left the television to come out to talk to me.

"What are you watching?" I asked.

"Just some programme."

"Is it any good?"

"No."

"Do you have any books?" He nodded. "Read one."

My growing impression was that the Chinese education system itself is largely responsible for how so many students finish school only semi-literate. Before they learn characters, they are taught pinyin, the alphabet-based phonetic system. That makes sense, perhaps, in terms of stressing standard Mandarin pronunciation, but an alphabetic writing system is a completely different concept from an image-based character writing system such as Chinese. I imagine the stress on pinyin at the beginning of the learning process when the real written language is made up of characters may slow down the process of becoming fully literate in Chinese.

I spent some time in Wushan with a ten-year-old boy who was in many ways typical, if a somewhat extreme case, in that he was remarkably unquestioning and non-inquisitive. I asked him which subject he liked best at school, and he had no answer. He had never thought about it. I asked if one of the subjects he studied at school was English and he said yes.

"How many letters are there in the English alphabet?"

"I don't know."

"There are twenty-six. How many letters are there in the English alphabet?"

"I don't know." His brain was not processing this.

"I just told you. There are twenty-six. How many letters are there in the English alphabet?"

"Twenty-six."

"Thank you."

The town was messy and, I was told, pretty lawless. "The law and order situation here is terrible," said a young man, who looked about eighteen years old. "There is a guy named Wang Xingping who was the mafia boss of Wushan, and he was arrested recently. But before that everyone knew he ran the casinos, the nightclubs, everything. It is said he and the county head had an agreement where he ran the dark side of Wushan and the county head ran the regular side. But when he was Laoda (the big guy), he could do whatever he wanted. People were knifed to death on Guangdong Lu (the main street of Wushan) and nothing happened." He told me the name of another guy who had already taken over as Laoda. "So I don't think things will change much."

I confess I didn't like Wushan too much and was glad to get out of it. Overall, you could make the argument that it is a town that should be left to shrivel. Many of the people were leaving, the tourists were passing it by and its role as a staging post river town had been reduced by the faster and bigger boats now cruising the Yangtze lake. Also, there were just too many steps.

I climbed the road through the town, from two hundred metres above sea level close to the river up to six hundred and fifty metres at the top of the town. The air was filthy and the traffic was pretty bad. I watched a boy cross the road at a run without looking the other way and a minivan taxi slammed into him. I raced over in horror, but he got up and said he was okay. "You have got to look before you cross the road!" I told him earnestly, in my new didactic mode. He nodded, took the dropped items I had picked up off the road for him and disappeared into the sidewalk crowd.

I passed a Christian church situated in a fairly new multi-storey building. Most of the building was occupied by a garage and auto repair shop. I looked, but could not see Jesus on the grille of any of the cars.

Before I knew it, I was out of the town and back on the old road heading vaguely west towards Fengjie, the next river town along from Wushan. The straight-line distance between the two is thirty-four kilometres, Google Earth informed me, and I desperately wanted to do the walk from Wushan to Fengjie along the river. The maps showed a road right through, but everyone said the maps were wrong and I had to take the mountain road, which was a seventy kilometre distance. Damn.

It started to drizzle, but I was prepared and had an umbrella. It was good to be out of Wushan; the air was cleaner and the people were friendlier.

I stopped at just about every farmhouse and sat in the doorway chatting for a while. As I walked along one stretch, a police car came towards me and the policeman stopped and rolled down his window.

"Where are you going?" he asked.

"Into the mountains," I said without stopping.

"Walking?" I nodded at this statement of the bleeding obvious, and he drove off, leaving me a little disappointed that China had become so blasé about a foreigner walking through the middle of nowhere.

Most of the people I met were older, and the few young people I spoke with were migrant workers who had come home on leave. There were signs on some of the mountain slopes saying the area was being allowed to return to wilderness. My feeling is that thirty to fifty years from now the central regions of China will be almost completely depopulated. The mountain areas will be released from agriculture and returned to Nature, with tourism on the side. The plains will be handed over to high volume mechanized agriculture with all the tiny family plots combined into massive fields. And the people will be gathered in dense cities along the coastal strip. Actually, it is not just a feeling – it is happening right now, and it is probably the best option.

I saw several signs painted on the sides of farmhouses warning that the cultivation of opium was forbidden and also not good for you, which meant of course that it was grown and smoked by at least some of the local farmers. I noticed a little frog hopping across the wet road, and as usual stopped to see if it would make it. A couple of vehicles passed but the frog hopped onwards through little puddles. Three girls huddling under an umbrella came over to see what I was looking at, and we followed the frog silently as it reached the other side. And then it turned back and hopped all the way back to where it had come from. Not an errand, evidently, just a Sunday stroll.

I headed up and west along a road that cut into the almost sheer northern wall of the valley directly to the north of the Yangtze River valley. Down below, I could see construction of the Fengjie-Wushan freeway, with four lanes, tunnels and long elevated sections. As I progressed up beyond the eight hundred metre line, the farmhouses disappeared and I was alone on the road except for the buses marked with their destination on the windshield – Hangzhou, Shanghai, Wenzhou, Fujian, Zhuhai. There was one almost every five minutes heading along this remote country road, taking the migrant workers out to the factories.

Then I came upon a traffic jam. It had been raining solid for more than a week and the mountain roads had become wet obstacle courses, with fallen rocks and landslipped piles of earth in many places under overhanging cliff walls.

Dozens of vehicles – minivans, SUVs, trucks and motorcycles – were backed up and waiting patiently. Around the curve of the mountain road, I could see a similar build-up coming the other way. I walked through the stationary traffic and reached the centre point, where a piece of cliff overhang had collapsed onto the road about an hour before, completely blocking the narrow road with boulders and a mound of earth up to two metres in height. A couple of dozen people were standing on and around the pile, occasionally eyeing the overhang above us to see whether or not another slab would break off, either burying us or pushing us off the cliff, which was an almost straight drop down of more than three or four hundred metres, with only a flimsy metal guard rail to hold us onto the narrow road.

An enterprising group of men had decided to try to create a path over the rubble by breaking up or rolling away the rocks and fitting slabs of stone into holes. They made some progress and one SUV revved its way over, but it was clear that most of the one hundred or so vehicles on each side of the collapsed wall – with more building up as the wait went on – would not be able to cross over. After about half an hour, the vehicles on one side were convinced to back up to create a path through to the front. A huge earthmover appeared with chained wheels and a confident young driver who rammed his shovel at the mound, scooped up dirt, then wheeled round and dumped load after load down the mountainside. After fifteen minutes, one lane was open and both sides rushed the gap. There was momentary confusion, but then one side prevailed and before long cars were racing away, making up for lost time by driving far too quickly along the little road. The incident showed how efficient China had become in so many ways. A landslip blocked a road more than an hour from the closest town but it was cleared and the road re-opened within two hours. I was also struck by the number of SUVs and the quality of the newer motorcycles waiting in the line – there was a new generation of all sorts of vehicles travelling the rural roads of China. My boots, however, remained the same.

The region between the river towns of Wushan and Fengjie is pretty much equidistant from Yichang and Wanzhou, the cities on the eastern and western limits of the Yangtze Gorges mountains and it feels very remote. The road veered up a long valley in the mountains, and then down another. In over forty kilometres I passed only one small village, and while there was a steady sprinkling of farmhouses along the way, there was almost nowhere to buy bottled water, which is an essential part of a walk across China.

The rain had come to an end and the summer heat was about to re-assert itself. But in the meantime, the spring world glistened in rain-washed clarity, the colours of the vegetation were bright, and the tones of the earth were deep and sonorous. Mist covered the valley as I trekked up the narrow road, with a cliff overhang on the right and a sixty-degree drop down to the valley floor on the left. I spent an hour moving in and out of rivers of mist, which climbed the mountainside in discreet flows.

I spent quite a bit of time looking at flowers. Purple and yellow hues dominated the area but the only type of flower I recognized were the daisies, and I was left with regret that I had never paid attention to categories and knew little of flowers beyond roses and tulips. What I did know was that the flowers cultivated so painstakingly in English gardens were largely transplants from wild places in China such as this.

The slogans scrawled on the farmhouse walls related mostly to fire, urging people to protect the forests, prevent fire, and were aimed at stopping farmers from deliberately burning sections of woodland in order to collect the ashes to use as fertilizer.

This road, still provincial Highway 103, was an uphill slog for this entire section. The fields, many at forty-five degree angles, contained corn, potatoes and sesame seeds. Most of the farmhouses were made of red brick; the older mud-brick houses were still there, high up on the slopes, but were already well outnumbered. I passed two men by the road, their motorcycles parked in the middle while they squatted on their haunches smoking and chatting. A girl stood nearby looking at the scenery. I said hello and kept walking, but a few minutes later, one of the motorcyclists drove up to see me with the girl, plump and overly made-up, sitting on the back of the bike. He asked where I was going and with that out of the way, I asked about him. His name was Wang Dejun, he was a farmer turned migrant worker from the Fengjie area to the west, and he was back home to get his child into a school in Wushan. Meanwhile, he had picked up the girl in a nightspot in Wushan and was taking her back to Fengjie for a few days of acrobatic companionship. His wife, he said as the girl listened, was also a migrant worker, currently in Chongqing city.

"You fancy her?" he asked – and this was a hard question to answer without embarrassing or insulting the girl who was quietly studying the ground. "You can have her if you like." I declined his kind invitation.

"Let's go to Wushan this evening," he continued. "I can show you some places. Totally safe. Only one hundred RMB for a girl, maybe three or four hundred for a good one. Don't worry, I will be there, so they won't cheat you."

His breath smelt of alcohol, which is not unusual for Chinese farmers in the middle of the day. He insisted the girl give me her mobile number so I could contact her next time I was passing through. "She can show you around," he said. The girl smiled uncomfortably.

I was seeing a lot of signs on farmhouse walls about drugs and opium – 'Growing drugs is illegal' said one on a telephone pole which had been signed by the local township government. I came upon a farmer who was rebuilding a wall that had collapsed during the rains. He was fifty years old, but looked much older; a peasant's life is tough. He told me he had four children, and the eldest son, aged fifteen or so, came out of the house to check out the foreigner. His father tried to get him to talk with me in English, but he was too shy to even respond to a slow and clear: "What is your name?"

I handed the farmer my name card but he pushed it away shyly, saying he was illiterate, then handed it to his son to read. He said he grew corn, potatoes and sesame seeds, and had two chickens and five pigs. He was healthy and strong and clearly proud of his son, even a little in awe of his ability to read. I asked him about opium, and he confirmed it was still grown up in the mountains, but when I asked if he ever smoked it, he shook his head, eyeing me carefully.

There were many butterflies around, large and small and all colourful. One black and yellow monster, much larger than a sparrow, paused long enough while tasting a purple flower for me to take its photograph. I saw a leopard-spotted butterfly almost perfectly camouflaged against a rock wall. Ants were out in force as well, carrying various insect roadkill goodies off to their dens.

I climbed to the top of the pass, reaching one thousand three hundred and forty metres above sea level and passed from one valley to another. This was the highest point I had yet reached on my walk from Shanghai, and the views down into the valleys, still partially filled with mist, were spectacular. Marching through the pass with me were electricity transmission pylons carrying power from the Three Gorges Dam towards the west. There was also a bilingual sign on an arch over the road that said in English: 'Wushan policemen wish you a nice trip!'

From there, it was downhill into a huge valley, roughly east-west with wide mountain slopes, occasional farms and fields visible, stretching from peaks of up to sixteen hundred metres down to the valley floor at less than three hundred metres. It was a majestic, secluded and peaceful valley, with a thin grey cloud layer that lapped at the peaks on the far side, making the whole scene seem very cosy. It was a pleasure to spend time in this space and allow my eyes the opportunity to track over such vistas.

I heard cowbells on the hillside as I made my way to Fengjie and later came upon four or five cows feeding in a spinney. I passed a boy by the road selling bright orange mushrooms as big as his hands from a wicker basket. There were more butterflies with bright red eyes and long black legs too drunk on nectar to care about the camera lens only inches away from them. Berries and plums hung from the trees beside the road, and a sign said: 'Love life, keep away from drugs'.

I passed several turn-offs that led to work sites where the China Railways Tunnel Group was building sections of the Wushan to Fengjie freeway and on occasion I could see tunnel mouths and concrete pillars that would carry the highway. I was much in favour of it – the highway, when finished, would remove the long-distance buses from my country road.

The Highway 103 route down the hillside involved all sorts of twists and bends, so when I spotted a path to the left that appeared to cut straight down from one level of the road to the next, I headed directly for it. I was overtaken by three children carrying firewood to a farmhouse below and I asked if it was possible to get down to the next level of the road. They nodded.

I arrived at the farmhouse, rounded a corner and walked into a quagmire of mud in the front yard, covered by a massive blue tarpaulin that the day before was keeping off the rain and today was simply keeping the mud wet. A number of old men were sitting around the doorway of the farmhouse; two of the men were banging metal rings onto crude, homemade paper sheets, making indentations about the size of a coin. I asked what it was for, and the answer was to create hell money to burn for dead people to spend on the other side.

There was a pause before I was invited to sit down, which was unusual. I talked with the people for a while, especially the children, and asked a seven-year-old girl called Wang Yan to write out her name for me, which she did pretty well.

I looked into the doorway and saw the room was dark with a candle burning on a table in front of an image of an old man. The old men were there because their friend had just died, which explained why this was just about the only time in the mountains that I was not offered tea

at a farmhouse door. I felt uncomfortable about crashing a wake, so I
stood up and asked for directions down the hill. They pointed into the
vegetation, but I could see no obvious path. I looked around and Wang
Yan was standing near me.

"Wang Yan, could you show me the way down?" I asked.

She looked round, her finger in her mouth and a woman said firmly:
"No."

And quite right too – I realized immediately that it was an entirely
inappropriate request. But they showed me the path entrance and threw
me a piece of bamboo to use as a walking stick and I clambered and slid
my way down the slope, through terraces of ripening corn and various
types of vegetables, and stumbled out five messy minutes later on the
next level of the road. I left the bamboo stick standing in between two
rocks at the entrance to the 'path' for the next person to use.

Sunflowers were much in evidence in this valley, but I did not find even
one that was pointing in the direction of the sun; many were pointing
at the earth, perhaps feeling depressed after all the rain and clouds. The
flowers were huge and bees were busy assisting in the propagation of
the species, working their way around the clock faces at the heart of the
flowers.

The sound of water was all around, little cascades coming out of the
rocks, with the liquid rumble of a major water flow coming from the
valley floor. There was a metal guard railing alongside the outer edge of
the road, beyond which the slope was sometimes almost perpendicular.
Chinese writing – black, flowery and barely legible, but calligraphically
interesting – began to appear on the railings and continued for
thousands, maybe tens of thousands of characters: at least two kilometres
of it. Unfortunately, at that point I was walking against the direction
of the writing, which made it hard to read the sentences and follow the
argument, but it was essentially a political rant. 'Out of 10,000 officials,
9,999 are corrupt' read one typical sentence. It went on and on, like
callers on talkback radio shows in more open societies, and I asked a

farmer sitting by the road who had written it. "He lives near here. He's about thirty years old. He keeps to himself," the farmer said.

The writing followed me and ended, or rather began, next to a cornfield where, as a preamble, the man had written on the railing: 'This corn is poisoned to stop thieves. Thieves please take note.' If it was poisoned, of course, then it would be useless to everyone else as well.

Down below near the river, I could see the luminous green of young paddy rice, the first I had seen for a long while. I passed a white painted slogan: 'Fight SARS', a reminder of that crisis in 2003 when the whole world wondered for a moment whether China had started another Black Death plague. 'Don't plant drugs in the forest' pleaded a sign.

I met an old peasant (there seemed to be no young ones) sweeping rocks and debris off the road. "Hello!" he said in English with a big smile, took off his straw hat and invited me to sit down. He looked up at the rock face and chose a shaded spot by the road that was unlikely to crash down upon us. "This will be safe," he assured me.

I asked him what he grew and he said corn and potatoes, which he called yangyu.

"That is tudou in Mandarin," he said. "What is it in English?"

"Potato," I said, and he repeated it back to me pretty accurately.

"I am speaking English with an Englishman!" he exclaimed with a big grin. "How do you say corn?"

His name was Mr. Li and he was in his late fifties and retired. He had three children, all still living in the area, which was rare – mostly children are off working elsewhere. He said he had travelled outside the mountains only once to visit his daughter while she was working for a time in Jiangsu province, but he hated it. "Their language is just impossible to understand," he said.

I asked him about opium and he said it was widely grown up to three years ago when the authorities started to crack down. "It was mostly used for medicinal purposes," he said. "Taking the seeds is good for stomach ailments. But it was also smoked."

He asked me if I had met any bad people on the road during my walk across China, and I said I had been lucky so far.

"But you went through Yichang, right?" he asked. "Yichang people are the worst. They will steal, and grab anything. You have to be very careful. But you are a foreigner so I suppose they are unlikely to touch you. Stealing from a foreigner would be a loss of face for the Chinese people."

"I don't think thieves are that concerned about face, but I have been lucky," I said. My own theory of why I had so far not had anything bad happen to me was that I was such a random phenomenon and I appeared and disappeared so fast that people with evil thoughts didn't have time to take action, even though the obvious conclusion was that I probably had a pretty substantial sum of money (in their terms) deposited in my pocket.

I later asked someone I knew from Yichang about what Mr. Li had said and he laughed. "You know, these people from Sichuan are really clannish and they used to be a real problem for us in Yichang." Clearly the feeling was mutual. "We call them the Sichuan gang and they caused all sorts of trouble on the wharves and ferry terminals. They and the local Yichang gangs would face off against each other. But law and order is better now, so it doesn't happen so often."

I imagined turf battles on the Yichang riverbanks stretching back through the decades and centuries. It was a reminder of the city's historical role as the gateway to the Gorges and Sichuan, the point where the plains and mountain cultures came together, evidently uneasily.

Later, another peasant told me I should be careful on the road and watch out for highway robbers from further west in Sichuan, who he said were bad.

"Where do you put your money?" he asked me. I pointed at my trouser pocket. "Not safe. You should be more careful." He showed me where he kept his money – he had on three loose shirts, each a different colour, and on the left side of the inside one there was a secret pocket in which he kept his little stash. He pulled it out and I would guess there was four hundred RMB there – not bad for an old farmer. The one thing that everyone, everywhere seemed to agree on was that people from their own area were fine, upstanding citizens and posed no threat.

As the road descended sharply, I saw a sign on a farmhouse wall saying 'For every cow or goat that goes into the mountains, compensation fine of between twenty and fifty RMB'. It seemed they were serious about letting the mountains recover from the trauma of agriculture and animal husbandry. The mountains to the north of the river, the mirror image of the ones from which I had just descended, were high and wild, layer upon layer of pristine greenness, and I applauded the decision to expand this huge lung in the centre of China.

Down below, I could see the town of Shuangtan, a couple of kilometres away as the phoenix flies, but six kilometres by the winding road in between. The problem was a little river cutting through the valley; the bridge over the torrent was a couple of kilometres upstream.

The bridge was right at the top of the valley, just where the river emerged from the thick mountains and the valley started to spread out. I watched the clear waters of a stream from a side ravine smashing into the main watercourse, diluting the brown water that had come a much longer way.

The road reached the base level of the valley by the river and proceeded westwards, with a brief stop at Shuangtan. It was a hot summer afternoon and everyone in the village was sitting around in the shade of the store and house fronts, playing cards or pool while a television costume drama droned in the background. I chose one shop, ordered a bottle of water and was invited in to take a seat. The children stole looks at me through their fingers, and the man next to me asked me where I was going. I asked him what he did for a living.

"I play mahjong," he replied.

"You make enough money at it to live on?"

"Sure!"

"What about you?" I asked his friend, who was shirtless and wearing flip-flops.

"Same," he said.

"In fact he's a doctor," interjected the first guy.

"A doctor? Where did you study?" I asked.

"Fengjie."

"For how long?"

"Ten years."

"How old are you?"

"Thirty-something."

"Thirty what?"

"Thirty-seven or eight."

"Thirty-seven or eight, which?"

"Thirty-seven or eight," he insisted.

It transpired he was not a doctor, but rather the operator of the sort of clinic in which I had seen so many people getting intravenous fixes in Hubei. I asked him what the most common ailments were, and he said colds and problems of the digestive tract.

"What happens if it is something more serious, like cancer?"

"Then I send them to the hospital."

He started to talk at me about international affairs from the knee-jerk clichéd mouthpiece perspective. "China is a country of peace," he said, as if it was an exception to the war-mongering rule. I decided to give him a break.

"Is there opium in this region?" I asked.

"Some in the mountains," he said. Then his eyes lit up. "The Opium Wars!"

I smiled.

Beyond Shuangtan, the valley widened out and on its southern slopes was the freeway-to-be – bridges and culverts all half-finished and with no sign of construction activity.

I found a farmer named Mr. Duan resting under a tree. He was seventy-three years old and had on a wide straw hat, a rather smart grey shirt, and traditional home-made straw sandals – all seriously retro cool gear, and all due to disappear with his generation. He had a small basket containing two plastic bags – one with small green plums, the other with green peppers.

"I am going to Shuangtan to sell them," he said. "Have a plum."

I tried to pay, but he absolutely refused. The plum was juicy and sweet.

I asked about his life and he said it was good. His children were all working, and he was in reasonable health for his age.

"At seventy-three, you must remember the Chairman Mao era very well," I said. He nodded. "How was life then?"

"Good!" More enthusiastic than the "good" about his life today. I probed why, and I got the sense that it was really because that had been the golden era of his own life. I stood up and he thrust a couple more plums upon me. I handed him his hat, which he had taken off while talking to me, and we went our separate ways.

At the other end of the political spectrum, I had a conversation that evening with a girl who had just graduated from high school and was waiting for her university entrance results. The brand of the beer on the table was 1958. "1958," I said. "The year of the Great Leap Forward."

"The Great Leap Forward?" she asked, puzzled. She had never heard of one of the greatest disasters in modern Chinese history, when Mao created so much upheaval that millions died of starvation. You really have to hand it to the Communist Party: their ability to make historical events disappear is – cliché alert! – Orwellian.

I came upon a lady walking in the same direction wearing one of the wonderful wicker-basket backpacks found throughout the Gorges region. She was plump and short and when I asked her age (after she had asked mine, of course) she said she was thirty-seven or thirty-eight years old – clearly a watershed age in these parts.

Her eldest child was sixteen and was at senior high school in Chongqing.

"How much are school fees?" I asked.

"More than ten thousand RMB a year. And a few thousand for the second child." I asked where the money came from, and the answer was that her husband worked on the freeway construction project on the other side of the valley.

"Three years they have been at it, and they said it would be finished in four years. Look at it. Do you think it will be finished next year?"

I shook my head. "No. But then from your husband's perspective, the longer the better, right?"

What it meant for the countryside, on the other hand, was that it would remain in a pretty tortured state for the foreseeable future. The new freeway being built along the valley's length was largely responsible for the mutilation, along with coal mines, gravel pits and some housing construction. There was a growing awareness amongst the farmers of the damage being done to the land. I asked one middle-aged man I met on the road what he did, and he replied: "I look after the planet." It was his cute way of saying "I am a farmer".

One of the towns I passed through was called Stone Horse (shi ma), and in a little market where farmers were selling fruits, I asked where the horse was.

"It died," replied one of the fruit sellers, and then he laughed at his own joke.

CHAPTER 23

ENVIRONMENTAL NUNS

The road heading down towards Fengjie town was busy with trucks filled with coal heading to the river, with empty trucks heading back into the mountains. Along the way, I passed through a number of small towns that all felt lively and prosperous.

As the valley flattened out I came upon a body of water – an outcrop of the great Yangtze Reservoir. The houses above the water line looked recently constructed but my impression was that most of the displaced farmers had been moved to the new and expanded county seat of Fengjie. "The majority of people who moved ended up poorer than they were before," one man told me.

I spotted the temple of Baidicheng, which has been one of the main attractions of the Yangtze Gorges for centuries. It sits on a hill, and I had passed it nearly ten years previously, before the waters rose, effectively turning it into an island. The locals told me it had been completely rebuilt and wasn't interesting any more, so I walked past the entrance bridge without going in.

Just beyond that bridge, however, was a very famous view – the view west into the entrance of the Kuimen Gorge on the Yangtze River, possibly the most beautiful of all the Gorges vistas. The bluish ten RMB note, the most ubiquitous of all China bank notes, features an image of the view, with the Baidicheng hill on the left, the perpendicular walls of the Gorge on the right, and a hook-like mountain in the background. It is spectacular in person, although of course not as deep and sheer as it once was.

I spent some time talking to a lady and her younger son who was fourteen years old. Her elder son was currently off on a three-year stint with the army. I asked how much he made as a soldier and her answer was: "Not much, maybe five hundred RMB a month."

"So why do it when there are other ways to earn more money?"

"It disciplines them, builds character," she replied. I asked where he was stationed and she said Fujian province.

"Protecting China from Taiwan businessmen?" I asked.

I asked the younger son what he would do when he left school, and the mother answered for him.

"He is not very good at his studies, so I think the army would be best for him too."

Later that same day, I met another mother and son, the son being a talkative and slightly drunk truck driver in his early thirties who had also previously spent three years in the army. "Well, at least he learned how to drive," his mother said.

His truck was parked opposite the little shop where they were eating lunch, while I was resting on the side sipping water. It was beat-up and filthy and fit perfectly into the scene. "Maybe I could drive it to England and work there," he said with a laugh. I tried to imagine this truck travelling up the M1. It definitely would have stood out.

Another man at the lunch table asked me how long I had been in China, and we discussed the many changes that had taken place since the 1970s. "In the old days, we could not even sell an egg to anyone but the state," he said. "But on the other hand, things have not changed at all politically. We elect the lowest levels of village officials, but all other levels are chosen by the Party. The so-called representatives to the National

People's Congress are not representatives at all." Such comments came up spontaneously much more frequently than in the past. It was part of the ponderous preparation process for whatever happens next in Chinese history.

The road wound down, and out of the mountains, eventually reaching a stream at the valley floor. I passed a government truck-weighing post. I stood on the scale and asked the man in the hut to tell me how much I weighed. "Sixty kilos," he said. He said they let all the trucks through whether they were overloaded or not but took a thirty RMB fine from every truck that was overweight. That would have been just about every truck coming down out of the mountains, mostly loaded with coal.

As I walked towards Fengjie town, the Yangtze River was once again visible. I kept touching it at the river towns, then being turned back into the mountains to get to the next river town. It was like a very slow rollercoaster ride. I sat for a while with a restaurant owner and his wife, eating beancurd and drinking a little beer as we talked. His wife had a cute three-year-old daughter on her knee.

"Can I come to Shanghai to work in your company?" she asked. "I will do anything. I'll be the cleaner. There is no work here at all."

"What about your daughter?"

"She will be living in school, no problem," she replied.

I hated the whole approach – children at that age should be with their mothers.

My dominant impression of Fengjie and its environs was children: huge numbers of babies and very young children everywhere. Every family had at least two children, and sometimes even four. There was definitely a population boom in progress here and I had never seen anything like it anywhere in China.

"The birth control policies are not strictly enforced here," said one man, who happened to be a Communist Party member in his spare time.

Fengjie was a dispersed mess of a place straggling along around ten kilometres of river bank, including several bits of the old town that were above the new water line. It was much bigger than Wushan.

I sat at a street stall restaurant in Fengjie and watched the coal trucks passing by, and also a few foreign tourists. Some of the Yangtze tour boats stopped at Fengjie overnight to let the tourists see the temple of Baidicheng. Other people joined us, including a couple who ran a knick-knack shop down the street, an orange trader who offered me a farm girl at a cheap price, and an unemployed man of fifty years old who was smart but bitter at the way life had treated him. He wanted to talk about Chinese medicine and Marxism, but mostly to bemoan his fate. He had no pension, he said, because he had been laid off at too young an age. His children gave him some help, but basically he survived by spending almost no money.

A girl stopped to talk to me in a restaurant and asked: "Why would you come to a crap place like this?" I protested that it didn't seem so crap to me.

The centre of the new Fengjie town was lively, and there appeared to be money here. People said the local economy was supported by three dragons – the white dragon of tourism, the yellow dragon of oranges and the black dragon of coal. Most of the money came from coal because Fengjie is the heart of the Gorges coal industry, sending barge after loaded barge down the river to Wuhan and beyond. I saw several Lexus cars on the streets, and I was sure there were some snazzy casinos somewhere in town.

Like Wushan, there was a slightly wild feeling about Fengjie. I asked a taxi driver about the law and order situation and he said: "Not so good."

"In what way?"

"There are a lot of fights. Mostly knives and handguns."

I discussed investment in the coal industry with a couple of people. It cost one million RMB to open up a new mine and two years to get a return on the investment. Not bad, but the uncertainties and risks of the business were also massive – the coal seams can run out suddenly, officials and policies can turn hostile and mine shafts can collapse, killing and injuring the miners.

"It's been quite bad this year for accidents," one woman told me.

In the countryside beyond Fengjie, I stopped to buy water at a small shop and sat for a while with a group who were enjoying the peaceful afternoon together in the shade of the little building. A boy in his late teens drew my attention and we chatted for a while about his life and hopes for the future. Before I left, I gave him the name card I use on the walk, which includes the Chinese name for the project: Graham's Travels to the West. This is a reference to one of the great classics of Chinese Literature, *Travels to the West*, in which the monk Tang Zeng travels to India to get the Buddhist scriptures. He is accompanied on the trip by the Monkey King and a pig named Zhu Bajie, who protects the monk along the way. An hour after I had left the shop, the boy called my mobile and said: "I would like to come with you. I will be your Zhu Bajie. I have no work, so I am available. I admire what you are doing and I have a problem with my leg too. Please let me come."

"Well, how about if we just walk together for a couple of hours tomorrow?" I proposed and he readily agreed, but the next morning he called me to say he had bad news: "My mother says I can't come," he said. "Sorry to have bothered you."

I finally spoke with someone who said he took opium occasionally. "It is great for toothache and digestion problems." I asked him about the preparation process and how it was taken. He showed me some opium poppy pods, which were dried, brown and cracked, around the size of a small egg.

"First you heat some water, then break two or three pods into the water and let it simmer for a few minutes. Then drink," he explained. "It makes you feel relaxed and comfortable."

I asked how often he drank the special tea, and he said a couple of times a week. "I don't want to do any more than that otherwise I might get addicted," he said.

I came across someone else who collected the pods and used them in soups. "They make soups really smooth and tasty," he told me. "You break a couple of pods into the soup tureen and let them simmer with the rest of the ingredients. Lovely. But I wouldn't do it too often."

My friend close to Fengjie asked me if I would like to try some of this special tea, and of course I had to take him up on his offer. It looked, smelled and tasted just like any other boiled Chinese medicine – a dark brown bitter brew producing a bit of a buzz, but nothing like the feeling I have heard accompanies smoking of the herb.

What was becoming clear to me was that the use of opium for low-level medicinal and soup enhancement purposes was still fairly widespread and a facet of the rural culture in this part of central China that had both preceded and followed the high-profile British excursion into the market in the 19th century.

The road from Fengjie to the next river town, Yunyang, followed a valley to the north of the Yangtze River that was one of the most beautiful stretches of country I had seen in central China. The scenery was enhanced by recent heavy rains that made the river race noisily down its steep gradient. Waterfalls cascaded off the cliffs at every turn. The vistas included the classic Gorges cliffs and steep terraced hillsides, and while it was on a slightly smaller scale than the classic Yangtze Gorges, it was more secluded. I would particularly recommend a walk east towards the town of Guojiagou, because then you have the sun mostly at your back during the afternoon.

While walking back into the mountains after passing through Guojiagou, a police car pulled up beside me and the passengers inside asked me what I was doing. They wanted to see my passport, which I handed over to them. I asked to see their credentials in return, but neither of them had them on hand. They said they would shadow me as I walked.

"Why?" I said. "I just want to walk along in peace, and enjoy the scenery."

"We want to be sure you are safe," said one.

"Is there a law and order problem around here?" I asked.

They handed the passport back to me and I walked on to the next village where their commander was waiting for me outside the Traffic Police office. "Come in and have a chat," he said.

I sighed. "It is getting late in the day and I would like to keep walking," I said, and I walked on. He didn't challenge me. But after a while, I started to regret turning down his invitation, so I returned to the police station and found the front now shuttered. I asked at the shop next door, and the shopkeeper said the policemen were upstairs. I asked him to go and tell them I would like to invite them for dinner, and the head policeman, a fellow in his mid-thirties, came out just as I was taking a photograph of a child.

"No photos!" he shouted.

"Of children?" I asked incredulously.

"No, of me."

I invited him and his colleagues to dinner – there was a restaurant just a few steps away. He declined. How about a cup of tea, then? "No," he insisted.

"But a while ago, you wanted to talk to me. Let's talk," I urged. He hesitated. "How about we go upstairs and we can chat?" He reluctantly agreed, took me to a formal meeting room, and brought me some tea in a paper cup. I asked him about the traffic and the village. He had only one question for me.

"What do you think of China?"

"I think… it is moving in the right direction. In the late 1970s, it came close to collapse, but then came Deng and now we have all this. There are many changes yet to be made, but the direction is right."

As he walked me out, I asked him what the biggest law and order problem was in the area. "No problems, really," he said.

"How about gambling?"

"Chinese people don't gamble much," he replied and I hid my smile.

Out on the road again, it was drizzling and autumnal grey. The mountains were shrouded in mist and there were few people out for me to talk to.

Many of the farmhouses had slogans on their walls urging young men to sign up for the army, which was not a bad option in a recession. 'Answer the call of the motherland, you hot-blooded boys!' one sign read.

Over two days, I walked from about three hundred and fifty metres above sea level to twelve hundred and twenty metres at the ridge, then back down to three hundred and fifty metres. So each day I walked about eighteen horizontal kilometres and also did around six hundred and fifty vertical metres. For comparison, the Jinmao Tower in Shanghai is four hundred and thirty metres in height.

The downhill stream, heading westwards, was crystal clear up to a point where a recent landslip had brought half a hillside down onto the road. From that point, the waters were muddy, and I watched with interest to see how long the mud would stay suspended in this stream, which consisted of a series of quiet pools interspersed with rocky rapids. The answer was about four kilometres, but just as the water had become clear once more, the stream hit its first village, and the first building on the outskirts was a small fertilizer factory, which of course was feeding gunk into the stream. By the second village, there were heavy growths of green vegetation in the waters, feeding off the unnatural richness, while the banks were covered with the usual detritus of modern Chinese civilization.

I came upon a shrine under a cliff by the road dedicated to Buddha in one of his more garishly Chinese forms. There was a plaque outside that said the shrine was named after the Purple Bamboo Buddha and had been in existence for hundreds of years, having been set up originally by a Taoist priest who had happened by and was enchanted by the view before him. It was tiny; the shrine itself was a grotto up a dozen steep steps occupying a space of only two metres square. There was a flame burning in a small oil holder in front of the image, with a small round kneeling cushion on the ground. There was no fresh incense to be had, so I took a half-burned stick and re-lit it, then did the usual obeisance to Buddha: kneeling on the cushion, holding the incense stick between my hands and waving it up and down three times. A woman and a boy had accompanied me up to see what the foreigner would do, and I asked them if they were believers. The woman said no, but the boy surprisingly said yes.

I am ambivalent about signs of religious belief. I am not religious myself but I like the continuity of tradition represented by the shrines and little temples still to be found in some corners of the Chinese countryside.

I met a young girl on the road named Peng Jingjing, who overtook me and asked if she could talk to me, so we walked together for a few kilometres. She was fifteen years old, and clearly extraordinary in that she was a farm girl taking the initiative to get to know a strange foreign man walking through the village. I asked her about the terraced fields on the hillsides around us, many of which had fallen into disuse.

"People have stopped farming them, it's not worth it," she said. "People plant enough to eat themselves, and then maybe some cash crop depending on what has a good market price at the time."

She had spent almost her entire life apart from her parents. She lived with her grandfather and lived most of the year at the dormitory at her junior high school. Her parents lived in Shenzhen where her father had a job as a driver.

"When did you last see them?" I asked.

"More than a year ago."

"Do you stay in touch?"

"Yes, they call me, maybe once or twice a month."

"Could you not go and live with them?" I asked.

"I went to Shenzhen once, but I hated it there." There seemed to be more to the story, but I did not press her for details.

Her dream, she said, was to get into a good senior high school, then a place in university to study Korean or Japanese to become an interpreter.

"What do you think of the Nanjing massacre?" she asked, in a strange segue from future to past.

"Hmm, it was bad, but it was also a long time ago, and has little or nothing to do with the Japanese people of today, just as I had nothing to do with the Opium Wars," I said.

She changed the subject again and said she was very proud of the Communist Party's leaders and was glad they had everything under control.

"But the corruption is terrible," she added in another weird juxtaposition. "All the money for improving schools in Yunyang, for instance, gets siphoned off, so our school gets none of it. We don't have even one computer and there is no library."

I asked her if she ever read novels, and she shook her head.

"They are not allowed, and we are not allowed to use computers either. There is an Internet café near my school, but the teachers come over every evening and get any students there to leave."

I am in a position to confirm that the road between Fengjie and Yunyang is both long and winding. On one particular day I walked around sixteen kilometres, and at the end of it, I was thirty seconds of longitude closer to Shanghai than at the start. But I didn't hold it against the road – this was the last real stretch of mountain country before the mountains of the Gorges region smoothed out into the Sichuan basin, and I was in no rush to move on. In fact, after racing impatiently across the Hubei plain in just six months in 2006, I had spent two years sauntering through the vast mountain region dominated by the Gorges.

I was approaching a little town with an offshoot of the Yangtze reservoir below me when I saw something that I had never before seen in rural China – a sight that was truly shocking in its uniqueness. Beside the road, next to some houses, were two people with brushes, sweeping up the litter! They were picking up bits of paper and putting them in a rubbish bag!

They were Buddhist nuns, dressed in orange-trousered robes, white socks and gloves, with shaven heads. As they busied themselves with basic tidying work, about a dozen ordinary people sat or stood around nearby ignoring them. I asked the nuns why they were picking up the rubbish. It was that extraordinary a sight.

"It is good to help people," one of them said.

"But shouldn't everyone pick up the rubbish?" I asked. "Why do you have to do it?"

"It doesn't matter who does it, as long as someone does. It is our honour," said the other nun, who continued to sweep as she talked.

The litter situation in rural China was dire; roadsides, hillsides and streams across the country were covered in the detritus of modern life. Plastic bags, rotting food, old clothes, saline drop bottles were sometimes dumped right next to the houses where people lived without any apparent thought to the consequences. Why was it that the first people I had seen actually fighting this tide of multi-coloured crap were two Buddhist nuns? I fervently hope that Chinese people do not need to get religion before they decide to pick up their rubbish.

The small space by the road being tended by the nuns turned out to be the entrance to an old market street, and it was also close to a temple, which was now only accessible by boat.

The local people were curious about my questions to the nuns, and several of them followed me as I walked into the narrow alleyway, with tarpaulins overhead, little shops and stalls pressing in both sides, stocked with plastic packed foods, eggs, simple clothing and footwear, kitchen implements, slabs of fly-enhanced meat and what may be the best-selling item in rural China – hair adornments for women. There were children sitting in wicker baskets on the backs of their mothers and grandmothers, and a young man with a cigarette hanging out of his mouth fired a shot with a small semi-toy rifle at a bird above us.

I stopped in the middle of the market and a crowd gathered around me, with them asking the obvious questions about who I was and where I was going, while they gave me the obvious answer to the question of how was life – poor, they said.

I took a photo of a man with a big smile on his face wearing pretty dirty clothes that nevertheless looked pretty comfortable, and I was berated for taking the shot by a woman wearing a vaguely fur-like coat that was stylishly out of place in a village market.

"His clothes are ragged, you shouldn't photograph him," she said.

"My clothes are not too clean either," I said, pointing to my slightly torn trousers and grubby work shirt. "Also, you are the most fashionable person here. Your coat is lovely." She smiled happily.

I walked out of the market with a middle-aged couple and they told me about how the village had a history of two thousand years, and that it was all that was left of the old Yunyang county seat, which had been below us.

"We were above the waterline, so we didn't have to move," said the woman. "We were lucky. Everyone else has moved to the new county town."

I could see why she was happy to stay. The valley was pretty even on a gloomy morning. Then we turned a corner and came upon a cement factory, the bane of China's rural environment. The air turned powdery and foul, and I hurried past, trying not to breathe deeply.

The road started to wind upwards, and at times I could see three or four stretches of road below me as it switch-backed up the mountain. I puffed my way up the steep grade, and the motorcyclists tried to get me to accept a ride, often for free, but I waved them away.

I came upon a field of half-mature rapeseed; the flowers were not yet fully open, but a family was busy harvesting it to presumably steal a march on the market. Four or five people cut and bundled the plants while their cow wandered around the patch chewing on selected flower tops. The family members laughed and talked as they worked steadily, and the cow seemed happy too. I stopped and absorbed this classic country scene for a few minutes, and left feeling that some of the peace had rubbed off onto me.

CHAPTER 24

THE BLUEST EYES IN CHONGQING

Chongqing is known, amongst other things, as the 'city of mists'. The mountains that sit two or three hundred kilometres northeast of the city proper – still within what is now known as Chongqing municipality – were shrouded in a wet white spring fog for a full two days, which made it impossible to see much of the countryside, but provided a muffled sense of peaceful isolation.

That is, until a bus roared unexpectedly out of the midday gloom.

I was walking mostly downhill through the mountains towards the Yunyang county seat, and there were few people on the roads. I stopped at a little shop where a dozen or so people of all ages were sitting and chatting, and bought a bottle of water to create an opportunity for them to offer me a seat. We talked for a few minutes, and one of them said, "So your Chinese is not very good, is it?"

I laughed. "Thank you for the directness," I said. "I try my best." A reality check is so much better than the usual lavish praise for saying "ni hao".

The countryside was a lavish green, having absorbed the rich moisture of the air, and while I was disappointed to have missed the yellow splash of rapeseed flower season by a week or two, I was there in time for the peach blossom season.

I passed many peach trees along the road, which sit anonymous for most of the year, then bloom into bright white smudges on the fields for a couple of weeks. The ground beneath the trees was covered with masses of delicate and decaying purple-tinged blossoms.

Shops were shuttered and there was little traffic on the road, not even the motorcycle ferrymen. Everywhere, everything was mist. I like to breathe deeply on my walks, to clean out the air of urban China, but I was warned by a couple of people not to breathe the mist in too deeply as it was unhealthy. Is that true, I wondered? Misty air holds moisture that could carry germs, but the air was still sweet enough that I shrugged my shoulders and filled my lungs anyway.

A couple of pigs trotted by, pulling along their owner, and through the mist, walking towards me on the same side of the road, I saw a man. What really caught my eye was that he was limping in exactly the same way I do – right leg slightly shorter than the left.

People who limp – I speak for myself at least – are unaware in normal circumstances of the fact they are limping, and I believe most people who know me don't give it much thought either, for the simple reason that I don't. But a meeting between two people limping forces both to remember what they would prefer to ignore. We limpers generally look away from each other, but this time I stopped and slapped my right leg. "Same leg," I said. The man grunted and walked on without stopping. It was not a conversation he wanted to have.

'For farmers to become prosperous they must read books', declared one slogan, followed by several more opium warnings, and then a slogan of relevance to one of the key themes in terms of the great Whither China question: 'Learn the law, know the law, protect the law, for you, for me and us all'. It was signed by the Shuikou local government and it sounded like they meant it. But what happens in Shuikou or anywhere else in China when the law is at variance with the interests of the Chinese Communist Party? Which takes precedence?

On a wall under a bridge, I saw that someone had pasted an A4 piece of paper with a printed message. The corner of the document was curled and there was a snail hiding underneath the curl:

'Notice,' it read. 'Over the past year, some non-local people without approval from our factory, have moved into the production areas of our factory and lit fires and slept. With regard to this, our factory has on numerous occasions made representations to the Shuikou people's government and called upon the non-local people to leave, but today some of these people are still in place. Due to the fact that during the production process, our factory needs to fire bricks, it is possible there have been incidents in which people have been poisoned and burned etc, with some people being injured and killed. In order to ensure the safety of production at our factory, as well as the personal safety of the staff, non-local people are not allowed to enter the production areas of our factory without permission, and if there are any accidents that occur as a result of such entries, our factory does not bear any legal responsibilities. (signed) Yunyang Xingwang Brick Factory, December 10, 2008.'

There was a story here of some sort, and I asked a few people but could not find anyone who knew of the situation. The notice raised so many questions. Who were these non-local people? Why had they moved to Yunyang and from where? Why were they squatting in the production area of a brick factory? Why did they not move away when production got underway? How many people had died? China, thankfully, remains a riddle wrapped in a mystery inside an enigma. Otherwise, what is the point of staying?

By now, I could hear the Yunyang county seat in the distance, but I couldn't see it because of the mist. I was eager to pass through it and move on to the next major town along the river – Wanzhou, or Wanxian as it has been known for most of the past couple of centuries. This was, and is, the largest town on the river east of Chongqing and west of the Gorges, and it was the place where my hero Isabella Bird, the intrepid adventurer of the late 19th century, left the river on her journey through western China in 1898 and struck out across the Sichuan basin for Chengdu. My intention was to follow her path as closely as possible, and to match my unworthy impressions against hers.

But first, I found I was in pipa country. Pipa is the name of a small apricot-like fruit found in the mountains of eastern Sichuan, and I happened to be passing through at the height of pipa season, which is in mid-May. All along the roads were little stalls set up by farmers to sell piles of pipa, but they were competing with Nature itself. I passed countless trees laden with the fruit right by the road, easy for anyone to pick. Business was brisk nevertheless, particularly in one village of the Bayang township, where I found the new middle class from Wanzhou taking a weekend drive out into the countryside in their new private cars to buy huge bagfuls of the fruit.

Price were low: only three RMB per jin (half a kilogram). I bought some from one stall, and the farmers at the adjacent stalls wanted me to buy more. "Next year," I said.

The Yunyang county seat, one of the main new towns on the Yangtze River, was built to house farmers displaced by the Three Gorges Dam. The town was not as large or as prosperous as Fengjie to the east, but it had better hotels. Dominating Yunyang was a hill topped with a tall pagoda, which I was told used to be the headquarters for a gang of outlaws. I couldn't get a clear reading from my farmer informants on the period, but it appeared to have been at some point after the communist takeover in 1949.

On the edge of town, I passed the campus of a privately-owned school called the Yunyang Foreign Language High School. The language concerned had to be English, and it was a smart selling point. I stopped at the school entrance and asked the guard if he could pass my name card to any of the foreign teachers. He looked at the card and said: "Well, there is only one and he is from the Philippines. And he is not here."

"So how do they teach foreign languages to so many students?" I asked.

"Chinese teachers," he said.

Clever idea. Pull in the customers with the name on the gate and cut costs to the bare minimum. I asked for the card to be passed to the Filipino teacher, but I did not hear from him.

In the centre of town, I stopped at a small restaurant for dinner. The restaurant manager had her son helping out, and tried to get me to buy the spicy prawns stewed with beef at a price of one hundred and eight RMB. It sounded like a disgusting combination, even discounting the fact that I don't eat meat. I asked her how her business was doing and she said it was best in the late evening.

"We stay open until the early hours of the morning," she said, and pointed to the row of establishments on the other side of the road, and on either side of her restaurant. They were all pink-lit massage and hairdressing places and the girls and the patrons would all be interested in late night snacks. The pink-lit hairdressers are a feature of all rural China towns. I have sometimes been told that Chinese are very discreet about illicit sex, unlike Westerners. Oh, really?

Yunyang town is basically composed of three roads along the river – upper, middle and lower – with a few steep linkage roads in between. I walked through the town along the top road and inspected the street signs, which featured three versions of each names – Chinese, pinyin and English. So Baiyun Lu was rendered as Cloud Road and Pingan Ti as Safety Stairs. Then I crossed a bridge that took me on to the west, leaving Yunyang behind me.

Back on the mountain road, with the river somewhere out on my left, I passed a house painted with the slogan: 'Give up your home, dedicate it to the Three Gorges Project'. I saw a small and very old stone bridge on a side road, a one-arched construction with a dragon-snake built into the design, with its head emerging from the stonework on one side, and its tail on the other. It was a work of traditional art with a practical purpose. Only the name was a bit of a clichéd disappointment – the Bridge of Eternal Peace – but was redeemed by the beauty of the calligraphic strokes of which the characters were composed.

The hills became gentler and I was happy to see rice paddies again – some terraced and some on flat land. I could almost smell the paddy-heavy Sichuan basin ahead of me.

I met an old woman with boyishly long grey hair meandering along the road with a walking stick, now on this side, now on that, but mostly blithely wandering down the middle of the road with no concern for the occasional trucks and buses that roared by. I said hello and the first thing she said was: "Eighty-eight! Double eight!"

"Congratulations!" I said. "Now, let's walk on the side of the road."

A little further along, a duck jumped out of a ditch beside me, waddled across the road, and proceeded in the same westerly direction as myself on the other side. We shadowed each other for probably two hundred metres in a repeat of the experience with the old lady, except the duck had nothing to say.

On the right of the old Yunyang to Wanzhou road I was on, higher up in the mountains, I could see the new freeway, which had opened just a few months ago. Fantastically long, high bridges stretched over the mountain valleys, each one a feat of engineering that twenty years ago would have merited the cover of *China Reconstructs* magazine, but now are just another unremarkable part of the country's national freeway network. China's infrastructural capabilities – road, bridge and tunnel construction – were phenomenal.

I heard a bird call which was a four-note song – high-mid-mid-low, repeated over and over. It was the same species of bird I had come across in the Anhui mountains, and had been told there that its call marks the start of the rice planting season. The bird was right on time: I passed peasants knee-deep in water, thrusting bright green rice shoots into the mud. The precise tones the birds used were slightly different than those in Anhui, but that was only natural; after all, the human dialects differed between Anhui and Sichuan too.

It was now the height of summer, and out on the road the temperatures approached and then exceeded forty degrees. I walked as fast as I possibly could from one patch of tree shade to the next but in that heat it was a real slog.

A lack of houses along the way meant that there were few opportunities for conversation. I decided to stop and rest out the hottest part of the day between noon and 1pm under the shade of a tree. But when noon arrived, I noticed that my shadow was still tending slightly ahead of me. As the road was heading exactly due west, this didn't make sense, and I puzzled over it for a little while before realizing that noon in Beijing, thirteen or fourteen degrees of longitude to the east, was in fact only 11am or so in real time in Chongqing / Wanzhou, and it would be another hour before the sun was directly over my head.

I stopped at a little storefront open to the road in which four women were playing mahjong on a table that automatically mixed the tiles and magically delivered fresh walls of tiles for them to play at the end of each round. It was the first time I had seen such a device in action and it was both amazing and a little disappointing. The process of manually mixing mahjong tiles, with all the noise and interaction involved, has its own charm.

Sitting at the side of the room was a middle-aged man whose face was distinctive in some way, but I didn't pay a lot of attention to him until one of the women pointed at him and said: "He's a foreigner too." The man had blue eyes – the only blue eyes I had ever seen on a Chinese person, and his skin and features had a relatively Caucasian or perhaps Turkic feel to them. The man was embarrassed and uncomfortable, but this was clearly what he had been dealing with all his life. I went over and sat next to him and chatted with him. He was both happy and unhappy about this.

"It does look like we are brothers," I said to him. "What is your surname?"

"My surname's Li," he replied with a thick Chongqing accent.

"Some foreigner did the act with one of his ancestors," said one of the women with a laugh. "He's a foreign bastard."

It was phrased in a friendly enough way, but he had been beaten down by what I imagined had been a constant thread of taunts and derogatory comments since he was a young child. Poor guy. He smiled sheepishly at the woman's remark.

"Do you have any idea how many generations back?" I asked.

He shook is head.

"How about your father?"

"Dead."

"Did he have blue eyes?"

"Yes."

We took a photo together. I guessed the blue-eyed ancestor who left his seed in this village was more likely to be a central Asian than a European, but who knows.

The valley widened out, the mountains became hills and tiny snails were out in force due to the rainy weather. I passed a peasant peeling them off walls and dropping them into an enamel mug.

"You eat them?" I asked. He nodded without even looking at me and continued his harvest.

CHAPTER 25

JOINING ISABELLA

Isabella Bird arrived at Wanzhou, then called Wan Hsien, in February 1898 after a journey by boat up the Yangtze River from Shanghai. She was planning to travel overland from Wanzhou to the capital of Sichuan province, Chengdu, and I planned to follow as closely as possible in the footsteps of one of the great adventurers and travel writers of the late 19th century.

Isabella, if I may be so familiar as to call her that, was sixty-seven years old at the time of her trip and Sichuan was seething with the anti-foreigner sentiment which would fuel the Boxer Rebellion two years hence. But on arrival at the river wharf, she typically ignored the danger and walked alone up into the town.

'I was much impressed by the good paving and cleanliness, and the substantial stone dwellings en route,' she said. 'Wan Hsien has a very large trade. Its shops are full of goods, native and foreign, and the traffic from the interior, as well as by junk, is enormous.'

The town I saw still had the sharp inclines and thriving shopping streets. But there were no buildings older than a couple of decades in sight, and the general sense of the city was almost the same as any one of hundreds of others across China. It was such a shame how every town in the country had had its individual charm ripped out of it.

This river port is the place where for many, many years – hundreds and even thousands – trade has met the Yangtze River, providing the connection for goods heading from the coast and central China into Sichuan, and goods from Sichuan's huge and verdant plains heading out to the world. In both directions, the primary point of shipment was not Chongqing city to the south, but Wanzhou, and still is to a great extent today, even though its role is challenged by the growth of the highway network.

Wanzhou had grown enormously since the mid-1990s due to the Three Gorges Dam with many farmer families uprooted and resettled in housing blocks in this city. I was told that it had a population of close to two million people.

Isabella's Wanzhou was a 'small, steep, and handsome' walled city. It had substantial suburbs extending beyond its walls. The countryside beyond the town 'is exquisitely cultivated, and is crossed in several directions by flagged pathways, carried over ascents and descents by good stairs. These usually lead to lovely villages, built irregularly on torrent sides, among a great variety of useful trees.'

The walls were gone, but the countryside was still exquisitely cultivated. I passed through several villages built beside streams, and I imagined they had once been pretty. I enjoyed particularly the river stretch of the village of Gaoliang, which I am sure Isabella was referring to in her comments.

I looked at the maps and satellite photos to try and figure out which route Isabella would have taken to exit Wanzhou, so that we could rendezvous for the trip across the Sichuan basin. I passed a turn-off at a huge flyover intersection which I was told was the main road west, and continued south past the countless truck repair shops and tyre graveyards that infest the town's outskirts.

Logic told me that she must have taken the valley stretching out before me to the west. It was the only way to get to the place I knew was her first stopover, a place named by Isabella as San Tsan Pu. In fact it was

Sanzhengpu, which is now referred to on freeway signs as just Sanzheng. I came to an intersection and asked if the smaller road west went to Sanzheng.

"You can get there on this road, yes," the man confirmed. "But why not take a car and go by freeway?"

Why not indeed? The official temperature on that day was 37 degrees Celsius, but it was definitely well into the forties on the road and with the naked sun blasting down it felt like a furnace. The ripe corn plants by the roadside looked exhausted by the effort of staying upright while waiting to have their cobs removed. I carried an umbrella and walked slowly along the dirt road, sweating mightily and relishing every inch of shade.

I took photos of scenes that I felt sure Isabella would have seen with almost no change, as she gazed out of her swaying sedan chair, coolies fore and aft jogging along in rhythm.

'The uniqueness of the neighbourhood of Wan consists in the number of its truncated sandstone hills', she observed, 'each bearing on its flat top a picturesque walled white village and fortification, to be a city of refuge in times of rebellion.'

The flat-top hills were still there, the same mighty slabs of earth as those in the Gorges region, but horizontal rather than jacked up at forty-five degree angles. They were remarkable, with rings of crops round their slopes, but they no longer had walled villages on them. The easily defended refuges had all been demolished.

Isabella said she took little with her for a land journey that would, in the end, cover more than 1,800 kilometres. 'The longer one travels the fewer preparations one makes, and the smaller is one's kit', she wrote. 'I got nothing at Wan except a large sheet doubly oiled with boiled linseed oil, and some additional curry powder.'

Her mode of travel, as mentioned above, was a coolie-carried chair.

'My light, comfortable bamboo chair had a well under the seat which contained my camera, and, including its sixteen pounds weight, carried forty pounds of luggage in addition to myself. It had bamboo poles fourteen feet long, and a footboard suspended by ropes', she said.

The stripped-down chair was suspended on bamboo poles and held up by a chair bearer at either end, rented from a travel operator in Wanzhou along with three chair bearers and four coolies – it was always good to have a spare coolie on hand.

'I may say at once that they behaved admirably; made the journey in two days less than the stipulated time; trudged cheerfully through rain and mud; never shirked their work; and were always sober, cheery, and obliging', she said.

She wore Chinese dress, which she felt 'certainly blunts the edge of curiosity'. I walked as opposed to being carried, but I also wore clothes aimed at melding into the scene: a simple work shirt and trousers that were often more ragged than the always Western clothes that the Chinese of this region now wore.

Isabella left Wanzhou 'early on a fine February morning, the air as soft and mild as that of an English April'. The road passed in open country 'on a good, flagged road, which was carried up and down hill by stone stairs'.

This road I believe to be a stretch of what is today National Highway 318. There was only one valley she could have taken, and it was so narrow that the highway – really a small two-lane road – must have been built on top of the flagged path Isabella travelled on.

'The road on which I travelled on that and two or three subsequent days has the reputation of being one of the finest in China' she wrote. 'It was built fifty-four years ago [i.e. in the 1840s], and is in splendid repair. It is never less than six feet wide, paved with transverse stone slabs, carried through the rice-fields on stone causeways, and over the bridges and up and down the innumerable hills by flights of stone stairs on fairly easy gradients, with stone railings and balustrades wherever there is any necessity for them. Streams are crossed by handsome stone bridges, with sharp lofty arches, and the whole is a fine engineering work.'

It is such a shame that this excellent path no longer existed, but to keep yearning for a past that has been destroyed has little value.

'The scenery,' she reported, 'is entrancing. The valleys are deep and narrow, and each is threaded by a mountain torrent. The hills are truncated cones, each one crowned by a highly picturesque fortified village of refuge, and there were glimpses of distant mountain forms painted on the pale sky in deeper blue. Everything suggested peace and plenty. The cultivation is surprising, and its carefulness has extirpated most of the indigenous plants. It is carried up on terraces to the foot of the cliffs which support the refuges.'

The scenery was still lovely and the threaded mountain torrents remained delightful. I walked along the valley that Isabella had traversed and came to a bridge over a stream that was of some antiquity, of at least the 1930s and probably earlier. I knew this because it had decorative stonework of a traditional Chinese nature, and typically, it had been smashed. Nevertheless, it was still a handsome stone bridge; Chinese people seem to have always had a talent for building bridges. There was of course no sign of the wonderful Wanxian bridge Isabella described in 1898. Alas, alas. But there were remarkable freeway bridges on massive scale that seemed to fit into the landscape by being so unconnected to it.

Isabella reported that the main crops visible in February were broad beans, rapeseed and opium. The road she describes sounds bustling: 'About every half-mile the road passes under a roof with food booths on each side. There were many travellers in shabby closed chairs with short poles, hurried along by two men at a shambling trot. There are so many temples that the air is seldom free from the odour of incense. We met two dragon processions, consisting each of 100 men, and the undulating tail of the dragon was fifty feet long.'

The road I saw was still busy, although quieter than it was a few years ago as the new freeway now drew away most of the trucks and buses. The introduction of the internal combustion engine meant the end of the food booths at half-mile intervals, but there were now small shops selling water, alcohol, cigarettes and nibbles every few kilometres.

I have so far not been as lucky as Isabella in regard to dragon processions. I have never seen even one in the countryside. I live in hope.

They passed a constant stream of baggage coolies, each with a bamboo pole over his shoulder and a package suspended at each end, for a total weight of 80 to 140 pounds. Those coming in towards Wanzhou carried opium, tobacco, indigo, or paper; while those heading west were loaded with cotton yarn, piece goods, and salt.

'These men, carrying the maximum load mentioned, walk about thirteen miles a day, and chair and luggage coolies about twenty-five,' Isabella said. 'Occasionally I made thirty miles in a day, as my men were carrying only seventy pounds each.'

On that first day out of Wanzhou, Isabella's chair bearers covered 27 miles. Trudging along Highway 318 just over one hundred and eleven years after she had passed this way, I was enjoying the same views but feeling the distance in a way she did not.

'Chair travelling is, I think, the easiest method of locomotion by land,' she declared. 'My one objection to it is the constant shifting of the short bamboo carrying pole on which the long poles hang, from one shoulder of each bearer to the other. It has to be done simultaneously, involves a stoppage, occurs every hundred yards and under, and always gives the impression that the shoulder which is relieved is in unbearable pain.'

The coolies accompanying Isabella each day chose a place for breakfast and a midday stop of one hour. Her description of the village restaurants, now frequented by the modern day equivalents of the coolies, the truck drivers, is more than vaguely reminiscent of some places I had seen on the road.

'The halting-place is a shed projecting over the road in a town or village street, black and grimy, with a clay floor, and rough tables and benches, receding into a dim twilight; a rough cooking apparatus and some coarse glazed pottery are the furnishings. On each table a bunch of malodorous chopsticks occupies a bamboo receptacle,' Isabella wrote. 'One or more exceptionally dirty men are the waiters. Bowls of rice and rice water or weak tea are produced with praiseworthy rapidity, and the coolies shovel the food into their mouths with the air of famished men, and hold out their bowls for more. People intending to be kind sometimes take pork, rice, or fish out of a common bowl and put it into yours, and to ensure cleanliness draw the chopsticks with which they perform the transference through their lips, giving them an energetic suck!'

Isabella came through this way in the month of February. In mid-August as I walked through the heat, the rice paddies on either side of the road were heavy with ripened plants. The screaming of the cicadas in the trees rose and fell in waves. I was delighted to see a slogan on a farmhouse wall, a variant on one of my favourites of the current Hu era, which could be read, depending upon how you cluster the characters and how warped your brain is, as 'Use the advanced sex education activities of Communist Party members to satisfy the masses'.

The coolies carried Isabella through the afternoon and into the dusk.

'Towards evening the hills became more mountainous, and were wooded with cypress and pine, and it was very lovely in the gold and violet light,' she observed.

More than a century later, those hills had been largely denuded of trees. But there were delightful stands of fast-growing bamboo along the way, and a few majestic and aged trees still arched out over the road in villages, with people gathered underneath in a semi-conscious homage to these wonderful artifacts of Nature.

The road followed a lovely river, crossed by simple stone bridges and roamed by flocks of ducks. I saw three coolies with burdens balanced on bamboo poles, one of them wearing a baseball cap, fording a stream. The corn had been harvested and was lying in broad sheets on the road to dry. The rice plants had turned yellow, ready to give up their ripened sustenance. A sign on a farmhouse said: 'If you want to not die from childbirth, the key is to stay in a hospital'.

Isabella described in some detail the wonderful arches she found in profusion spanning the road:

'These arches, or paifangs, are put up frequently in glorification of widows who have remained faithful to the memory of their husbands, and who have devoted themselves to the comfort and interests of their parents in law and to good works,' she said. 'The whole affair lends some éclat to the town or village. Many of these arches are extremely beautiful. Chinese carving in stone has much merit, even in such an intractable material as granite. The depth and sharpness of the cutting and the undercutting are remarkable, and the absolute realism (but) I never saw a bit of sculpture which showed a trace of imagination.'

That sounds a little unfair, but it is impossible to take a categorical view on the quality of the artistic work as all the paifang were demolished in the 1950s by the Communist Party. They have been replaced today by paifang carrying advertisements for baijiu brands or property developments. I am just glad the concept of paifang has survived the transition into the modern era in any form at all.

'We halted for the night at the large village of San-tsan-pu, where, though I had travelled for seven months in China, I had my first experience of a Chinese inn, and I did not like it,' Isabella said.

The village she called San-tsan-pu is indeed fairly large, strung along the road for a kilometre or more. I wanted to find the location of the inn in which she stayed, and as I walked into town, I came to an intersection, which is often the centre of a settlement. I asked a couple of old guys sitting by the road where the old inn used to be, but they pointed down the road further west, so I kept walking, and came to a narrower, more built-up, older part of the village. There was a small inn there called the Peace Hotel in a recently constructed four-storey building, but no one could help me on the location of the inn Isabella stayed at. I sensed, however, that a location on the street now occupied by an agricultural market and an Internet café was most likely the place where Isabella had bedded down for the night.

She was carried in her chair through the hotel restaurant that fronted onto the street, and into a paved yard behind 'where, in the midst of abominations, was the inn well. My chair was set down, and, after extricating myself from it according to the rules of etiquette, I was attempting to see it unpacked, when I was overborne by a shouting crowd of men and boys, which surged in after me, and I had to retire hastily into my room'.

The descendants of these individuals who were driven by curiosity or fear of foreigners to such impoliteness towards the formidable Ms. Bird were calm and pleasant towards me. One man, who said he was almost eighty years old, invited me to sit with him. He told me he had joined the Communist Party in the 1950s and repeated several times during the conversation that one should "do more good things and less bad things." I found the second half of the sentence more revealing than the first.

A fifteen-year-old boy, whose albino father was playing mahjong in the convenience store he owned, said his family had lived in Sanzhengpu for at least five generations, which could have put his great-great-great grandfather in the inn yard with Isabella. I asked the boy if he went to school and he said, not any more. I asked him if he read books. "I have done," he answered carefully.

The room Isabella stayed in was 'long and narrow, and boarded off from others by partitions with remarkably open chinks, to which many pairs of sloping eyes were diligently applied; but I was able to baffle curiosity by tacking up cambric curtains brought for the purpose.'

The roof was sloping, the walls were black with dirt and crawling things, the floor was damp and irregular, and on the other side of the outer wall was a pigsty 'which was well-occupied, judging from the many voices, bass and treble'. The room contained two rough bedsteads on which the coolies laid down wadded quilts, and sleep four or more on a bed. 'It is needless to say that these beds are literally swarming with vermin of the worst sorts.'

Isabella arranged herself as best she could: 'Between two of the bedsteads there was just space enough for my camp bed and chair without touching them. The oiled sheet was spread on the floor, and my "furniture" upon it, and two small oiled sheets were used for covering the beds, and on these my luggage, food, and etceteras were deposited. The tripod of my camera served for a candle stand, and on it I hung my clothes and boots at night, out of the way of rats. With these arrangements I successfully defied the legions of vermin which infest Korean and Chinese inns, and have not a solitary tale to tell of broken rest and general misery. With absolute security from vermin, all else can be cheerfully endured.'

This reminded me of a sleepless night I once spent with a number of rats in the Jinjiang Hotel in Shanghai in 1979.

The Sichuan inns, she said, were 'worse than the Persian ordinary caravanserai, or the Kurdistan khan, or even the Korean hostelry.'

Times had changed in this regard. My main interest was finding a hostelry that provided broadband Internet access. As in all of provincial China, hot and cold running whores were a given. Chinese hotels and inns now almost always have electricity and hot tea in the early morning. I, however, like to begin the day with coffee, and that is still a way off for most places in China.

On this day, Isabella was awoken at 7am by her servant with the information that there was no fire, and therefore no breakfast and no tea. She was not pleased. I could relate.

CHAPTER 26

BUFFALO IN WINTER

It was the heart of winter, but the weather in the eastern part of the Sichuan basin was still fairly mild and the mountains were still a wonderful green, even though the paddy fields were brown and silent. The nights and early mornings were still very cold, and mists covered vast regions through noon and beyond, causing transport problems, but also adding a delightful sheen to photographs of rural scenes.

I walked from the top of one of the mountain fingers in the region down into the valley beyond. The region was covered in bamboo forests and judging from the trucks loaded down with cut bamboo trunks, bamboo harvesting appeared to be a significant industry. I hoped it was being done in a sustainable way, but I wasn't optimistic.

My main problem as I strolled along was the fact that the quiet was constantly shattered by trucks carting coal out of the Sichuan basin to the Yangtze River to the east for shipment into central China. The mountain road was far too small to handle so many huge trucks, and I constantly had to lean to the edge to let vehicles pass each other beside me.

But the drivers I had contact with were all solid guys, and I exchanged greetings with many of them as they drove by. One stopped right in the middle of a steep stretch of road with another truck barrelling down behind him to offer me a cigarette as a way of initiating a chat. They always think I am just being polite when I refuse the smoke.

I was sitting on a stool outside a house on the road, close to the top of the mountain, that also sold water, cigarettes and instant noodles, photographing a cat and chatting with the store owner and his wife who were sure England was paradise.

"We are so poor, and England is so rich," the man said.

"You have fantastic views in front of you, the freshest air to breathe and clean food," I replied. "You're doing okay."

A coal truck pulled up, fully loaded, and the driver and his girlfriend got out for a rest. The wife bustled about preparing instant noodles for them, the driver pulled out a cigarette and sat down beside me. Meanwhile the shop owner clambered up onto the top of the coal truck and started raking it back and forth.

"Why is he doing that?" I asked.

"To smooth out the coal," explained the driver.

"Ah, he's doing it to thank you for your next visit," I said. "He wants you to stop here again."

The driver nodded, then smiled. "That's right," he said. "I stop here every time."

I asked him about business and he said it was slow. The economic crisis was to blame, he said.

The road was mostly muddy, not because it had been raining, but because the trucks all pour water out onto their brakes as they rumble down the slopes to stop them from overheating. At one point I came across a path leading down from one level of the winding road to another, and I took it. The first part was slippery, but then it became quite well-constructed and stepped, with proto-flagstones that I guessed pre-dated the road by quite a long time.

I passed a truck stopped on the road with the driver and his mate doing a tyre change.

"Where are you from?" asked one of them.

"From England."

"Do you have a president?"

"No," I said. "A queen."

"We have a president," he replied. "And the Communist Party."

"I had heard that somewhere," I said.

"So what are you doing here?" he asked me.

"Checking on trucks to see if they are over the load limit. Are you?"

"Yes!" he said instantly and I am sure truthfully.

There were quite a few water buffalo on the road, going to and from the fields. They padded patiently by the terraced fields, with the setting sun glinting through the mist onto the placid paddy waters. I watched one female water buffalo being led along followed by her young calf, and a dog which nipped playfully, actually lovingly, at the calf's legs as it walked along. Water buffalo are easily the best-natured animals I have ever come across.

Just as the sun was setting, I met a man standing beside a field wearing a bright red jacket. He said he worked for China Petroleum.

"What are doing here?" I asked. "Looking for oil?"

"No! I just came to look at this area for my own interest. I live in Qiqiao," he replied, referring to the town to the east of the mountains through which I would later pass.

I gave him a name card, and the following day he sent me the longest text message I have ever received, offering to take me to see all the amazing places he had found in Liangping County, of which this was still a part. He listed them all.

"Liangping is a second Shangri-la!" he enthused, exclamation points scattered through the message like trees in an orchard. "Beautiful Liangping!"

He also declared that one of his life's goals was to write a long poem in English called Ode to the Globe, and said he would come and visit me in England if he was awarded the Nobel Prize for Literature. There's no way I could make that up.

The next morning, I was out in the fields by 7am, and it was only just getting light. The views out over the paddies and hills were monochromically mysterious, bathed in a pearly glow. I stood there shivering, snapping photos, and absorbing the sounds of the early morning fields. The experience only lasted fifteen minutes or so, and then the growing lightness of the sky added commonplace colour to the scene and it was time to move on.

CHAPTER 27

TOBACCO ROAD

Occasionally, I came upon a stretch of country that made me say: this is the most beautiful and spectacular scene I have seen. The region to the west of Wanzhou on the eastern slopes of the Sichuan basin was one of those.

The road followed the river southwest to the town of Fenshui, in between two of the mountain fingers that spread out over the Sichuan plain like the hand of Buddha. At Fenshui, the roads of past, present and future separate. The original stepped path that was for centuries the main way between Wanzhou and the Sichuan capital of Chengdu crossed the finger at Fenshui, while the highway builders of the 1950s decided to route Highway 318 further west along the valley and across the finger at a lower point. The new freeway, which has liberated Highway 318 from much of the heavy traffic, follows closer to the original path.

But the old path was also turned into a road capable of taking vehicles in the 1950s. I knew that because a seventy-seven-year-old farmer named Mr. Hou who I met on the road told me so as he was on his way to gather firewood, wearing very cool – in both senses – homemade straw sandals.

It was one of the quietest and most memorably scenic pieces of road I have ever had the pleasure to walk along, through immaculately cultivated farmland interspersed with spinneys of pine and bamboo.

The fields were planted with rice and also the first tobacco I had seen on my walk – tall, voluptuously green plants topped with delicate pink flowers. The vast hillside spreads of tobacco would, in Isabella's day, have been planted with opium, and I saw several slogans painted on farmhouse walls in the area warning that the cultivation of opium was illegal.

"It's a foreigner!" shouted a child as I walked into view, and all the people seated in front of the little shop turned to look at me. "Hello, everyone," I said. "I would like to buy some water."

One young man took up the opportunity, and asked where I was from. I told him I was born in England, and he said: "London is your capital, isn't it?"

"It's the capital of England, yes," I said.

"And the English pound is much more valuable than our currency," he continued. "Around thirteen or fourteen RMB to one pound."

To hear this from a farm boy of twenty years old in the middle of nowhere was amazing. Where does this level of awareness of the world come from, for someone living in such an isolated place?

"I worked for a few months in Ningbo," he said. "In a button factory. Then the global economic crisis hit, and I came home." He now drove a motorcycle to make money. I asked him what his ambition was. "I want to travel abroad. But it is very difficult to get an exit permit." He was smart and lively, and I gave him my card and told him to call me if he ever visited Shanghai.

The exchange brought to mind Isabella's experiences with the ancestors of my friends at the store. She would not get out of her sedan chair when the bearers stopped for a rest, staying immobile in her seat. She could not speak Chinese, and so could not converse with anyone except her servant, Bedien.

'I sat in my chair in the village street, the un-willing centre of a large and very dirty crowd, which had leisure to stand round me for an hour, staring, making remarks, laughing at my peculiarities, pressing closer and closer till there was hardly air to breathe, taking out my hairpins, and passing my gloves round and putting them on their dirty hands, on two occasions abstracting my spoon and slipping it into their sleeves, being in no ways abashed when they were detected', she wrote.

As to the discussion on the value of the pound, Isabella faced significantly greater payment problems than I did.

'Money annoyances began early, and never ceased,' she said. 'Before leaving Wan Hsien, I bought 10,000 cash, brass coins, about the size of a halfpenny, inscribed with Chinese characters, and with a square hole in the middle. By this they are threaded a hundred at a time on a piece of straw twist, and at that time (for the exchange fluctuates daily) the equivalent of two shillings weighed eight pounds! The eighteen shillings in cash with which I started weighed seventy-two pounds, and this had to be distributed among the coolies.'

By contrast, I was able to pay for bottled water and batteries at small stores with small paper renminbi notes.

'We passed through rich and cultivated country, with many noble farmhouses with six or eight irregular roofs, handsome, roofed, entrance gates, deep eaves, and many gables of black beams and white plaster, as in Cheshire,' Isabella wrote. 'Next pine-clothed hills appeared, and then the grand pass of Shen-kia-chao (2900 feet) lifted us above habitation and cultivation into a solitary mountain region of rock, scrub, torrents, and waterfalls.'

Isabella travelled through the region before the spring thaw and traversing the area in late summer provided for me a feast of aural and olfactory experiences she would have missed. The sound of cicadas, cooing doves and bleating month-old goats, the smell of fresh rice stalks being burned off, the wind in the pines and bamboo, the scent of ripe tobacco being roasted in roadside furnaces. And – a new development – Chinese disco booming out of the stereo systems of passing motorcycles.

The place name given as Shen-kia-chao is in fact the village of Sunjia, which is some distance from the pass, but the mountain country is still much as she described.

'The road ascends the pass by 1140 steps on the edge of a precipice, which is fenced the whole way by granite uprights two feet high, carrying long granite rails eight inches square. Two chairs can pass along the whole length,' she observed.

I think I know the section she is referring to, just to the north of Sunjia. The path has been widened to a two-lane road, and has steel cable fence along the outer edge, but it is still spectacular.

'The pass is grand and savage. There were brigands on the road, and it was patrolled by soldiers, small bodies of whom I met in their stagey uniforms, armed with lances with long pennons and short bows and arrows,' she said.

No brigands today. None that I saw, anyway. But then again, I did pass a house sporting the following slogan: 'The people of the entire county should motivate themselves to fully open up the struggle against robbers.'

The consequences of being caught as a robber in the time of Isabella were not pleasant.

'At one point on the pass where there were some trees, three criminals were hanging in cages with their feet not quite touching the ground,' she reported. 'The chai-jen said that they were to be starved to death. Not far off were two human heads which looked as if they had been there for some time, hanging in two cages, with a ghastly look of inquisitive intelligence on their faces.'

For me, the road from Fenshui to Sunjia was closed for repair for a stretch of around seven kilometres, which was fine – it meant the only traffic was an occasional motorcycle. Far below, just outside Sunjia, I saw a huge prison to which today's robbers are sent.

The rice fields were mostly harvested, with the rice plants bundled and lined up in little pyramids along the curved terrace field walls, looking to me like an audience at a concert. But it was the tobacco plants that really dominated the scene.

I stopped at a small 'factory', where a dozen women were sitting under an awning processing the already richly brown roasted tobacco leaves.

The ovens nearby carried 'China Tobacco' signs, in English.

"How's business?" I asked.

"Not too good this year," said the only man there, the supervisor. I asked where the tobacco went, and he said Wanzhou. After that, I guess it goes into the national tobacco machine from which emerge the foul-smelling cigarettes we all have to put up with. What a shame. It smells so lovely in the hills of Sichuan.

The road followed a stream downwards, then another stream upwards, through well forested stretches interspersed by intensively cultivated valleys. Rice paddy until just recently, today vegetable plots had just been planted to keep the land engaged during the coming winter. I was still on the route taken by Isabella Bird. It had taken her three days of travelling to get from the river town of Wanzhou west to the county seat of Liangping; it would take me a total of six days of walking to cover the same distance, meaning that I was sauntering lazily, travelling only half the distance each day than her coolies managed to carry her.

On her last day's journey to Liangping, Isabella makes no reference to anything of note having happened or being seen. I had a similar experience: it was just a very pleasant stroll through the hills of the eastern Sichuan basin.

The river valley contained many rocks, large and small, that had fallen off the cliffs at some point and rolled down. One of the largest had a big tree growing on top of it, which helped give some indication of how long it had been since it had become dislodged. One rock had a slogan written on it saying: 'Firmly attack the electrocution and dynamiting of fish'.

I passed a magnificent old stone bridge that crossed the stream near some houses. It was called the Wan An Bridge – ten thousand peacefuls – and while it had a short span, it rose about twenty metres above the water and was covered in dangling vines and vegetation that reached down to the stream. I asked how old it was and a lady said "more than one hundred years", but it was a guess on her part. I was hoping for a date earlier than 1898, which would make it the only construction that both

Isabella and I had seen – mud brick farmhouses don't last more than a few decades.

I finally descended from the last valley and started walking across the first really flat country I had traversed on the walk since I left the Hubei plain in late 2006, many hundreds of kilometres to the east. It was a strange experience not having mountains and hills in sight as I walked along Airport Road, which is an absolutely straight stretch of at least six kilometres. The airport referred to is a military airfield right next to Liangping town that, I was informed, had not been used for a number of years.

Isabella arrived in Liangping late in the afternoon in 1898 and described it as 'an imposing city… on a height, approached by a steep flight of stairs with a sharp turn under a deep picturesque gateway in a fine wall, about which are many picturesque and fantastic buildings.'

This hill is just to the south of today's Airport Road, and is now the centre of a much more sprawling town. Isabella entered the town gate and started along the main street, 'fully a mile and a half long, and not more than ten feet wide, with shops, inns, brokers, temples with highly decorated fronts, and Government buildings "of sorts" along its whole length.'

But the locals then were as violently antagonized by her presence as they were largely indifferent to mine:

'I had scarcely time to take it in when men began to pour into the roadway from every quarter. The crowd became dense and noisy; there was much hooting and yelling. I recognized many cries of Yang kwei-tze! (foreign devil) and "Child-eater!" swelling into a roar; the narrow street became almost impassable; my chair was struck repeatedly with sticks; mud and unsavoury missiles were thrown with excellent aim; a well-dressed man, bolder or more cowardly than the rest, hit me a smart whack across my chest, which left a weal; others from behind hit me across the shoulders; the howling was infernal: it was an angry Chinese mob. There was nothing for it but to sit up stolidly, and not to appear hurt, frightened, or annoyed, though I was all three.'

She and her sedan chair coolies made it into an inn courtyard, and the innkeeper pushed her into an inner room, but the mob surged into the inn after her.

'There was then a riot in earnest; the men had armed them-selves with pieces of the doorway, and were hammering at the door and wooden front of my room, surging against the door to break it down, howling and yelling. Yang-kwei-tze! had been abandoned as too mild, and the yells, as I learned afterwards, were such as "Beat her!" "Kill her!" "Burn her!"'

She sat near the door with her revolver in hand, 'intending to fire at the men's legs if they got in'. The mob tried to ram open the door to her room, and the upper part of the door had begun to cave in when suddenly soldiers arrived and the mob scarpered. The riot had lasted an hour before the local officials intervened.

'I was half inclined to return to Wan [Wanzhou], but, in fact, though there was much clamour and hooting in several places, I was only actually attacked once again, and am very glad that I persevered with my journey,' Isabella said.

Today, the walls of Liangping feature many slogans about drug use. I asked an eighteen-year-old boy if the drug situation was serious.

"Oh yes, there are lots of drugs here," he replied. I asked what the local poison of choice was.

"Baifen." White powder.

"Heroin?" I asked.

"Yes."

"How do they take it?"

"Smoke it."

"Well, don't you touch it," I said sternly to my young friend.

"Oh no, I wouldn't," he said.

The air in the town was filthy and the people looked dulled by the shabby environment. I passed a stream course that possibly set a new record in terms of the concentration of rubbish and filth. Then I reached an intersection, marked by one of the strange abstract post-socialist metal sculptures that rural Chinese officials seem to like, turned right and I was back with my old friend, Highway 318, the road I first took out of Shanghai in 2004.

The first photo I have of a Highway 318 milestone is the thirty kilometre mark. I finished this particular walk at precisely the one thousand nine hundred and thirty-nine kilometre milestone. Nearly two thousand kilometres. The distance as the phoenix flies from Shanghai to Liangping is roughly fifteen hundred kilometres, so all the twists and turns in the road added an extra five hundred kilometres to the distance.

Then the town dropped behind and the fields re-asserted themselves beside the road. All rice paddy, and as rich as any I had seen; as rich and fertile as any in China, I would imagine.

'Jiang Demei, you are a stinking little thief', read a chalked message on a rock by the road. 'Believing in you has taught me not to be gullible'.

'Xiong Ling is a good student and got 100 marks for his homework' said another message on a wall. Good for him.

CHAPTER 28

YOU'RE WELCOME

It was winter and raining in the eastern part of the Sichuan basin, but after a brisk walk it only felt mildly cold. I shed my jacket and continued along in my shirt, puzzling some of the well-padded passers-by.

The land in this part of China seems to be left to sleep during the winter months. It is almost entirely made up of paddy fields, surely amongst the most fertile rice lands in the country, but the fields were all water-logged and silent as I passed by, except for the flocks of white ducks, heads down in the muck, sucking up the goodness.

There were many signs strung across the road. Here is a selection from one section of highway: 'Being conscripted is the honourable right of every citizen'; 'Fully plan a solution to the population problem, the merit attaches to this age, the benefit lasts for 1,000 autumns'; 'Seriously implement scientific development, and unhesitatingly follow the road of Socialism with Chinese characteristics'. There were many, many more.

As on my previous walk, I was struck by the substantial number of signs and slogans along the road warning people not to take drugs. From what I could tell from my conversations, the drugs come into Sichuan from Yunnan, and are distributed at a local level by people who must have some measure of protection. Chinese villages and towns are so transparent that it would be difficult for a local police chief or village chief to miss something as obvious as drug dealers plying their trade; the assumption therefore is that if the drugs are there, it is known and a blind eye is being turned.

I fell into step alongside a twelve-year-old boy who was walking into the little town of Jugui to buy a pen so he could do his homework. I felt like buying him a whole box of them, but controlled myself. I asked him about the anti-drug signs.

"There are lots of drugs here," he said. "But less than before. They had a crackdown on crime last year, around October National Day. Before that, it was terrible. There were robberies and even kidnappings. A boy I know was kidnapped in return for a ransom, but he was released and is okay now."

Pretty scary stuff. I really have no idea of the situations through which I am walking. I passed the Jugui Communist Party headquarters and wondered if they had experienced any personnel changes in recent months. I hoped so.

I didn't have a particularly warm or fuzzy feeling for the officials of the area, but I was very impressed by the hospitality and goodwill of the ordinary people. I was bombarded with invitations for tea and meals and offers of lifts by passing motorcycles and cars; truck drivers waved and saluted me.

I stopped to eat with a family that had two sons aged seven and nine. The two boys asked me lots of good questions and the seven-year-old showed me the game he was playing on his dad's mobile phone, which seemed to be a mix between Super Mario and Loderunner. I handed them both sheets of paper from my notebook and pens and asked them each to write me a letter. They sat earnestly at the table next to me for fifteen minutes composing their letters, of course in Chinese, while I chatted with their parents.

"Dear English uncle," read the nine-year-old's letter. "I very much hope you can come to our school to teach English. When you have finished walking across China, I will invite you to come to our home and you can be a family English teacher. Wishing you good health, Respectfully, Jia Meiwen."

The seven-year-old's letter said: "Today I met a foreign uncle. I am very happy."

I ripped pages out of my notebook and started to write a reply in English, but after three words I stopped, realizing it was too much for them, and wrote simple Chinese letters to them instead, urging them to study hard and learn lots of words in Chinese and English. In my letter to the nine-year-old, I made a point of including some traditional characters.

"I can read some traditional characters," he said.

"Learn more," I replied.

He held the letter tentatively. "Can I keep it?" he asked.

"Of course! It's yours."

He folded it carefully and put it in his pocket.

If you look at a map of east Sichuan, you will see four fingers extending southwest out of the Gorges mountain region, like Buddha's hand. On this day, I walked through the town of Qiqiao (seven bridges), which is the second finger. The plain from which it protrudes is around four hundred and twenty metres above sea level, and the middle of the finger rises to around nine hundred metres.

I was able to note the exact point where the mountains began and the plain ended, an experience I also had in Hubei at the western edge of the Dabie Mountains. The road angled up and I was back in mountain territory.

There was a factory gate to the left and I took a photograph of it for no particular reason and wandered on. A minute or so later, I heard a shout from behind, and became aware of a man standing in the street outside the factory gate looking at me. I feigned deafness and walked on.

Up a little further, I passed a lovely reservoir with blue waters. I chatted with a few truck drivers on the shore who were waiting to cart away the gravel that was being ripped out of a hillside above us. They were very nice and told me that their business was doing badly because of the global economic crisis. I asked if they had children. They all did. I gave them name cards and said I'd be happy to teach their children some English if they contacted me by email.

Then I saw a pall of smoke hanging over the northern end of the reservoir and made my way with a heavy heart along the road towards yet another cement factory in the middle of pristine mountain countryside – the bane of rural China's environment. It was filthy, and as it was on the shores of the reservoir I had no doubt it was discharging all sorts of disgusting waste into the waters every day.

It was a Cultural Revolution-era monstrosity, and outside on a wall was a slogan from the early 1980s that I had almost forgotten: 'Long live Marxist-Leninism Mao Zedong Thought Deng Xiaoping Theory'. What a damning justification for such pollution.

I walked up the steep hill and passed the factory gates which displayed a sign that said: 'Chongqing City Tiansheng Cement Company Ltd'. The factory buildings stood along the left side of the road, with thick grime-laden smoke pouring from twin chimneys above the furnaces. As usual, I took photos of the scene.

As I passed the last of the grimy outbuildings and coal dumping bays, a man called out to me from the road below. I glanced back and kept walking.

"What are you doing?" he asked loudly.

"Looking at the scenery," I said.

He looked like he was in his thirties, had a Bluetooth mobile earpiece in his left ear, short cropped hair and wore a fur-lined black jacket. I assumed he was security of some sort. I smoothly removed the flash memory card from my camera and slipped it into my pocket as I walked.

"He says he's looking at the scenery," he shouted to someone further down the road. I kept walking at the same pace. I could feel him hesitating, unsure of what to do. I was sure he was unhappy about those photos, but he did nothing more. Or so I thought.

The road became steep and sharply winding up the mountain, and was close to eight hundred metres at the top. I was chatting with some people waiting for a bus when a police van pulled up ahead of me and out stepped a senior policeman in a very smart uniform and a younger man in plain clothes, who I sensed was the one who was making the decisions.

"Hi," said the uniformed cop in lilting English. He then asked in Chinese if I spoke Chinese. I said I did.

"What are you doing here?" he asked.

"Just looking around," I replied.

"Looking at the scenery," he offered, and I immediately knew what was going on.

The cement factory management, concerned about an outsider taking photos of their filthy polluting plant, had made a call, hoping to get those photos or at least find out who the hell I was. The police responded, as they would have to if the ownership structure of the cement factory was as I suspected.

"Do you have a visa?" the uniformed policeman asked.

"How could I be here if I didn't?"

He asked me where I lived, how long I'd been in China ("Since before the third Plenum of the eleventh Congress," I said), and some other questions. I looked him straight in the eye and never hesitated as I answered him politely and truthfully. He didn't know how to handle it. He asked to see my passport, and I showed him the relevant pages without ever letting go of it.

I knew the plain-clothed officer wanted to just grab my camera and remove the damn photos, but the triumph of China today is that within the context of that moment, it was not possible for him to do it.

I turned to look at him. "Your region is very beautiful," I said. "There is no problem, is there?"

He looked at my camera, then at me.

"You're welcome," he murmured.

I put the passport back in my pocket, said goodbye and walked on, marvelling again at the how far China had come since I first moved here.

Progress: visible. Outlook: hopeful.

It is early 2010, and the walk continues, usually once a month for several days. I have walked every step of the way, from the Bund in Shanghai to Sichuan (in fact, there is a small possibility that I missed about five metres just east of the city of Tongling in Anhui, but don't tell anyone).

I have changed during the walk. I have learned so much from sharing a few moments with so many strangers. The world of rural China is so different from my usual world that I have a much clearer sense of who I am and what I am doing thanks to the contrast provided by the paddy fields and the farmers. If I had to name one thing I have learned on the journey, it is that we are all the same, no matter who we are, no matter where we live, no matter how much money we have. People everywhere have the same hopes and fears, the same basic needs, the same basic goodness. Every time I say hello to yet another stranger in the fields and get a smile in return, I know we human beings are basically good.

China has changed too, and it continues to change at a fantastic pace, for better and for worse, in a myriad ways. It is an honour to be able to watch and experience it, and even play a small role in the middle of it.

My original plan, conceived in that Japanese restaurant in Shanghai in 2004, was to end the walk in Lhasa, but increasingly I feel… no. It would be exhilarating to walk across the Tibet plateau, with the crystal clear air, and the magnificent mountains, but the purpose of the walk has been to talk to people and explore the state of the China heartland. On the Tibetan plateau, there is almost no one to talk to, I do not speak Tibetan, and I am not really very interested in Tibetan culture. I am in no rush to end the walk. I enjoy sauntering along the open Chinese road, breathing in the fresh air and having random conversations with the farmers too much to stop after all these years. So my current plan is to walk into the mountains west of Chengdu to a place where there are Tibetan-speaking residents, and declare victory on my Shanghai-to-Tibet project, then turn south to Guiyang, five degrees of latitude south of the route I have taken west, and then head back east to the coast.

And when I hit the coast, I could turn left again and walk up to Shanghai, hopefully arriving in time for afternoon tea.

ABOUT THE AUTHOR

Graham Earnshaw was born in England and has lived most of his adult life in the China world. He speaks Cantonese and Mandarin and his translation of the Jin Yong kung fu novel *The Book and The Sword* into English was published in 2004 by Oxford University Press. He has been a journalist, writer and publisher. Other books he has written include *Life and Death of a Dotcom in China*, published in 2000, and *Tales of Old Shanghai*, published in 2008.